The Reformation
Towards a New History

This book recasts the story of the Reformation by bringing together two histories: the encounter between Europe and the western hemisphere beginning in 1492 and the fragmentation of European Christendom in the sixteenth century. In so doing, it restores resonances to "idolatry," "cannibal," and "barbarian," even as it moves past such polemics to trace multiple understandings of divinity, matter, and human nature. So many aspects of human life, from marriage and family through politics to ways of thinking about space and time, were called into question. Debates on human nature and conversion forged new understandings of religious identity. Debates on the relationship of humanity to the material world forged new understandings of image and ritual and of physics. By the end of the century, there was not one "Christian religion" but many, and many understandings of the Christian in the world.

Lee Palmer Wandel is Professor of History, Religious Studies, and Visual Culture at the University of Wisconsin–Madison. She is the author of *Always Among Us: Images of the Poor in Zwingli's Zurich* (1990); *Voracious Idols and Violent Hands: Iconoclasm in Reformation Zurich, Strasbourg, and Basel* (1994); and *The Eucharist in the Reformation: Incarnation and Liturgy* (2006), all with Cambridge University Press. She also co-authored (with Robin Winks) *Europe in a Wider World, 1350–1650* (2003) and co-edited (with Walter Melion) *Early Modern Eyes* (2009).

The Reformation

Towards a New History

LEE PALMER WANDEL
University of Wisconsin

CAMBRIDGE UNIVERSITY PRESS
Cambridge, New York, Melbourne, Madrid, Cape Town,
Singapore, São Paulo, Delhi, Tokyo, Mexico City

Cambridge University Press
32 Avenue of the Americas, New York, NY 10013-2473, USA

www.cambridge.org
Information on this title: www.cambridge.org/9780521717977

First published 2011

Printed in the United States of America

A catalog record for this publication is available from the British Library.

Library of Congress Cataloging in Publication data
Wandel, Lee Palmer.
The Reformation : towards a new history / Lee Palmer Wandel.
p.   cm.
Includes bibliographical references and index.
ISBN 978-0-521-88949-0 (hardback) – ISBN 978-0-521-71797-7 (paperback)
1. Reformation.   2. Church history–16th century.   I. Title.
BR305.3.W36   2011
270.6–dc22   2011015715

ISBN 978-0-521-88949-0 Hardback
ISBN 978-0-521-71797-7 Paperback

Contents

List of Figures and Maps

Figures

Maps

Preface

I grew up in California, in a landscape dotted with the missions established by Junipero Serra, eighteenth-century Franciscan settlements that did not figure in my elementary school's textbooks, with their narratives of the westward expansion of a Protestant nation. Those material presences of a different Christianity on the west coast of North America invite us to consider how the history of the Reformation has been told, how the histories of the western hemisphere and of Christianity have been cast, and the implications of those histories for how we see ourselves today. Histories of Protestant triumph or the "westward expansion" of Anglophone churches speak from only one of many understandings of Christianity, one that was forged in the sixteenth century and itself claimed the triumph that now shapes so many of the histories we tell.

This book began with one invitation. In 2004, Bethel College invited me to give the Menno Simons Lectures. I am especially grateful to my host, Mark Jantzen, to Keith Sprunger and the other members of the Lecture Committee, and to the students of Bethel, who offered me a gentle and generous environment in which to begin rethinking how we have told the story of the Reformation. And it was realized in another. In 2008, Cambridge University Press invited me to write a short history of the Reformation. I am grateful to Beatrice Rehl, my editor, for the opportunity to think through what we have learned and to recast the narrative.

The Bibliography is at once an invitation to further reading and an introduction to some of the work that informs these pages. Steve Cantley, Erin Lambert, Robert D. Sack, Domenico Sella, and Lindsay Starkey have been the best of readers. My conversation with tms is older than this book and informs every page. Even more than for his willingness to read infinite drafts, I am grateful for his thinking and his acute listening.

This book, the history it seeks to tell, is for my students.

Introduction

In the Name of the
Father, Son, and Holy Spirit
The First Book
From the Arrival of Christ,
our savior and a fundament of the one true and
original
faith.

As I have undertaken to describe the history and the working of miracles in this present time, so shall I report the same in truth, and foremost what God the Almighty has done out of abundant grace and mercy for the proclamation of his healing Gospel, against the arrogant papacy whose power is solely human, and which many in our time call the Antichrist.

Johannes Kessler, *Sabbata*[1]

Thus begins one of the earliest efforts to tell the story of the Reformation. Johannes Kessler was born in 1502. The events he described occurred in his lifetime; many he witnessed himself. But he did not seek to narrate "what happened"; he did not see his task as to set some kind of pattern, some order, some meaning, to change that reached into every corner of human life in the sixteenth century. Kessler numbered among those who called themselves *evangelicals*: those who found in the printed and spoken text of the Bible the definitive authority for human life. For them,

---

[1] *Johannes Kesslers Sabbata*, edited by Emil Egli & Rudolf Schoch [Historischen Verein des Kantons St. Gallen] (St. Gall: Fehr'sche Buchhandlung, 1902), p. 18.

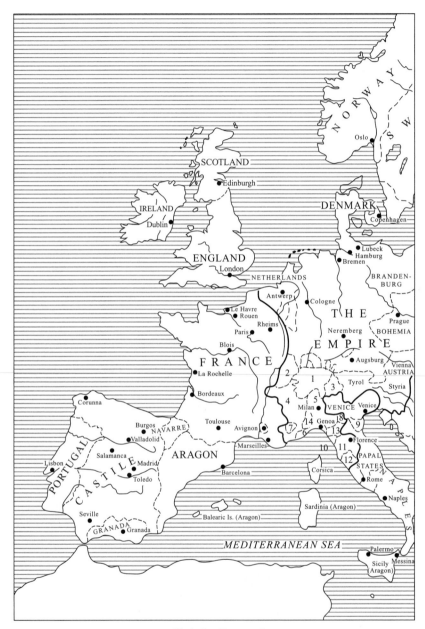

MAP I.1. Christian Europe in 1500.

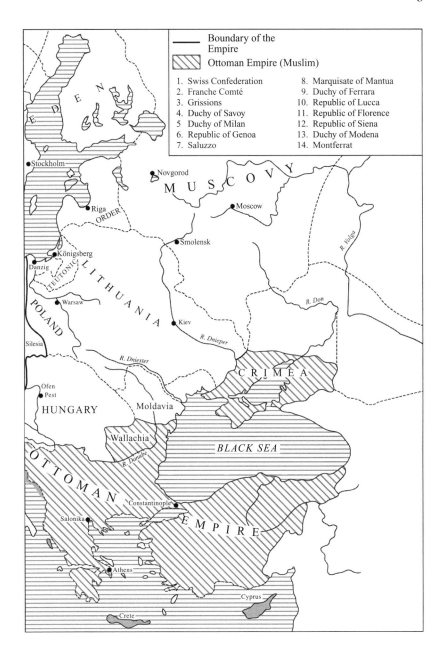

Boundary of the Empire

Ottoman Empire (Muslim)

1. Swiss Confederation
2. Franche Comté
3. Grissions
4. Duchy of Savoy
5. Duchy of Milan
6. Republic of Genoa
7. Saluzzo
8. Marquisate of Mantua
9. Duchy of Ferrara
10. Republic of Lucca
11. Republic of Florence
12. Republic of Siena
13. Duchy of Modena
14. Montferrat

the enterprise of writing history was to tell the story of God's revelation. For them, the story was one of not human choices or human acts, but divine design and divine agency.

Following his specific understanding of revelation, Kessler began his chronicle not with Adam or Moses, the Torah or Old Testament, but with Jesus Christ and the New Testament. He opened with a brief account of the person whose teachings and life had been the wellspring for any definition of "Christianity." Broadly, those who sought to "follow" Christ – the way he conducted his life, his parables and sermons, his commands – called themselves *Christians*. It was an ancient name, encompassing many different sorts of persons. By 1500, the overwhelming majority of Europeans called themselves Christians: Jews were a persecuted minority; Muslims an even smaller minority; no other religion had a discernible presence in Europe from the Atlantic coast to the expanding border of the Ottoman Empire.

For Kessler, the sixteenth century had its origins in the person of Christ, but there was no continuum from Christ's life to his own. From the life of Christ he turned to a brief "epitome" of Christianity in Europe from the first century to his own. He summarized the proliferation of offices, incomes, benefices, and practices such as fasting and pilgrimage – all of which he attributed to papal initiative. For Kessler, as for other early evangelical chroniclers, between the life of Christ and his own adulthood was a period of a turning away from Christ. In all those years, evangelicals held, Europeans who obeyed the Pope failed to conform their lives to the teachings of Christ as they were set down in the text of the Bible. For evangelicals such as Kessler, the Bible was the written record of God's will, now ever more accessible in the form a new technology made possible: the printed codex. Medieval Europeans, in failing to orient their lives to that text, were deviant – so Kessler and others constructed the story.

When Kessler turned to his own time, he framed it in terms of the revelation of God's will and design for humankind. The frame of revelation shaped the story that he and other evangelical chroniclers told. It defined their choices: which acts were meaningful, which not; which persons were significant, which not. This is how Kessler introduced Martin Luther:

> The landlord said, 'You are not [Hutten], but Martin Luther'. Then he laughed with such pleasure: 'They take me for Hutten, you, for Luther. I shall soon become Marcolf.' After such a speech, he raised a glass of beer and, speaking in the local idiom, said, 'You Swiss, let us share a friendly drink, in blessing.' And as I was to receive the glass from him, he changed the glass

and ordered a measure of wine for it, saying, 'This beer is strange to you and unfamiliar; drink the wine.' Then he stood up, threw his soldier's cloak over his shoulder, and took his leave, gave us his hand and said, 'When you get to Wittenberg, give my greetings to Dr. Hieronymus Schürpf.' We said, 'We will do it willingly, but what should we call you, that he will understand your greeting?' He said, 'Say no more than, "He that should come sends his greeting." He will understand you immediately.' Then he took his leave and went to bed.

Johannes Kessler, *Sabbata*[2]

So Kessler introduced a man he held to be an instrument of God's design, evoking Gospel accounts of Jesus. Luther shared that sense of himself, as a tool God had taken up in order to realize divine purposes, divine providence. Evangelicals shared a sense of human agency: Whatever change human beings effected, they effected not through any ability on their own part, but because God had chosen them as crude instruments of his will – no different from hammers or hoes. And those who were not God's instruments did not figure in the story: Their choices were unimportant, their actions no expression of divine design.

The frame of revelation also shaped evangelical conceptualizations of time itself. They divided their own time from that immediately preceding it, their own childhoods from what they witnessed as adults, sorting all of human history into four segments defined in terms of their relationship to revelation: the oldest, from Genesis to Anne, the mother of Mary, herself the mother of Christ, encompassing all time before Christ, as it was recorded in the Christian Old Testament; the second period, the time of Christ's life, of which the New Testament was the testimony; the third period, a time of deviance; and their own time, the last period. Those segments, moreover, divided into pairs that paralleled one another. The time before Christ was, like the millennium and a half after Christ, a time of laws and a plethora of practices. At two moments in human history, 1,500 years apart, God had chosen to make manifest his purposes for humankind: at the moment when God chose to become human; and Kessler's own lifetime, when God's Word – the Bible – once again circulated in material form, this time, not a physical person, but the object, the printed codex.

Not all sixteenth-century Christians construed the events of their lives in these terms. Those whom we now call Catholics quite consciously rejected such a sense of time, and, equally consciously, placed themselves in a tradition they saw as reaching in a continuum all the way back

---

[2] *Johannes Kesslers Sabbata*, p. 79.

to the life of Christ. For them, the time between Christ's life and their own was one not of a single note or of a rigidly enforced orthodoxy – both caricatures evangelicals circulated – but of multiple voices who formed a consensus over time. More importantly, for us, Catholics imagined a very different geography for the events of their lives. Whereas evangelicals focused geographically on those places where God's chosen instrument was to be seen and heard – Wittenberg, Zurich, Strasbourg, Geneva, London, Leiden – Catholics encompassed the globe in their thinking. For them, the "discovery" of "the New World" – themselves European perspectives – meant theaters in which God's glory might be demonstrated through the missionary work of their most devout.

Polemics and Reformation History

Sixteenth-century polemics abide to this day. Many still divide sixteenth-century Christians into two groups, Protestants and Catholics, using two terms that acquired their modern definition in the sixteenth century – the first did not exist before 1529; the second was an adjective, not a noun, prior to the sixteenth-century. Sixteenth-century characterizations have shaped how generations since have told the history of the Reformation. One of the most influential books of the twentieth century, Max Weber's *The Protestant Ethic and the Spirit of Capitalism* (1904/1922), took as one of its fundaments sixteenth-century Catholics' claim to traditional Christianity, a Christianity that reached all the way back to the life of Christ and his disciples – though sixteenth-century Catholics thought that a positive attribute and Weber, concerned with "modernity," found it a negative one, one of the key reasons why, he argued, capitalism could only arise from Protestantism.

Sixteenth-century evangelical chroniclers have shaped in more ways and more deeply how the history of the Reformation is told. If their Catholic contemporaries saw themselves in a continuum and evangelicals as breaking with the past, evangelicals severed their age structurally from its immediate past, a structure that abides in both textbooks and the organization of university courses on European history. There are good reasons, as I hope this book will show, why the division makes sense: The sixteenth century witnessed change that reached from the most intimate of relations to the most public, that redrew the map of Europe in a number of different ways, that altered the relationship between religious and civic authority, that changed what it meant to be "a Christian" – for evangelicals and Catholics. But their own sense, that their age was the antithesis of the age of their own childhoods, at once deforms the Christianity of their childhoods and distorts the Christianity of their own day.

Sixteenth-century evangelicals posited a single authority, the text of the Bible, for the definition of Christianity: If a *doctrine* – that which was taught – or a *praxis* – that which was rhythmically done – was not to be found in Scripture, then, for them, it was "not Christian." That definition of Christianity, as derived from a text and as defined by the canonical Bible, led them to cast their ancestors as biblically illiterate. And yet, as medievalists have shown, while the majority of medieval Christians probably could not read, that did not mean they were biblically illiterate: The walls, columns, chapels, and altars of their churches were filled with visualizations of Christ's life; sermons might take a moment in Christ's life or one of his sermons or parables as their focus; plays enacted moments in Christ's life. The Bible's relationship to medieval Christianity was complex, rich, and multiform.

Evangelicals' emphasis on the biblical text also distorts the Christianity of their own day. It shaped their story at many levels. For them, the text's internal conflicts, its mysteries, its puzzles resided not in the text, which was unified, but in the reader. For them, the text was not vulnerable to multiple readings.[3] For them, there was no diversity of readers – of different experiences, expectations, understandings brought to bear on the words of the Bible. For them, there was God's Word, which was understood or not – an insistent bipolarity running through their debates on so many questions. So many evangelicals, including Luther, claimed that the Bible was self-evident, its meaning, in his word, "clear," and yet, individual evangelicals read that text in ways that divided them not only from Catholics, but from each other. Their sense of the Bible, as a coherent unity of self-evident meaning, continues to shape the history of the Reformation. It led them and later historians to characterize different understandings as "misunderstandings" – though the century is replete with testimonies of the text's multivalencies, ambiguities, elusiveness, and evocative power. It led them to deny the sheer protean power of the text to inspire diverse visions of true Christianity and the multiplicity of positions each of which is rooted in the text. And it obscured the different understandings of the person of Christ evangelicals brought to bear on that text.

[3] Thomas M. Green, *The Vulnerable Text: Essays on Renaissance Literature* (New York: Columbia University Press, 1986).

Sixteenth-century evangelicals' emphasis on the printed codex of the Bible as the physical location where humankind should look to find God drew attention away from one of the bitterest battles of the sixteenth century: the nature, import, and implications of the *Incarnation*. The Incarnation is what sets Christianity apart from Judaism and Islam. For Christians, the Incarnation is when the monotheistic God of Judaism who had been such a jealous God chose to become human, Jesus Christ, in the words of the Apostles' Creed – a text that both evangelicals and Catholics trusted:

> conceived of the Holy Spirit, born of the Virgin Mary, suffered under Pontius Pilate, was crucified, died, and was buried; he descended into hell. On the third day he rose from the dead; he ascended into heaven, sits at the right hand of God the Father Almighty.[4]

As we shall see, for medieval Christians the Incarnation invited both representation and *mimesis*: the conscious effort on the part of many different Christians to bring the living of their lives into an enactment of something they saw in Christ's – his poverty, his suffering, his humility, his itinerancy. In the sixteenth century, European Christians divided on what it meant for God to be born, to suffer, to die, and to be resurrected. Perhaps the most difficult concept of all, God-become-man, the Incarnation called into question, powerfully in the sixteenth century, what exactly was it, to be "divine"? What exactly was it, to be "human"?

Sixteenth-century Christians had grown up in a world filled with representations of Christ, the Son of God: as infant in his mother's arms or lap; as child in a temple; as young man preaching; as teacher surrounded by his disciples; most often, as a body broken and bleeding on a cross, executed in the Roman practice of crucifixion – literally executed on a cross. As evangelicals turned to that text they held to be the materialization of God's will, as we shall see in their debates, their understanding of Christ's person was not restricted to what the text said. It could not be: The text itself was filled with mysteries and puzzles that, in turn, eluded consensus or a single unifying reading.

Sixteenth-century evangelicals' emphasis upon the biblical text also obscures the importance evangelicals themselves accorded *praxis* – the regular and consistent enactments, using their own bodies, of their faith.

---

[4] *Creeds and Confessions of Faith in the Christian Tradition*, edited by Jaroslav Pelikan and Valerie Hotchkiss, vol. I: Early, Eastern, & Medieval (New Haven: Yale University Press, 2003), p. 669.

The emphasis on the biblical text called attention away from the physicality of the Reformation and the many different ways that Reformation implicated human bodies: All bodies in the institutionalization of the Ten Commandments; women's and children's bodies in the formation of Christian families; the body of each faithful Christian in the moment of communion, when he or she took a piece of bread, a sip of wine, and, in that moment, came closest to God – physically as well as spiritually. It silences the preaching from street corners as well as pulpits, the singing in workshops as well as churches. And it obscures the violence.

According to the testimonies and memoires of those who lived through it, violence of many different forms ran through the sixteenth century. For many, it felt a time of extraordinary and exceptionally volatile violence. Indeed, it could be argued that the sixteenth century and the twentieth had far more in common than not – something of that thinking informs the chapters that follow. Mothers reported daughters to authorities who in turn executed those daughters for *heresy* – a word whose violence may be harder to hear today than then. Heresy, from an ancient Greek word, means a kind of stepping away from a path; formally, in relationship to the doctrine of a Church, it means a stepping away from orthodoxy – that which is the straight path. In the sixteenth century, for thousands of European Christians, the word heresy had as its consequence their arrest, their torture, their execution or exile. It was a word of corporeal consequences. Rulers executed subjects for the crimes of heresy and blasphemy – the assault on God or Christian practices or doctrine; Catholic rulers, their subjects for iconoclasm, the destruction of images. Neighbors stabbed, bludgeoned, burned in their houses, neighbors. The concept of "heretic," that person who deviated from the true path, led not simply to legal violence, but to the most personal and intimate: mothers and daughters, husbands and wives, neighbors and co-workers. "Heretic" is a question of perspective: For Catholics, all evangelicals were heretics; for evangelicals, not only all Catholics, but other kinds of evangelicals were heretics. And for each, that perspective authorized violence, whether the violence of legally constituted authority or the violence of person against person.

Towards a New History of the Reformation

Even as sixteenth-century polemics continue to shape narratives, an extraordinary flowering of archival research in the years since the Second World War has increasingly revealed the distortions of the polemics.

Studies of lived Christianity, social relations, forms of political authority, and its jurisdictions have brought new voices, new perspectives into
the story. Close studies of a number of evangelicals have revealed their
interconnections and dialogues with one another, as well as defining
more precisely where they divided. George Hunston Williams, in seeking
to document the many different "sects" of what he called "The Radical
Reformation," delineated dozens of different understandings of Christianity that were all evangelical.[5] John O'Malley has argued for a notion
of early modern Catholicism, which, in turn, another body of scholarship
has shown to have been vibrant and multiform.[6] Interdisciplinary work
on devotional images has revealed their complex role in late medieval
Christian life – different models of human cognition, different conceptualizations of representation, a deeply different sense of the image than
we have today. Utterly different worlds have come to light.

This book, then, seeks to do two things. It seeks to craft a new narrative
of the Reformation that integrates what we have learned. And it seeks to
narrate a history in which no one position defines the positions of others –
free of polemics and its conceptual consequences. As such, it is a history
neither Catholic nor Protestant. So, too, readers will find no traces of
divine design – this history is firmly and exclusively a human history of the
Reformation. It narrates human choices and human actions, intended
and unintended consequences.

This is a history of Christianity as European Christians redefined it in
the sixteenth century and the consequences of that redefinition for all
aspects of their lives. In 1500, Christianity was not a "belief." We have
no evidence of what the great majority of European Christians thought:
Their voices are largely mute. But that evangelical sense of Christianity
as defined by a text denies the Christianity that surrounded them – the
architecture, the temporal rhythms, the enactments of many different
kinds, the objects, and all the different ways that persons might manifest
Christianity: in the dress of monks and nuns, in the acts of flagellants
and pilgrims, in plays and gestures that sought to imitate the person of
Christ. Christianity was not a statement in 1500; it was a world.

In holding Scripture the sole authority to define what Christianity
was, evangelicals called that world into question. No aspect of human

---

[5] George Hunston Williams, *The Radical Reformation* (Philadelphia: Westminster Press,
1962), Third Edition (Kirksville: Truman State University Press, 2000).
[6] John O'Malley, *Trent and All That: Renaming Catholicism in the Early Modern Era*
(Cambridge, MA: Harvard University Press, 2000).

life went unexamined. None was untouched. Little remained unaltered. The violence that evangelical and Catholic chroniclers construed within the frame of a divine drama erupted in every area where that test of Scripture called for change. The violence is, among other things, a dramatic signal that Christians did not agree; they did not divide into two cleanly defined groups; they did not form stable or definable groups until well into the second half of the century. For more than fifty years, every aspect of human life was called into question: the relationship of birth to Christian identity, the age of adulthood, marriage, family, political authority, the relationship between the home and the place of worship, charity, sexual relations, ethics, work, and human creativity.

The story begins not in 1517, the date that Martin Luther posted ninety-five theses for debate on the door of the ducal church in the small town of Wittenberg. It begins with late medieval Christianity, the ways in which it inscribed the landscape of Europe, dominated that landscape visually and spatially, organized time for all Europeans – Christians and Jews – through the ringing of church bells to mark liturgical time, and was visible in objects, structures, and persons everywhere, from the most remote crossing to the largest cities. So, too, it begins with what we shall call the Encounter, when Europeans first discovered that the world was a third again as large as they had held it to be, that the world encompassed continents, in the plural, that their classical authorities had not known, and peoples, innumerable, they could not even have imagined. Columbus first set foot on an unknown island in the westernmost reaches of the Atlantic in 1492; Europe grappled with the implications of that "discovery" during the same years as evangelicals were casting Scripture as the sole authority for Christian lives. And the story begins with a technology, printing, that made it possible for evangelicals to imagine a text might ground each Christian's understanding of Christianity, with material objects that engendered new kinds of reading, new kinds of preaching, and a portable site from which one could determine, what was Christian, what not.

It is a story of fragmentation. The world of Kessler's childhood was indeed lost to him. That same world was lost to his Catholic contemporaries. Christianity had been dominant in medieval Europe. The same year that Columbus set sail, his patrons, the Catholic monarchs of Spain, completed what they called "the Reconquista," the reconquest of the Iberian peninsula; by that, they meant that they had conquered the last lands held by Muslim rulers. Those lands had been home to Muslims, Jews, and Christians. Within six months of conquering Granada, Isabel

Of Castile and Ferdinand II of Aragon called for the forced conversion or expulsion of all Jews; nine years later, Muslims faced the same choice. In 1500, European Christians looked across a landscape that was ever more emphatically Christian: Entire domains had expelled Jews – England, France, parts of the Holy Roman Empire, Spain. Within twenty years, peoples of the western hemisphere and printed Bibles were leading Europeans to ask, what is it to be "Christian"?

Their answers did not simply divide theologians or even preachers. Their answers, as the mothers' betrayals testify, divided European from European intimately, viscerally, deeply. Their answers divided families: husbands and wives, parents and children, siblings. They divided subjects, vassals, and lords. They overthrew a delicate balance of competing claims of jurisdiction between the medieval Church and different rulers, including the Catholic monarchs of Spain, and divided the political landscape of Europe as it had not been divided before. Those answers led to thousands of deaths and tens of thousands of exiles. By the time European Christians had formed stable groups, what we shall call Churches, the world of medieval Christianity was gone. While universal Christendom had always been a myth, it was a powerful myth, one that Isabel and Ferdinand believed, one that Columbus believed. By 1600, it was gone. The name "Christian" would never again signal something obviously shared.

And amid that fragmentation, European Christians rethought what it meant to be a Christian, what a Christian place of worship should look like, what the relationship between things made by human hands and worship was to be, and how God was to be present in a world in which his presence was no longer taken for granted, in a world in which God might be absent in this place, in this community, in that place, among those Europeans. "Religion" changed in its meaning in the sixteenth century. In medieval Europe, laws formally recognized "the Christian religion" and "the Jewish religion." In 1555, in a transient peace, the parties legally recognized two forms of Christianity; it was the first time since the western church had split from the eastern in the eighth century. Within western Europe, it was the first time that two forms of Christianity were legally recognized. Until then, there had been Christianity and heretics, Christianity and Judaism – in each case, an opposition. The transformation this book seeks to trace is not a "return" to an earlier Christianity, but the emergence of an understanding of Christianity, among all European Christians, as something spoken, as something one believed and expressed from that belief, no longer residing in buildings or objects, bells or crucifixes, but within persons – something they said, which in turn shaped conduct.

Faith

In the shadow of the twentieth century, it is easier to view sixteenth-century violence as one of many ways persons gave expression to faith. Faith is a difficult concept in the modern world. It is treated with hostility by those such as Richard Dawkins or Christopher Hitchens, who hold it to be irrational – following the Enlightenment assault on religion, which one of its core texts, the *Encyclopedié*, equated with "superstition." For them, faith is emotional, something that unthinking persons "hold," like an idea, in order to explain a confusing world.

For others, whom we now call "fundamentalists," faith is the foundation of all knowledge. For them, it is an orientation, from which one looks out at the world. In ways that echo sixteenth-century evangelicals and Catholics, faith gives them certainty: certain knowledge, not just of their God's existence, but of his will, his intent, his commands for all humankind. And in ways that also echo that earlier century, it organizes their world, sorting humankind between those who "share" that faith and those who do not.

The word names different things for different people. A witness to sixteenth-century violence, Michel de Montaigne (1533–1592) offers a definition particularly useful when we approach the sixteenth century. In what he called an "essay," a kind of foray – in explicit opposition to the diatribes of his age – "The Apology for Raymond Sebond," he presented a critique of the claim, so rampant among his contemporaries, to "know God," as they said, the claim to know what God (as they defined that God's person, power, and agency in the world) intended, what God willed, and with that, to authorize their own violence against those who did not see the world as they did. But Montaigne did not call for atheism as the response to that claim for certainty. At the very end of the essay, he posits that the knowledge of God is in its fundaments different from any other kind of knowledge. For Montaigne, God existed, but human knowledge of God, he argued, was located in unique beings – no two of whom were identical. That knowledge could and should not become normative. Though as real as any experience a human being might have, each person's knowledge of God, he argued, was shaped by that person's essential individuality. No two human beings, for Montaigne, knew God in quite the same way.

That spirit informs this book: at once a recognition of the possibility that human beings know God and a rejection of the claim that any individual's knowledge of God is exclusive or definitive. Indeed, the word "God" connoted many different attributes, different natures to different Christians in the sixteenth century; in this book, the word connotes what all held in common: a person who was eternal, immortal, ineffable, and, in their own term, "uncircumscribable." In this book, faith is a human experience, and, as such, various: different persons' understanding of their God's presence in their lives. Faith took many, many different forms in the sixteenth century, from the cloistered passion of Teresa of Ávila to the violence of Uli Anders, a Swiss peasant who smashed a crucifix and paid for it with his life. The history of the Reformation that follows is both Teresa's and Uli Anders', as each grappled with the question, what does it mean to be a Christian? It is a study not only in the agony of human difference but also of its protean power.

PART I

BEGINNINGS

1

Christianity in 1500

On January 2, 1492, Queen Isabel of Castile and King Ferdinand II of Aragon entered the ancient city of Granada. For them, it marked the completion of the "Reconquest": to bring all of the Iberian peninsula under Christian rule, a meaning affirmed in the title, "Los Reyes Católicos" or "The Catholic Kings," Pope Alexander VI bestowed on them in 1494. They moved quickly to make Granada "Christian." In the Edict of Expulsion, of March 31, 1492, Isabel and Ferdinand gave all Jews in all their dominions and possessions – which subsequently would come to include vast stretches of the western hemisphere – until July 31, four months, to convert or to be expelled from all their lands. In 1499, Cardinal Francisco Ximenes de Cisneros began the forced conversion of the Muslims of Granada. In 1501, "The Catholic Kings" offered the Muslims of Granada much the same choice as they had offered Jews in 1492.

But what did it mean, to be "Christian" in the year 1500? Within the Iberian peninsula, it meant, as much as anything else, that one was not Jewish or Muslim – one did not publicly or, increasingly, within the walls of one's own home, observe the dietary laws, forms of dress, practices of prayer and reading sacred texts, or rituals of Judaism or Islam. To be "Christian" in 1500 required no knowledge of the Bible, the Church Fathers, or decrees of church councils or popes. To be Christian in the year 1500, as Isabel and Ferdinand's edicts make clear, meant that one belonged to a legally constituted majority, which encompassed both popes and peasants, monks and merchants, the most devout of religious women and the most cynical of courtiers. In fact, in 1500, to be Christian was relatively simple: One had to be baptized. To be a Christian in good standing in the eyes of the Church, one was also required to confess, do penance, and take communion once a year. Nothing more.

The forced conversions offer important insights into what Europeans understood "Christian" to be in the year 1500. Ferdinand and Isabel gave Jews four months "to convert." Here was no careful process of learning theology, no measured inculcation of creed, no catechesis of any kind, but the notion that one could go from one religion to another abruptly, without preparation, without consideration, and that that "conversion" would be durable. Europeans learned otherwise over the course of the sixteenth century, as earlier forced conversions proved deeply problematic, generating an ever greater sense of clandestine or hidden religious belief, a belief that could no longer be seen in dress, praxis, or collective rituals, but remained hidden beneath a façade of conformity. But in 1500, rulers such as Isabel and Ferdinand held that being Christian was a relatively simple thing.

Perhaps they believed it because so much of European life was Christian: from a geography inscribed as parishes and dioceses and dotted with pilgrimage sites, such as Santiago Compostella in the Iberian peninsula, through urban landscapes dominated by churches, usually both the largest and the tallest building in a town, to the measurement of time – the tolling of liturgical hours, the colors of liturgical seasons, a week set to Sunday rather than Friday or Saturday. They were not creating Christians, in that sense of portable individual identities, but forcing a minority into the culture of the majority: its spatial organization, its temporal rhythms, its understanding of person and community.

In 1500, Europe was Christian physically, geographically, spatially, in its organization of time, work, and family. Over the course of the sixteenth century, each would be called into question, rethought, overthrown by some, abandoned by others, reinstituted by still others. Let us, then, begin with how Europe was Christian in the year 1500.

Boundaries

Queen Isabel and King Ferdinand belonged to a tradition reaching back at least to Charlemagne in the eighth century. That tradition equated the expansion of Christianity with the extension of the boundaries of a kingdom. It claimed the right over all the peoples within a domain to force conformity with the religious majority and to execute or expel those who did not conform. The intertwining of the boundaries of secular sovereigns' jurisdiction with Christianity reached its apex in the sixteenth century. But it had shaped all Europeans' lives for more than seven hundred years.

It had shaped how Europeans approached religious difference. Christians, such as the Albigensians in France or the Lollards in England, whose understanding of Christianity diverged from that of the majority, may have been accused before and prosecuted in ecclesiastical courts, that is, courts of the Church, but they were executed by secular authorities. By 1500, heresy and treason had become intertwined both in law and in practice. So, too, sovereigns had long claimed the right to expel from their jurisdiction religious minorities, most spectacularly Jews – wealthy merchants and poor peasants, men, women and children, all of whom were collected under the rubric, "the Jewish religion." Edward I of England had expelled all Jews from his kingdom in 1290; Kings of France, definitively in 1394; and within the crazy quilt of jurisdictions in the Empire, the rulers of Austria, Bavaria, Franconia, and Swabia as well as a number of cities expelled Jews from within their borders. In 1516, the Venetian government instituted the first ghetto in Europe; in 1555, in the papal bull, *Cum nimis absurdum,* Pope Paul IV called for all Jews in Rome to be gathered in a single area, which would become the Jewish ghetto in Rome. The rest of each city was open to all those who had solely in common that legal designation, "Christian."

Within the boundaries of the domains of the kings of England from 1290, of France from 1394, and of Castile and Aragon from 1501, all subjects were to be "Christian." In these lands, "Christendom" was coterminous with the monarch's sovereignty. In the Empire, a patchwork of jurisdictions led in places such as Austria to destruction of the Jews, in other places to expulsion, in still other places to the articulation of clear legal boundaries, dividing "Christians" from "Jews" in terms of legal rights and economic and social privileges. Nowhere in Europe was religion autonomous from political jurisdiction. Even in those places where Jews were not expelled, governments divided subject populations according to broad categories, the "Christian and Jewish religions."

The Geography of Christendom

In 1501, with Jews and Muslims expelled, Granada was organized spatially in ways familiar to Christians across Europe: It was divided into parishes. Parishes were the local level of administration for "*the Church*" – a term that referred both to a hierarchy of authority with its apex in the office of the Pope, the most articulated bureaucracy in Europe, with its headquarters in Rome; as well as to all its members, Christians in good standing. From the perspective of both the hierarchy of authority and the bureaucracy, the *parish* was a geographic entity, at the center of which was a building, also called a *church* – in this book distinguished by small-case "c" – some rudimentary, many simple, some large and elaborate. Those Christians who lived within its boundaries were under the immediate care and jurisdiction of the priest assigned to that parish. It was his responsibility to celebrate the Mass, hear confession, assign penance, and offer communion to his parishioners. It was also his responsibility to address the moral transgressions of the parishioners – adultery, envy, violence against kin or neighbor – to investigate accusations, to allocate blame, to assign compensation where a victim was involved and to impose penance for the transgressor.

In 1500, boundaries of parishes were neither so fixed as they would come to be nor so solid. Town dwellers in particular might go to a church in another part of the town to hear an exceptional preacher, such as Savonarola in Florence or Geiler von Kaisersberg in Strasbourg. And in much of Europe, parishes were not yet centers of record keeping, as they were in England. Parish priests differed widely, from local sons, who might never have learned Latin, the language of the Mass, to men of exceptional learning, such as Leo Jud in Zurich, who read Greek and Hebrew as well as Latin. The character of parishes differed: Whereas remote rural parishes might see their priest but once a month, urban parish churches, by 1500, were usually staffed with deacons, assistants, and priests, a number of whom, increasingly, had as their sole responsibility celebrating Masses for the dead.

Even as parishes were variegated, some more porous, some isolated, they were the most meaningful spatial unit of Christendom for the majority of European Christians by the end of the fifteenth century. Most Europeans' knowledge of "the Church" was through the person of their priest and within the parameters of their parish. They worshiped in their parish church, confessed to and received communion from their parish priest, were baptized, married, and buried within their parish and by their parish priest. The dangers of travel, the demands of work, and the instabilities of communication together meant that most European Christians were baptized, confirmed, married, and buried in the same parish.

If most European Christians experienced Christianity within their parishes, for the Church hierarchy of authority, the *diocese* – the most ancient geographic unit of Christendom – was the most important. The church of the diocese was called the *cathedral*, that is, the "cathedra" or seat of the *bishop*. As the *episcopal* (the bishop's) seat, each diocese encompassed multiple parishes. The bishop was the point of connection between the papal court in Rome and ordinary Christians. He was responsible for the supervision of parishes – both the conduct of their priest and the practice of their Christianity, individual and collective – a responsibility the Council of Trent moved to strengthen. So, too, the bishop in each diocese was to promulgate and enforce papal bulls and the decrees of councils. The bishop ordained priests for each parish under his jurisdiction. In medieval Europe, the bishop might also promulgate and disseminate within his diocese his own *missal*, the text for the celebration of the Mass, for each Mass throughout the year – an authority the Council of Trent would rescind in 1564.

By 1500, two different sorts of jurisdiction had been inscribed across the landscape of Europe, the one "temporal" or "secular" – that is, of this world – the other "spiritual" or, as we shall call it, "ecclesiastical": the jurisdiction of the Church. Of the two, the ecclesiastical was more complete and defined in 1500. By the sixth century, the Bishop of Rome had won the right to call himself "Pope," and with that, to claim preeminent authority over the Church. By 1500, the pope, who resided in Rome, was recognized as the head of western Christendom. The nature of his jurisdiction over western European Christians, no matter how far they might live from Rome, was disputed; the fact of his jurisdiction was not.

The pope was elected to his office. Certain Italian families tended to be elected more often than others, and Italians tended to be elected almost exclusively; nonetheless, blood did not determine who was to be pope. Unlike monarchs throughout Europe, whose authority was dynastic, received through bloodlines, the pope's authority resided in the office: Whoever was pope was head of all Christendom. Different popes construed their authority differently, from Boniface VIII's claims of universal sovereignty in the fourteenth century, to the humility of Adrian VI in the sixteenth. In the sixteenth century, different popes were differently taken up with those lands, known as the Papal States, over which originally the Carolingian rulers Pepin and Charlemagne had granted popes full sovereignty. Machiavelli detailed Alexander VI's ruthless pursuit of the expansion of the boundaries of the Papal States, while Erasmus remarked on Julius II's use of war to reassert papal sovereignty over those states. For the popes of the early sixteenth century, excepting Adrian, their office comprised both the more abstract jurisdiction over universal Christendom and the more immediate jurisdiction over lands in the Italian peninsula.

At the center of both those jurisdictions was the city of Rome. In 1500, Rome was the most sophisticated city in Europe. Within a few years, "sophistication" would designate for many European Christians a negative value, but in 1500 it still conveyed attributes that elevated Rome above all other cities. By 1500, Rome had become the administrative hub of the most extensive bureaucracy in Europe, encompassing thousands of souls across hundreds of miles of different monarchies, principalities, and townships, who spoke more than a dozen different languages. With Columbus's landing in the western hemisphere, Rome became the first global capital, where, over the course of the sixteenth century, Jesuits from China and Goa and Franciscans from New Spain would report what they were learning of places unimagined a century before.

As the center of an administration that reached into the farthest corners of Europe, the most remote villages, and across the Atlantic and Indian Oceans, Rome was a magnet for talent: Greek scholars such as George of Trebizond, Latinists such as Pietro Bembo, as well as the polymaths Michelangelo, Gian Lorenzo Bernini, and Galileo. Some of that talent was, in the eyes of contemporaries, questionable in its "piety" – Bembo or Bernini, for example – and yet, Pope Leo X, the head of all Christendom from 1513 to his death in 1521, called Bembo, as well as another gifted Latinist, Jacopo Sadoleto, and the poet, Bernardo Accolti, to serve as papal secretaries and place their talents in service to how the papal court expressed itself. The Basilica of Saint Peter, the most famous and influential Christian church in the west, received its monumental scale, the cadences of its walls, and its dome from Michelangelo and, from the artist whose piety is most suspect, Bernini, not only the colonnades that reach out to all Christendom, but the baldachin over the high altar. Each Christian who visits Saint Peter's Basilica sees the work of Bernini and Michelangelo; thousands, by their own testimonies, have found that work wondrous, commanding exactly the piety denied to its creators.

In 1500, the Basilica that now dominates the Christian portion of Rome did not yet exist. Rome was, nonetheless, a city of wonders. In part, its wonder lay in the singular density of history within its walls. The Colosseum, the Pantheon, as well as obelisks, columns, porticos, and mosaics marked the former capital of an empire sixteenth-century monarchs sought to emulate, even as popes supported the collection of its "antiquities": pieces of architecture, sculpture, glass, jewelry – the material remains of everyday life. Only the Holy Land exceeded Rome in the density of sites meaningful to western European Christians: ancient churches, sites of martyrdom, paths of discipleship, relics – the material remains of holy lives. For all Christian pilgrims, the city contained within

its walls the history of Christianity: wondrous relics from the time of
the apostles – pieces of the true cross; the remains of Peter and Paul;
streets that Peter and Paul had walked; churches marking sites of early
martyrdoms; layer upon layer of material reminders of events, persons,
and pious lives that constituted "Christianity" in 1500. In one place, the
devout could walk where apostles had walked, touch the physical remains
of dozens of individuals who had embodied extraordinary piety, and visit
the seven churches that together gave the pilgrim forgiveness.

Architecture

In Rome, churches formed sites for pilgrims, from Saint Peter's, where
the relics of the apostle Peter were entombed, to San Lorenzo, built
over the catacombs where the Christian martyr Laurence's remains were
buried, to Santa Croce in Gerusalemme, where pilgrims might view a
piece of the true cross. Across Europe, church spires were usually the
first sight travelers had of a village or town, built to rise dramatically
above the towers of fortifications and civic government. As in Rome,
the spires marked for Christians a place of an exceptional density of
meaning: a locus for worship; a site where relics could be seen, touched,
contemplated; and a place where any Christian might reenact important
moments in Christ's life.

Long before 1500, the interior spaces of churches had come to be
differentiated from the world outside. Insofar as it was possible, churches
were built on a west-east axis, "orienting" – literally directing eastwards,

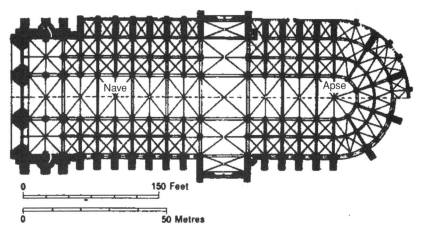

FIGURE 1.1. Floor Plan of Notre Dame, Paris.

towards Jerusalem – the faithful. Through a formal ritual, the local bishop consecrated the space of the church to the worship of God. Following that ritual, the space within the walls was qualitatively different from the space outside. The primary entrance into churches was usually on the western end; the faithful moved from "the world outside" into consecrated space, facing towards the eastern end of a church, where the greatest density of meaning was to be found.

Unlike modern construction, medieval churches were built in close collaboration among theologians, architects, and craftsmen, as well as between clergy and laity. Architects, such as Villard de Honnecourt, brought their technical expertise, and theologians, such as the Abbé Suger, participated actively in the design. Thus, churches presented to European Christians multiple layers of meaning. Even the simplest rural church had a "portal" – marking a particular sense of the boundary between the "outside world" and the sanctuary inside the walls, that consecrated space. The importance of that sense is visible in churches in the Swiss Alps, along fjords in Norway, and in the French countryside, where one often finds over the western portal a tympanum depicting Christ in Judgment: at times alone, at times surrounded by his apostles, dividing the souls of the dead between heaven and hell.

By 1500, churches were visually denser and more complex than any other structures in Europe. Cathedrals presented the greatest density of images on their exteriors. In addition to tympana, the portals might be populated with figures of saints, virgins, apostles, prophets, and Old Testament Kings; depending on the wealth of the church, sculpted figures of saints, apostles or kings might also fill niches in the buttressing of the walls. On walls, in niches, surrounding portals, along rooflines, European Christians could see individuals whose lives embodied in various ways the sanctity that the Church taught.

In crossing the threshold, the devout entered a sacred space to which different theologians had given different metaphors: a ship of souls, the body of Christ, the cross. Even as they demarcated a boundary between consecrated and profane space, the walls also confounded any absolute division between "secular" or "this world," the world of commerce and politics, and consecrated space. Even in the poorest churches, which could afford no glass, let alone stained glass, the stone walls were pierced by openings. Even in the poorest churches, one encountered the interplay of materiality and light, of enclosure and illumination. Wealthier churches commissioned stained-glass windows to cover those openings. Artisans crafted images illumined and illuminating: As light shone through them, viewers could see simultaneously the narratives and figures they represented in blue, red, yellow, and green glass, in black line and leading, and the patterning of that light on the floor of the church. As they entered such a church, they entered a space lit like no other – neither civic building nor workshop nor home – illumined, according to the Abbé Suger in the twelfth century, with mystical light.

Within each church was spatially articulated the fundamental division of Christendom, of the *laity*, the great majority of Christians, from *clergy* – those whose dress distinguished them "from the world" as having taken vows, for most, of chastity, obedience, and poverty. By 1500, poor rural churches might have retained their ancient and simple rectangular plan, but most urban churches were organized on a cruciform plan, in which space was divided into a nave in the western end, a transept or crossing, and an apse at the easternmost end of the church. The great majority of European Christians – the laity – were restricted to the nave, the ship of the church, which was separated from the apse by the transept. In the nave, one might find the most devout of goldsmiths and the most skeptical of peasants. By 1500, in many communities, the nave itself had become liminal – not fully "spiritual," used exclusively for worship, but neither fully "secular," that is, belonging to the world of markets and politics. Christians might conduct their business in the nave, discuss local politics, gossip. But as Christians approached the altar, they moved from the world of exchange to a site of extraordinary density of meaning. By 1500, the apse or choir was restricted to the clergy and, in many churches, was distinguished visually and physically from the rest of the space of the church by a choir screen.

Images

Reformation, revolutions, and world wars have altered or destroyed thousands of churches from Scotland to Marseille, from Warsaw to Bordeaux – during Reformation and revolutions, it was precisely the density of meaning within the walls that drew the violence that was directed against images and altars. As with windows, so, too, with images, churches varied widely. The poorest churches might have murals painted on their walls, a crucifix on or above their sole altar, perhaps a carved altarpiece over that altar, though churches for the poorest Christians could not themselves afford an object of such skill and work. So, too, did individual images differ from church to church: While many churches were dedicated to Mary or to the cross, different churches had different patron saints – local

FIGURE 1.2. Pieter Neefs the Elder, Church interior. Musée des Beaux Arts, Valenciennes, France. Photo credit: Giraudon / Art Resource, New York.

or major, apostle or martyr – and those dedications informed many of the images donated or commissioned for a church.

By 1500, churches in towns and cloisters were rich in imagery of many different kinds. The Cathedral of Our Lady in Strasbourg, for example, the seat of the bishop, or episcopal see, in a medium-sized town in the borderlands between France and the Holy Roman Empire, had more than forty altars, including a high altar behind one choir screen, another set into a choir screen at the entrance to the nave, and one in the Chapel of the Holy Cross – each one of which seems to have had its own altarpiece or retable, a large folding image above the altar. The altar dedicated to Mary, in its own chapel dedicated to her, had a particularly beautiful and skillfully crafted retable atop it. Like other churches Charlemagne had favored, the Cathedral possessed an enormous cross – according to some, of gold, to others, of silver – which disappeared in the 1520s. The Cathedral also possessed a life-sized, three-dimensional Garden of Gethsemane, where Christ prayed as his apostles slept the night before he was crucified. The parish church of Saint Lawrence in the commercial center of Nuremberg had fewer altars than a cathedral, but benefitted in many different ways from the church's location in one of the great centers of artistic production in the Empire. On the north side of the apse was the twenty-meter-tall stone tabernacle Adam Kraft had designed and carved, a singular creation. Tabernacles held consecrated *hosts* – the thin wafers of wheat and water used in the Mass – that had not been consumed. Most tabernacles were a quarter its size. This one, supported on the backs of four carved artisans, included figures of apostles and a sculpted image of the Last Supper, as well as delicate tracery work. In 1516–20, Veit Stoss carved and painted a life-sized wooden crucifix that still hangs above the main altar, with the wounded and bleeding Christ directly above the site of the eucharist. In 1517–18, the patrician Anton Tucher commissioned, also from Stoss, an extraordinary wooden Annunciation, some three meters in diameter, which hangs in the apse. In 1521, the Imhoff family commissioned an altar and altarpiece dedicated to John the Apostle, which incorporated an earlier image of the Last Supper into its predella. These families, as well as guilds and other corporations, had also commissioned individual stained-glass windows, as well as other altarpieces, panel paintings, sculpted figures and their niches, and murals.

Each urban or cloister church was likely, by 1500, to have certain things. Moving from the west portal to the apse, one found, at the entrance, a basin to hold holy water, water the priest had consecrated, which Christians used to cross themselves upon entry. Standing just inside the entry, one could see multiple altars, many – perhaps all – of which would have an altarpiece or retable on them; panel paintings hung along the walls and on columns in the nave; murals on some of the walls; often, a larger-than-life mural of Saint Christopher with the infant Christ on his back. A baptismal font, usually of stone, could normally be found to the side of the main altar. In many churches, a life-sized crucifix hung over the main or high altar. Choir stalls for the clergy attached to the church who sang parts of the Mass lined the inside of the apse. Most churches also had objects that were brought out for specific occasions: a missal, a book, frequently bound in a gilded cover with semi-precious stones embedded in it, read in each Mass; a monstrance for carrying the host in Corpus Christi processions; reliquaries, each of which might be carried in a procession on the day of its saint; as well as the vestments of the clergy, which changed with the liturgical season and were as elaborately stitched as the church's wealth permitted.

Images did not "represent" in our modern sense of the term. Their relationship to the devotional life of European Christians was more complex; their relationship to the space more dynamic than a modern museum.

It is more accurate to say, they participated in a complex visual culture encompassing panel paintings, stone figures, silver *reliquaries* – containers shaped variously to hold the *relics*, the physical remains, such as bones, hair, or clothes, of holy persons – as well as processions, plays, and other kinds of performances. Like the Cathedrals of Paris, Strasbourg, Chartres, or Lübeck, for instance, the Cathedral of Tournai was dedicated to the Virgin. In 1089, the Cathedral became a refuge for people fleeing a plague. In 1090, the bishop led a procession around the Cathedral to honor the Virgin for protecting her people. In 1205, relics of the Virgin were housed in a beautiful new reliquary Nicholas of Verdun designed and crafted in gold. In 1566, the relics were removed and destroyed. But the reliquary remains, as does the procession, which is still held every year in the Cathedral.

Throughout Europe, bishops in cathedrals and priests in parish churches led processions honoring a saint or Mary who had intervened at one or more moments in the life of the place, whose "presence" was active, palpable, and remembered. The church might house relics of that saint or Mary, which would then be carried in the procession. Given the particular relationship of Mary or saint to the community, the church was also very likely to house at least one image of that patron, possibly more, which rendered in stone or marble or pigment events in that life that made it especially holy. For Mary, the moments increased in number as her life became the focus of more intense devotion: her birth and mother, her childhood, the Annunciation, her meeting with Elizabeth, the Nativity, the flight into Egypt, the infant Jesus, and then her own death and Assumption. Images of saints depicted their charity, their faith and its steadfastness in the face of persecution, their miracles, and their martyrdom. On a specific saint's day, his or her particular life might well be there, rendered on panel or mural, perhaps invoked in sermon, and commemorated with a procession bearing his or her relics around the church, perhaps throughout the town.

The interiors of churches held before the eyes of European Christians a multitude of images: of Christ's birth, life, suffering, death, and resurrection; of Mary's life and assumption; of the apostles, with Christ and in their different martyrdoms; and of men and women held to have lived lives of holiness. Those images did not simply rest on walls as they do now, but were linked variously to performance, word, chant, and song. Various plays, which were performed both within churches and in public spaces outside the church walls, were linked through gesture, costume, and narrative to images within the churches. Christmas and Easter plays,

FIGURE 1.3. Anonymous, 15th century, The Mass of Saint Gregory. Oil on wood, 60 × 39 cm. Louvre, Paris, France. Photo: J.G. Berizzi. Photo credit: Réunion des Musées Nationaux / Art Resource, New York.

for instance, drew on narratives that might be painted on the walls or on panels in the parish church. Acts of holiness that had marked the lives of saints were rendered in paint or stone, recounted in homily, and commemorated in liturgy.

Altars

At the center of that devotional life was the altar, or, more precisely, that to which the bishop consecrated the altar: the Mass. Each church had at least one altar, normally situated at the crossing or in the apse, at that end nearer to Jerusalem. By 1500, most urban and cloister churches had multiple altars. It was not unusual for cathedrals, such as Strasbourg, Paris, Amiens, Cologne, Salisbury, or Antwerp, to have forty altars or more: on individual columns in the nave and in side chapels along the nave and the outer wall of the apse. In churches of multiple altars, the altar situated in the apse served as the main altar, where the Mass was celebrated for the entire congregation. In churches such as Strasbourg, which had two altars consecrated to the regular celebration of the Mass for everyone, the "high altar," the one closest to the eastern end, was the site for the celebration of holy days, such as All Saints' Day or Epiphany or Easter; the other altar, normally situated in the nave, was the site for the daily celebration of the Mass. The side altars – those along the nave and apse – were usually endowed: an individual, a family, a corporation of some other kind having provided funds to build an altar, perhaps also to commission an altar retable, and to support a single priest saying a Mass once a day at that one altar, on behalf of those who had endowed the Masses. In large churches, the Mass was celebrated several times in a single day, at multiple sites, at the high altar for the entire parish or diocese, at the side altars for those who had endowed the Masses in perpetuity.

By 1500, many altars had come to be shaped like a Roman sarcophagus: of stone more often than wood, foursquare, rectangular, and solid. Their form participated in the many layers of meaning of the Mass. Other objects, too, signified another dimension of meaning, the singular linking of the worlds of matter and spirit that occurred within the Mass, at once affirming the singular importance of this one ritual and themselves acquiring religious significance for their participation in its layers of meaning. Each altar was covered by an altarcloth. Atop many altars were candelabra of gold or silver and a crucifix, also of gold or silver. Atop the more important altars was an altar retable, some rising as high as ten meters – elaborately carved, gilded, and painted. By 1500, the high altar and the main altar, if separate, were frequently partially hidden behind a carved choir screen. With each celebration of the Mass, the priest – or, if he had a staff, his assistants – carried to the altar cruets, a paten, and a chalice. These objects were made as beautifully and with as precious materials as were possible for each church. They held the *elements* of communion: the *wine* in a cruet and the *host* on the paten. Beginning in the twelfth century, Europeans had crafted other objects signaling the singular importance of the elements: a flabellum to fan away flies, a pyx to hold the host enclosed against mice or insects, a cover for the chalice to protect both against insects and spilling, embroidered cloths for paten and chalice, and a tabernacle.

In the sixteenth century, the multiplicity of objects, the skill with which they had been made, the richness of their materials – gold, silver, precious and semi-precious gems – all came under attack. But the preciousness of materials, the care in the making, the multiplicity of objects testify to the importance of the ritual for European Christians and intimate something of the complexity and density of its meaning for many different sorts of Christians: lay and clerical, male and female, urban and rural, rich and poor, northern and Mediterranean. Those objects also help us remember the ways in which "the Mass" was not a single ritual performed in different places, but deeply local, embedded within the visual and material culture of specific places, each with its own history of patron saints, processions, devout lay men and women, relics, images, and the endowment of altars. As Pope Pius V acknowledged in 1570, the dioceses of Milan, Lyon, Toledo, Braga, Lièges, Trier, and Cologne had each published their own missals anchored to ancient traditions within their diocese, not to what was being done in Rome.

At the center of the ritual was the eucharist, a moment of singular importance for Christians across Europe. While the specific parts of each Mass differed, according to liturgical calendar and local tradition, each Mass moved through a preparation, an oblation or offering, to consecration and communion, before sending the faithful back to their worlds. At the consecration, following the Fourth Lateran Council, *transubstantiation* – a term that first appeared in the Constitutions of that council in 1215 – took place. As he held up the host, the priest spoke the Latin words, "hoc est enim corpus meum," [for this is my body]; in that moment, the wafer became the body of Christ. As he held up the chalice of wine, he spoke the words "hic est enim calix sanguinis mei" [for this is the chalice of my blood]; at that moment, the wine became the blood of Christ. In the moment when the priest spoke those words, the Church taught, the bread *became* Christ's body, the wine *became* Christ's blood: Christ was "present" each time the bread and wine were consecrated. When, therefore, the faithful "received communion" – and a piece of the consecrated host was placed in the mouth of each Christian in good standing – each Christian received, in the language of the theologians, "Christ's real body." Christians in the sixteenth century would divide bitterly over what precisely that meant, but for the faithful in the year 1500, altar, priest, words, and elements were bound together in making the God who took on human flesh and blood present in the here and now.

Over time, the Mass, Christ's death on the cross, the atonement it offered for human sin, and the office of the priest had become deeply interconnected. In 1215, the Fourth Lateran Council declared that only a priest could effect transubstantiation. Images of the Mass of Saint Gregory placed Christ, wearing the crown of thorns, upon the altar, the priest at the center of the action, and linked the priest, through the cross on the back of his alb, to Christ's crucifixion. Not until the Council of Trent, in 1562, did Rome articulate a formal doctrine of the sacrifice of the Mass. In the preceding centuries, images, the movements and vestments of the priest, and Christ's body on the paten and the blood in the chalice wove together a many-layered understanding of sacrifice, even as the church also taught Christ's atonement for human sin and required the faithful to confess and do penance before receiving Communion.

Embodying Christ

In 1500, in Europe, Christ – variously conceived and symbolized, signaled, represented, indicated, evoked, and imitated – was everywhere to be seen. The cross – symbol of his Crucifixion, death, and resurrection – could be seen in the wilds of the Pyrenees; thousands of times in the urban centers of Rome, Vienna, Prague, Lyon, Paris, or Antwerp; hanging from the belts of monks and the necks of clergy; on crowns and tiaras. No other symbol approached it in pervasiveness across the landscape of Europe or sheer numbers of representations: in gold, silver, gems, marble, stone, limewood, oak, ebony, ivory. Christ was invoked with every wayside cross on every road, at intersections of trade routes, and atop steeples marking the landscape from Trondheim to Valencia. Christ was invoked in the very shape of the floors of churches. And Christ was represented – as infant, small child, youth, young adult, and

FIGURE 1.4. Rosary bead. Metropolitan Museum of Art, New York. Photo credit: Art Resource, New York.

man – in thousands upon thousands of images, not only on the exterior and interior walls of churches, but also in images that pervaded the lives of Europeans individually and collectively, from miniature crucifixion scenes within pods carried on the belts of devout laity to his works or moments of his life painted or carved into the face of a house.

Christ came to life for Europeans in the year 1500: riding an ass into a town or a church, preaching in the piazza of Venice or Florence, begging for alms at the door of the church, speaking the words, "For this is my body." From Granada to Trondheim, each spring, details of Christ's Passion – from his entry into Jerusalem to his resurrection on Easter Sunday – were called forth in word and image, enacted, given voice, movement, life. On Palm Sunday, the Sunday before Easter, congregations followed a carved wooden ass upon which was seated a figure of Christ – in some places, through the town, in others, within their church – as they sought to reenact Christ's entry into Jerusalem the Sunday before Passover. On the Thursday of the week between Palm Sunday and Easter, Holy Week, in many places bishops washed the feet of congregants, in explicit mimesis of Christ, when he washed the feet of his disciples. On Saturday of Holy Week, devout Christians kept vigil, their churches darkened, a temporary tomb set up, where they waited for the resurrected Christ.

Prior to the sixteenth century, many different devout sought a *mimesis* of Christ: More than a mechanical imitation, mimesis sought to make visible with the human body attributes Christ had taught and himself embodied, such as humility or poverty. Many different Europeans, both in groups and individually, in their in gesture, conduct, and dress, sought to live specific facets of the person of Christ as they understood him. By 1500, many of those embodiments were a part of daily life in towns. Many towns had at least one house each of the Order of Preachers (or Dominicans), founded by Saint Dominic in 1216, the Order of Friars Minor (or Franciscans), founded by Saint Francis in 1221, and the Augustinian friars, whose order was formally constituted around 1243. All three were mendicant and preaching orders: They consciously invoked Christ's peripatetic preaching, frequently moving from their own churches, which usually had halls designed specifically for the hearing of sermons, into the public spaces of such major commercial centers as Florence, Venice, or Augsburg. The Rule of Saint Francis, in addition, called for those who joined the Order to "observe the holy gospel of our Lord Jesus Christ, living in obedience without anything of our own, and in chastity." The Order, as many European Christians knew in 1500, was to embody, make visible, tangible, perceptible, in their conduct and simple dress, Christ's poverty and humility.

Lost to us is the sheer diversity of representations of the person of Christ in late medieval Europe. Each *Order* – group of people constituted according to a rule that governed their conduct – wore a specific dress, a *habit*. Each habit signaled a particular understanding of Christ's person, works, and message: The black habit of Benedictines was meant to signal a life removed from the world, in obedience to God; the brown habit of Franciscans, a life of poverty and abject humility; the black-and-white habit of Dominicans, a life of preaching and austerity; the white habit of Cistercians, a life of silent prayer and radical simplicity. In the sixteenth century, each of those Orders was challenged, at the simplest level, for the failure to live the life the habit signaled. More deeply, however, Europeans debated the relationship between mimesis – a notion that engaged that sense of enacting, embodying, bringing to life – and Incarnation. Could any human being, with his or her body, in any way approximate, represent, invoke, Christ's person, which was perfection itself?

The office of the *priest* developed within this context – of images, altar, and mimesis. If various religious orders sought in their conduct and dress to evoke Christ's humility or poverty or submission, the Church consciously articulated a very different role for the priest. The priesthood was an "office," according to the church, conferred through a sacrament, a sacred act, called *ordination*. The Church traced the office to Christ, who had bestowed upon his apostles the authority to baptize, to forgive sins, to absolve, and to offer communion. Each man, in receiving the sacrament of orders or ordination, was transformed. In the words of the Council of Florence (1439–41), three sacraments – baptism, confirmation, and ordination – "imprint indelibly on the soul a character, that is a kind of stamp which distinguishes it from the rest"[1]; the effect of the sacrament of ordination is "an increase of grace to make the person a suitable minister of Christ."[2]

Between the Fourth Lateran Council in 1215 and 1500, the human landscape of Christendom changed and with it, the place of the priest in Christian life. Popes and Councils reiterated again and again the ideal that each parish would have an ordained priest – a man upon whom the bishop had conferred "the office of the keys" – to minister to its

---

[1] *Decrees of the Ecumenical Councils*, edited by Norman P. Tanner, S.J. (London: Sheed and Ward, 1990), vol. I, p. 542.

[2] *Decrees of the Ecumenical Councils*, vol. I, p. 550.

faithful. More important from the perspective of the sixteenth century was the official demand, voiced in the decrees of Fourth Lateran, that an ordained priest celebrate the Mass. Beginning perhaps as early as the twelfth century, but increasing dramatically in popularity over time, lay patrons endowed Masses to be said at family and corporation altars, engendering a demand for ordained priests whose sole function was the celebration of Masses for the dead – perhaps as many as two to an altar in cathedrals such as Strasbourg. By the fifteenth century, the Council of Florence, in its "briefest formula" regarding the sacraments, could anchor the efficacy of all the sacraments to the presence of an ordained priest – a priest was to preside over the major moments in each person's life: within three days of birth for baptism; at the formal transition from childhood to adulthood with confirmation; at marriage; and at death. As the numbers of priests, parishes, and parish churches increased, with the Christian settlement of Europe, the Church could call for its faithful to bring their infants, their seven-year-old children, and their young men and women into the consecrated space to receive sacraments marking these transitions in their lives, even as its priests entered homes to be with the dying in their final moments.

Sacraments

Augustine (d. 430) offered perhaps the most influential definition of a *sacrament*: "a visible form of invisible grace." His definition engendered more than a millennium of discussion, at times quite bitter, of the nature of a sacrament. At the center of those debates was the question: What is the relationship among the world of matter, the divinity of Christ, and the words he was recorded to have spoken?

For Augustine, sacraments were not finite in number. He held the possibility that God might work through any matter he chose. Over time, the Church came to fix the number of sacraments, at seven, formally decreed at the Council of Florence. All Christians shared five sacraments, three of which were to occur only once in each life. *Baptism* initiated a person into Christianity. *Confirmation* initiated a person, usually at the age of seven, into adulthood as a Christian. The *Last Rites* prepared a Christian for death, that portal from this world to the next. Two sacraments the Church required of each Christian at least once a year to remain in good standing as a Christian. *Penance* comprised the contrition of the individual, the confession of his or her sins, the atonement that the priest named to be fulfilled for those sins in order to offer absolution of them. *Communion*, the reception of Christ's body in the eucharist of the

Mass, nourished each Christian, body and soul, over the course of his or her lifetime, from confirmation to death. One sacrament divided clergy from the laity: The sacrament of ordination transformed a man into a priest. After ordination, the Church had come to hold, a man could not marry. One sacrament, *marriage*, was enacted by the laity.

The sixteenth century revealed both the centrality of certain sacraments in the lives of ordinary Christians and the absence of consensus among the faithful as to their nature, their efficacy, and their necessary components. The Church, following Thomas Aquinas (d. 1274), had taught that they were "signs." Deep shifts in Europeans' understandings of epistemology and language called into question that simple word in the sixteenth century, and with it, a way of speaking about the most important legacy of the Incarnation – a world in which divine grace might be communicated through matter.

By 1500, sacraments were received within the world we have been traversing, a world in which crosses marked the intersections of roads traveled by (fewer and fewer) pilgrims and (more and more) merchants; in which each town, no matter how great commercially, was still architecturally dominated by ecclesiastical structures, the towers of churches and the sheer expanse of monasteries; in which images of Christ were to be seen on walls, in homes, and on persons; and in which various embodiments of Christ's teachings and actions walked roads and city streets. For clergy and laity alike, they were experienced not within white walls, but layers upon layers of representations of Incarnation. And for all Christians, the sacraments were inseparable from the experience of time. They marked the transitions of each human life: birth, adulthood, death. They also were embedded in liturgical time, the annual cycle of Christ's birth, death, and resurrection, as each Christian prepared her- or himself, through confession and penance, to receive the eucharist on the day of Christ's resurrection.

Time

Time as much as space was Christian throughout Europe. Throughout Europe, every Sunday – in an ancient conscious distinction from the Jewish Sabbath – was set apart from the rhythms of market and daily life. Well into the sixteenth century, imperial secretaries, town councilors, and princes recorded dates according to a liturgical calendar. That Christian liturgical calendar was structured visually and aurally into European collective life. Within churches, colors marked the liturgical "seasons" – Advent, Christmas, Lent, Easter, and Pentecost – dividing the year according to defining events in Christ's life: birth, forty days in the desert, death, resurrection. Colors also signaled days commemorating events in Mary's life. And colors distinguished the single feast days, such as All Saints' Day on November 1 or Corpus Christi in early summer, as well as the dates set aside for honoring the apostles, such as the Feast of Saints Peter and Paul on June 29, other major figures in the foundation of the church, such as Saint John the Baptist's day on June 24, and saints, such as the Feast of Saint Francis on October 4. Altarcloth and vestments signaled not only season but linked specific seasons and feasts:

> Advent, to Christmas Eve: black or violet
> Christmas Eve, if Sunday: rose
> Christmas Day: white
> Epiphany: white
> Lent to Maunday Thursday: violet
> Good Friday: black
> Easter: white
> Pentecost: red
> Trinity Sunday: white
> Corpus Christi: white
> Trinity to Advent: green
> the feasts of Mary: white
> the feasts of John the Baptist, John the Evangelist, All Saints' Day: white
> the feasts of the other Apostles and Evangelists: red

Each church marked time in ways that extended far beyond its walls to the surrounding countryside. One or more bells, depending on the stature of the church, marked the liturgical "hours" of each day – times when monks would pray: Matins (middle of the night), Lauds (morning), Terce (midmorning), Sext (midday), None (midafternoon), Vespers (evening), and Compline (night). The hours were not uniform in length, but adjusted according to daylight: Lauds, Terce, Sext, and None all were daylight hours; Vespers, eventide. Church bells also marked feast days and called Christians to each celebration of the Mass.

Above the high altar, increasingly, was a bell, which was rung at the elevation of the host. Thus, no matter where one was within hearing of that bell, sound marked the moment, each time, when the host was transformed, following the teaching of the Church, into the body of Christ. For Christians, the bell marked the precise moment when Christ was physically, corporeally, present in that particular space. Sound signaled presence, the moment of mystery, of Incarnation, at the very center of Christians' lives.

2

"The New World"

Encounter

Thursday, 11 October.... All the men I saw were young. I did not see one
over the age of thirty.... They are the colour of the Canary Islanders (neither
black nor white). Some of them paint their faces, some their whole bodies,
some only the eyes, some only the nose. They do not carry arms or know
them. For when I showed them swords, they took them by the edge and cut
themselves out of ignorance. They have no iron.... and I believe they would
easily be made Christians, for they appeared to me to have no religion.

...

Wednesday, 17 October.... During that time I walked among the trees,
which were the loveliest sight I had yet seen. They were green as those of
Andalusia in the month of May. But all these trees are so different from ours
as day from night and so are the fruit and plants and stones, and everything
else.

Bartolomé de Las Casas, Digest of Columbus's Log Book
of the First Voyage[1]

Just after daylight on October 12, 1492, the Genoese entrepreneur
Christopher Columbus set foot on an island somewhere in the Atlantic.
It was the first land he or his crew had seen since departing the Canary
Islands, to the south and west of Spain, September 9. Modern scholars
think that the island was probably Watling Island in the Bahamas, but
they cannot be sure: Columbus was quite literally out of his reckoning.

According to his log book, he thought he had landed on islands off
the coast of Asia, within the kingdom of the Great Khan. He thought he
was looking at subject peoples of the Khan. He noted their nakedness,

---

[1] *The Four Voyages of Christopher Columbus*, edited and translated by J. M. Cohen (Penguin,
1969), pp. 55–6, 66.

which did not correspond with his expectations of a famously luxurious land. He found in those first encounters no silk, no spices, and very little gold – all of which he took to be not any absence of natural resources, but markers of the transmission of tribute to a powerful political and commercial center he had not yet seen.

The voyage had, dangerously, proven longer, landfall more distant, than he had expected. His ships were running low on food and water, his crew close to mutiny, when they sighted land. Columbus had spent years, according to his own account, culling all the available knowledge in preparation for this enterprise. He had drawn on late medieval geographical and navigational knowledge to calculate the distance between Palos in the recently reconquered Granada, his port of departure, and the East Indies, his projected point of contact. Drawing on the system of calculation the second-century Greek geographer, Ptolemy, had developed to graph the surface of the earth, and adjusting to accommodate more recent information, Columbus calculated the earth's circumference to be no more than 18,000 miles. In fact, it proved to be 24,830 – 30 percent larger than he had expected. Columbus expected to encounter the coast of what is now China thousands of miles closer. The "earth" Ptolemy had graphed had as its center the Mediterranean and encompassed the three continents of Europe, Asia, and Africa. Ptolemy's earth did not include the continents of North or South America, Australia, or Antarctica.

None of the trusted classical and medieval sources, from Aristotle, Pliny, and Ptolemy through the great Summae of the thirteenth century, offered any indication that these lands existed. None. Columbus had no notion at all of any land mass between the easternmost coastal islands of Asia and the westernmost coastal islands of Europe.

Columbus seems to have employed all the technology developed for navigation: the quadrant, the astrolabe, the plumbline, and sandglass, as well as the compass. But, in 1492, no one had tested that technology for navigation across a body of water of unknown expanse and extension, in the midst of a moving ocean, of waves, winds, and currents. There was no system, either navigational or cartographic, by which Columbus might locate exactly where he was in that ocean Ptolemy had set on the margin of his earth.

There is tantalizing evidence that earlier Europeans – the Phoenicians, the Vikings – had crossed the Atlantic and touched some shore of the North American continent. Gonzalo Fernández de Oviedo recounted a story of a ship's pilot, near death, who had come to Columbus's home, where he had told the Genoese of his ship, driven westward over days,

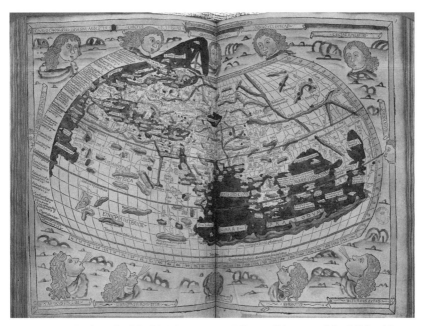

FIGURE 2.1. Ptolemy's World Map; copy Ulm edition, 1486. Bibliothèque Nationale, Paris, France. Photo Credit: Erich Lessing / Art Resource, New York.

far off its European course, ultimately to land on one of many islands clustered together, inhabited by naked people. According to the story, the pilot was able to calculate latitude – though the means to calculate longitude, that westward distance, was not yet available. None of these earlier ventures provided sufficient information to chart the Atlantic.

Columbus was the first one to leave us a written record: of the course he charted across the expanse of the Atlantic Ocean; of the coasts he either saw or landed on; and of what he thought he was seeing, in those lands that had never been recorded on a European map. He looked with a merchant's eyes. He saw goods that would have value in European markets: gold, feathers, plants of potential medicinal use, unfamiliar animals, and human beings whose value as servants he calculated as he met them. His log books also testify that he knew he was seeing plants, animals, and persons for whom there were no categories in traditional European knowledge. Plants could only be described by analogy, in relation to known vegetation in Andalusia. Human beings could be described by contrast to peoples from Africa or Europe – neither black nor white – but there were no words to name the color of their skin, the texture of their hair. They had, he recorded, no iron and "they appeared to me to have no religion." He looked at them not simply through European references, but according to conceptual categories he had brought from his experience on the other side of the world: Andalusian palms, Portuguese slaves, Genoese merchants, metal technology, and an unexamined idea of "religion."

Columbus himself cast his story in a number of ways. In one letter to Ferdinand and Isabel, he framed his voyages as fulfilling the prophecy of the twelfth-century mystic, Joachim of Fiore, that someone from Spain would effect the restitution of the temple of Zion. He signed at least one document as Christoferens, "Christ-bearer." Even as he was calculating the market value of the plants, animals, and persons, he sought to situate that strange world within a Christian universe. Even as he was naming islands, signaling his possession in the name of the Catholic monarchs of Spain of places he had not even imagined, he was also seeking to locate those places within the matrices of the world he had left – to make them not new. That move, to situate what he was seeing within the late medieval Christian map of knowledge – to name new islands after European saints, to locate persons of nameless color within the narrative of Genesis, to integrate the "discovery" within the arc of Christian time – would be echoed in European account after European account.

The New World

In 1507, the cartographer, Martin Waldseemüller, relying on the report of another explorer, Amerigo Vespucci, inserted a new land mass on his own version of a Ptolemaic map of the world, naming it "America," a land apart from China or the Indies. In 1540, another cartographer, Sebastian Münster, set two land masses between Europe and the eastern coast of Asia, labeling the southern land, "the New World." Throughout that time, Columbus's accounts were circulating in Europe, as were the accounts of others who accompanied him on his second, third, and fourth voyages. In 1526, Oviedo wrote in his *General and Natural History of the Indies*:

> No writer ever knew about most of the animals living in those parts, including the ones I mention here, since they are in a region and a land which was unknown until our times and was not mentioned in either Ptolemy's cosmography or any other until the admiral Christopher Columbus made it known to us.[2]

---

[2] *Christopher Columbus and the Enterprise of the Indies: A Brief History in Documents*, edited by Geoffrey Symcox and Blair Sullivan (Boston: Bedford/St. Martin's, 2005), p. 57.

FIGURE 2.2. Martin Waldseemüller, World Map, 1507. Staatsbibliothek zu Berlin, Stiftung Preussischer Kulturbesitz, Berlin, Germany. Photo Credit: Bildarchiv Preussischer Kulturbesitz / Art Resource, New York.

Before the Encounter, all known cultures existed in a single hemisphere – whether one lived in the western or the eastern. And in 1587, it would be another cartographer, Gerardus Mercator,who rendered as a map that sense of two discrete worlds of knowledge, divided by an ocean: two halves, two half-spheres, spatially two separate worlds.

The Encounter transformed Europeans' diet, material culture, politics, economy, social relations. No aspect of European life went untouched by the Encounter. Europeans saw and brought back to Europe avocados, blueberries, corn, peanuts, potatoes, sweet potatoes, tobacco, tomatoes, sunflowers.[3] New foodstuffs such as chocolate altered the cuisine of Europe, as well as the social practices surrounding those new foods – pots for chocolate and coffee, then houses for the drinking of coffee and chocolate. Certain cities emerged as political and commercial "capitals," centers of "global" empires. New wealth and new kinds of wealth restructured social relations. And entrepreneurs like Columbus planted commercial crops as never before. Before the Encounter, coffee was Arabic, not Brazilian, woolens were European, and cotton was an expensive and rare cloth.

---

[3] Symcox and Sullivan, p. 32.

FIGURE 2.3. Rumoldus Mercator, after Gerardus Mercator, *Orbis terrae compendiosa descriptio*, 1587. Library of the University of Amsterdam.

European Christianity participated in these transformations, from questions about the morality of coffee to a central role in the expansion of empires. The "New World" also confronted European Christianity directly. It was not simply the influx of new information – though the stunning array of previously unknown plants and animals ultimately eroded Genesis's botanical and zoological authority, as well as circumscribing Pliny's and Aristotle's. Nor was it simply the utter absence of anything resembling Judaism, Christianity, or Islam in the western hemisphere. The "New World," in being precisely that, challenged European Christianity, even more than it challenged the Greek and Roman authors whom Europeans had held as authoritative. It confronted European Christianity with understandings of time, the human person, and social relations, which were, in the words of sixteenth-century Europeans, "new."

That word, "new," so familiar in the modern world, was far less in use in the fifteenth century, and its valences were different. It was not, as it became in twentieth-century consumer culture, a self-evidently positive value. Nor was it necessarily a negative value. But it marked for European Christians a tension, something of a break, not simply from "tradition" – another word whose valences have changed in the wake of the Encounter – but from the momentum of the world that God in his wisdom had set in motion. "New" did not exist simply in relationship to human practices. For European Christians, the word most famously marked a rupture in divine time: the "New Testament."

Genesis

In 1494, the "poor friar of the Order of Saint Jerome," Ramón Pané, accompanied Columbus on his second voyage. Fray Pané was sent to live among the peoples of those islands Columbus had landed on his first voyage, to learn their language, to record what he saw of their way of life, and to convert them to Christianity. He was particularly attentive to what he thought were religious questions, such as the origins of humankind (chapter 1), the difference between men and women (chapters 2–8), or the sea (chapter 9):

> There was a man called Yaya, whose name they do not know; and his son was called Yayael, which means son of Yaya. Because Yayael wanted to kill his father, the latter sent him into exile, and thus he was exiled for four months; and afterwards his father killed him and put his bones into a gourd and hung it from the roof of his house, where it was hanging for some time. It happened one day that Yaya, desiring to see his son, said to his wife: I want to see our son Yayael. And she was glad, and taking down the gourd, she turned it over to see the bones of their son. And many fish, large and small emerged from it. Whereby, seeing that those bones had been changed into fish, they resolved to eat them.[4]

Pané's text has served as the earliest record of a culture that disappeared within a generation. It is also an artifact of "encounter" between a person who saw himself very much as a Christian and a people about whom he had known nothing only two years before. As Pané's readers would have known, the stories the Tainos told him have no counterpart in either biblical or classical narratives. It was not simply that they were unfamiliar. These stories were utterly new – without resonance, without association, without analogy. They were not so much "alien" as outside the mental landscape of late medieval Europe.

As later Europeans, such as Michel de Montaigne, recognized, Pané's questions had framed his viewing of the Tainos in categories deeply embedded in European life. Pané asked after the "origins" of the earth and humankind. For Pané, as for most European Christians, the Genesis

---

[4] Fray Ramón Pané, *An Account of the Antiquities of the Indians*, edited by José Juan Arrom, translated by Susan C. Griswold (Durham and London: Duke University Press, 1999), p. 13.

text was foundational in a number of different ways. It posited a notion of "origin":

> In the beginning God created the Heauen and the Earth.
>
> 2 And the earth was without forme, and voyd, and darkenesse was upon the face of the deepe
>
> Holy Bible, King James Version[5]

The particular conceptualization of origin that Genesis posited was, by the end of the fifteenth century, pervasive throughout Europe. Genesis posited a single point of "beginning" – not a multitude of simultaneous generations, as the Tainos' stories suggested – but a sequence of discrete acts of creation. Before that point, there was nothing. That particular construction of origin grounded Europeans' conceptualization of time as linear, with a point, a single solitary point of "beginning," after which time was structured according to the generations of humankind, father and mother to sons and daughters. Jews, Christians, and Muslims all shared that sense of time as linear, though the moment at which each began counting the sequence of years differed.

Genesis narrated explanations for a number of questions that pervade medieval texts. From whence do we come? Whence the stars? Animals and plants? The sun and the moon? Why are men's and women's bodies different? What makes them different? What is the meaning of that difference? What should the relationship between men and women be? What should the relationship of humankind to the earth be? To animals? To all Creation? Why does time divide between darkness and light? Why must we die? The questions inspired by and answered in Genesis were infinite.

So, too, Genesis had long provided Europeans with a sense of how things were "in the beginning," foremost the relationship between men and women and between humankind and knowledge. The Genesis text grounded discussions of the relationship between the sexes, the gendered hierarchy of authority in both domestic and political life. Well into the sixteenth century, it suffused debates about the relationship between humankind and knowledge, casting a shadow over discussions of "curiosity."

And Genesis narrated a story of "The Fall," in which evil seduced innocence, a woman either misled or seduced a man, and "paradise" was lost. Like the structuring of time itself, this story had permeated

---

[5] Unless otherwise noted, all quotations are from *The New Oxford Annotated Bible*, Third Edition, edited by Michael D. Coogan (Oxford: Oxford University Press, 2001).

FIGURE 2.4. Genesis, Frontispice Depicting the Creation, Luther Bible, First Edition, 1534. Private Collection. Photo Credit: Art Resource, New York.

European Christian society, shaping conceptualizations of human nature, of women, of proper and improper relationships between men and women, of proper and improper approaches to knowledge. Clothing – the absence of which Columbus had noted from his first sighting – was the direct consequence of the Fall, Adam and Eve's self-consciousness of their nakedness the marker by which God discovered that they had taken the forbidden fruit of the tree of knowledge.

Against all of these ways that Genesis had so shaped Europeans' sense of themselves and the world, the Tainos' stories, and those of other peoples, which came to circulate in the sixteenth century, were "new." The Tainos, the Aztecs, the Inka posited stories that bore *no* relationship to Scripture or classical texts. We can now see that this makes perfect sense: How could they know the Bible, Aristotle? And yet, that capacity to see, to acknowledge the two worlds that Mercator could represent, is the direct consequence of the Encounter. Before it, Genesis was not one of many different, let alone equal, ways of conceptualizing. While we have some evidence of other conceptualizations of origins, Genesis pervaded the lives of European Christians. Hundreds of images in churches, psalters, prayerbooks rendered moments of the story of Genesis. Week after week, preachers addressed "original sin" and the sins that followed upon it, such as pride. The very act that made one a Christian, baptism, was rooted in a notion of "fallen" humankind. Before the Encounter, Christianity was not one "system of belief" among many, but the epistemology, the points of reference, the structures that organized the lives of all European Christians – from their conceptualization of time itself to their sense of themselves as "fallen" as well as "lords of all the earth."

Paradise

... It has been discovered that with [the Tainos] the earth, like the sun and the water, is common, nor do "mine and yours," the seeds of all evils, fall among them. For they are content with so little that in that vast earth there is an excess of land to farm rather than a lack of anything. Theirs is a golden age: they do not hedge their estates with ditches, walls or hedges; they live with open gardens; without laws, without books, without judges, of their own nature, and they cultivate what is right. They judge he is evil and wicked who takes pleasure in inflicting injury on anyone.

Peter Martyr of Anghiera, *The New World*, 1511[6]

---

[6] Peter Martyr of Anghiera, "On the Tainos, Caribs, the Flora and Fauna of the Indies, and the Golden Age of Life According to Nature," Symcox and Sullivan, p. 171.

As Columbus's log book reveals, Europeans looked at the lands of the western hemisphere through lenses ground in their education and experience in Europe. As his writings more generally reveal, individual Europeans might look through multiple lenses – commercial, Christian, colonial, imperial – that, in Europe at least, did not always sit comfortably together. A number, echoing Columbus's log book, saw in the peoples of the islands of what is now called the Caribbean what human beings looked like before Eve took the apple. They saw paradise.

European Christians grappled with the question of whether the peoples they had encountered in the western hemisphere were "prelapsarian," that is, human beings who had not fallen or become sinful. Within that question were potent challenges to the Genesis narrative. The first was the challenge of time: If Adam and Eve "fell," how could anyone – since all humankind descended, according to Christian thought, from those first two human beings – not be fallen? According to the linear time of generations in Genesis, everyone came temporally after Adam and Eve. How could there exist a people outside of the linear descent of fallen humankind? Europeans tested a number of answers to that question, culminating in the great debate at Valladolid in 1550–51 on the questions of conversion and slavery in the Spanish lands of the western hemisphere. In the first half of the sixteenth century, "prelapsarian" was not an esoteric question, but bound up with the fates of millions of persons in the western hemisphere.

The possibility of paradise in this world posed a series of challenges to European Christians' understanding of human nature. Following Genesis, all human beings were born into a state of sin – they were "fallen" from birth. Even children were encompassed in that understanding of human nature. Pride, greed, anger, lust, envy, gluttony, sloth – these were natural to human beings, sins against which every person should, according to Christian doctrine, be vigilant, but sins towards which every human being, by his or her nature, was prone.

That sense of human nature was the underpinning of the complex penitential system of late medieval Christianity. At least once a year, Christians were to confess to their priest, a practice which had at its heart the presumption that every Christian had something to confess, that every Christian had fallen, now in the more immediate sense, into sin, whether it was envy of a neighbor's prosperity or sexual promiscuity or any of the many mundane manifestations of sin. By 1492, the Church had differentiated between two kinds of sin, deadly or mortal, which put a soul in peril, and venial, relatively minor. In sermons, visual images, and plays, the Church taught European Christians how to recognize these sins. In the sacrament of penance, the Church offered a complex ritual in which each Christian was to examine oneself for all the different manifestations of these sins, to name them out loud to a priest, and, from that priest, to receive either a simple absolution – itself a powerful notion – if the person was penitent in proportion to the sin, or directions for the act of penance required to restore that person's life to grace. The penitential system, with its tripartite process of confession, penance, and absolution, bound European Christians in cycles of transgression, confession, contrition, penance, and absolution, a cycle that had proven psychologically and emotionally extraordinarily powerful.

If the Tainos were "innocent" (as neither Jews nor Muslims had ever been in European Christian eyes), then what was the relationship of the penitential system to human nature? Prior to 1492, that penitential system had been, for European Christians, the necessary counterpart to a nature prone to sin. Over the sixteenth century, European Christians worked to missionize the peoples of the western hemisphere, to bring them into that cycle, but in the early years, as those first accounts circulated, the possibility of human innocence opened worlds.

Utopia

In 1516, the English humanist, Thomas More, published a best seller. In 1518, a revised edition was published, bearing the title, *Concerning the Best State of a Commonwealth and the New Island of Utopia* and Ambrosius Holbein's woodcut rendering of the island. It opened with a chance encounter between More, who narrated the first part and closed the second, and

> a stranger, a man of quite advanced years. The stranger had a sunburned face, a long beard, and a cloak hanging loosely from his shoulders; from his appearance and dress, I took him to be a ship's captain.
>
> ... This man, who is named Raphael – his family name is Hythloday – ... took service with Amerigo Vespucci. He accompanied Vespucci on the last three of his four voyages, accounts of which are now common reading everywhere; but on the last voyage, he did not return home with the commander.[7]

The first part of the book posed the question of the usefulness of the knowledge Hythloday had acquired through his travels for European

---

[7] Thomas More, *Utopia*, edited and translated by Robert M. Adams (New York: Norton, 1992[1975]), pp. 4, 5.

FIGURE 2.5. Sir Thomas More. "De optimo reip. statu, deque noua insula Utopia." [*Utopia*] Apud inclytam Basileam [1518]. Woodcut by Amrosius Holbein showing the island and the facing page of text. Rare Books Division. The New York Public Library. Photo Credit : The New York Public Library / Art Resource, New York.

rulers. Hythloday's experiences in other lands led him to be sharply critical of European, and specifically English, laws, customs, and practices.

> The Utopians marvel that any mortal can take pleasure in the weak sparkle of a little gem or bright pebble when he has a star, or the sun itself, to look at. They are amazed at the foolishness of any man who considers himself a nobler fellow because he wears clothing of specially fine wool. No matter how delicate the thread, they say, a sheep wore it once, and still was nothing but a sheep. They are surprised that gold, a useless commodity in itself, is everywhere valued so highly that man himself, who for his own purposes conferred this value on it, is far less valuable.[8]

In the second part, Hythloday offered More an account of a remote island, called Utopia, which he had reached after leaving Vespucci and the coast of Brazil – by 1516, itself a coast Europeans were charting. Like Columbus, Hythloday offered details of another world sorted according to categories Europeans found meaningful: the geography of the island, with particular attention to harbors and rivers; buildings; clothing; meals; and the presence of precious metals. Like Pané, Hythloday also offered

[8] More, *Utopia*, p. 48.

information of a more complex character – no longer simply what his European eyes saw, but what he learned by "living among" the people of the island: their political organization; work and leisure; social relations; travel; trade; moral philosophy; notions of pleasure; learning; slavery; health care; marriage; law and punishment; and diplomacy and warfare. Like Columbus or Pané, Hythloday presented his account in contrast to European customs. Unlike them, he did not speak in terms of absences of European goods or practices. He presented a way of life that freed human beings from the sins of pride, greed, anger, lust, gluttony, sloth, and envy.

Sloth was given no place and no time in Utopia:

> ... there is no chance to loaf or kill time, no pretext for evading work; no taverns, or alehouses, or brothels; no chances for corruption; no hiding places, no spots for secret meetings. Because they live in the full view of all, they are bound to be either working at their usual trades, or enjoying their leisure in a respectable way. Such a life style must necessarily result in plenty of life's good things, and since they share everything equally, it follows that no one can be reduced to poverty or forced to beg.[9]

The foundation of Utopian life was what Hythloday called a "Commonwealth," in which everyone took his or her turn working the land to produce the food and goods necessary to collective life, and no one owned anything. Not the land they worked. Not the food they ate together in large communal meals. Not houses:

> Every house has a door to the street and another to the garden. The doors, which are made with two leaves, open easily and swing shut automatically, letting anyone enter who wants to – and so there is no private property. Every ten years, they change houses by lot.[10]

Nor wealth of any kind. They had no need of money. And, in one of the most memorable descriptions, placed no value on metals or stones that Europeans called "precious":

> While they eat from pottery dishes and drink from glass cups, well made but inexpensive, their chamber pots and stools – all their humblest vessels, for use in the common halls and private homes – are made of gold and silver. The chains and heavy fetters of slaves are also made of these metals. Finally, criminals who are to bear through life the mark of some disgraceful act are forced to wear golden rings on their ears, golden bands on their

[9] More, *Utopia*, p. 45.
[10] More, *Utopia*, p. 34.

fingers, golden chains around their necks, and even golden crowns on their heads.[11]

Sufficiency of food and shelter dispensed with the sins of gluttony, envy, and greed. The elimination of envy removed a primary source of anger. The Utopian attitude towards gold, silver, and gemstones eroded the ways in which those natural materials had become implicated in European displays of pride. So, too, the Utopian approach to clothing accorded no value to any of the markers of social place in European dress – everyone wore leather work clothes, woolen cloaks of the same color, and linen cloth of natural color. No silks, no colors, no textures such as velvet or brocade visually differentiated one person from another, set one person over another in a hierarchy of display.

By the sixteenth century, the vice of "lust" – which was set forth in the last two of the Ten Commandments – had come to be construed largely in terms of sexual desire. In Utopia, that vice was addressed in law:

> Premarital intercourse, if discovered and proved, brings severe punishment on both man and woman, and the guilty parties are forbidden to marry during their whole lives, unless the prince, by his pardon, alleviates the sentence.... The reason they punish this offense so severely is that they suppose few people would join in married love – with confinement to a single partner, and all the petty annoyances that married life involves – unless they were strictly restrained from a life of promiscuity.

and custom:

> In choosing marriage partners, they solemnly and seriously follow a custom ... Whether she is a widow or a virgin, the bride-to-be is shown naked to the groom by a responsible and respectable matron; and, similarly, some respectable man presents the groom naked to his future bride. We laughed at this custom and called it absurd; but they were just as amazed at the folly of all other peoples.... in the choice of a mate, which may cause either delight or disgust for the rest of their lives, people are completely careless.[12]

In contrast to Europe, marriage was not a sacrament. What bound two people together into old age was not a sacred act, but compassion: One did not leave another human being as he or she aged and became infirm.

Before 1516, the word "utopia" did not exist – the word is a compound of the Greek words for not, "ou," and place, "topos." Like other accounts such as Pané's, *Utopia* presented European readers with descriptions – of economic practices, social relations, political arrangements – of

[11] More, *Utopia*, p. 47.
[12] More, *Utopia*, pp. 60–1.

"another world," a place constituted according to different principles, in which all relations were different, from those between men and women to those between persons and things. Unlike those other accounts, however, Hythloday drew on his travels to critique Europe, to state with the knowledge of experience that things could be otherwise – not simply that they did not need to be as they were in Europe, but, far more potently, that things could be better in Europe were they to be organized according to the principles of that other world. As no other before it, the book engaged with the conceptual power of "the New World," its potency, to present Europeans with other ways of thinking about the most fundamental aspects of their lives: what they valued and why; what the purpose of work was; how they bound themselves to one another. And, as those very first accounts of "innocent" Tainos implicitly posed, so *Utopia* directly questioned: What if human beings were not, by their nature, proud, greedy, angry, lustful, envious? What if it was not nature, but the particular fusion of commercial and courtly culture of Europe that inculcated these vices?

Utopia is fiction. And yet, to say that is to miss its play in the imagination of early-sixteenth-century Europeans. Many, many of them took it to be a true account, of real people, in a real place. They were not naïve to do so, though More certainly peppered his account with small absurdities that might have warned more astute readers. They lived, after all, in a time of dozens of such wondrous accounts, of places constituted utterly differently from anything they held to be familiar. In such a world, what could be "common" sense?

At the end of his account, Hythloday turned to religion. At the beginning of a lengthier description of their religious practices than he had offered for any other aspect of their life, he observed:

> But after they had heard from us the name of Christ, and learned of his teachings, his life, his miracles, and the no less marvelous devotion of the many martyrs who shed their blood to draw nations far and near into the Christian fellowship, you would not believe how they were impressed. Either through the mysterious inspiration of God, or because Christianity is very like the religion already prevailing among them, they were well disposed toward it from the start. But I think they were also much influenced by the fact that Christ had encouraged his disciples to practice community of goods, and that among the truest groups of Christians, the practice still prevails.[13]

[13] More, *Utopia*, p. 73.

At the end of *Utopia,* More posed the possibility that one could be "Christian" without being baptized, that to live as a Christian one did not need the ecclesiastical hierarchy of Europe. He offered a vision of Christianity deeply in harmony with that of his dear friend, Desiderius Erasmus, as something one lived, in accord with the simple life of Jesus and the apostles. That Christianity required neither church nor altar, neither priest nor penance nor Pope.

Many stories of the New World circulated in European courts in the years immediately after the Encounter. As they were retold on European soil, the referents shifted. While the accounts might speak in terms of absences of European values and things, some Europeans, such as Thomas More, heard affinities with the world of the apostles. The juxtaposition of the absence of private property and the absence of religion in Columbus's accounts of the islanders translated, once on European soil, to two deeply destabilizing possibilities: that human beings could be Christian without the complex sacramental system of the late medieval Church; that the absence of much of late medieval ecclesiastical and courtly culture could in fact foster the Christianity of the apostles.

Conversion

Columbus saw himself as carrying Christianity across the ocean. But what did he understand Christianity to be? Columbus claimed to see "no religion" among the peoples of that first island. He could not speak with them. He did not know what they thought. All he could see in that first encounter was the absence of those visible signs of Christianity in Europe: structures for worship, persons distinguished by special dress, rituals accorded singular dignity. For Columbus, Christianity could be transported, from a place where it was to a place where it was not.

Europeans divided almost immediately over how to convert the peoples of the western hemisphere. Columbus and Pané represent two models for conversion that would compete well beyond the sixteenth century. In claiming the islands for the Catholic monarchs, Columbus saw himself as "carrying Christ," extending the boundary of Christendom across that great expanse of water. For Columbus, as for the conquistadores who crossed in subsequent voyages, the jurisdiction of their monarchs corresponded with the jurisdiction of Christianity. Much like Charlemagne's conversion of the Saxons, Spanish soldiers drove thousands into rivers where priests spoke the words of the liturgy of baptism in Latin, a language those thousands had never heard before. This model, which came to be called forced conversion, was concerned with jurisdiction. Like Charlemagne in the eastern marches, Isabel and Ferdinand in Granada, it was predicated on the notion that bringing peoples within the boundaries of Christian Europe was the necessary first step in making them Christian. It made them subject to the laws of Christian Europe, even as Europeans were building churches, importing liturgical books and objects – importing as they could the material culture of Christian Europe.

Pané offered an account of one of the very first conversions in the western hemisphere:

> When I was at that fortress [the Magdalena, built by Columbus], in the company of the commander, Artiaga, under orders from the aforesaid Governor Don Christopher Columbus, God was pleased to illumine with the light of the holy Catholic faith an entire household of leading citizens of the said province of the Magdalena, which province was then called Macoris, and the lord of it was named Guanáoboconel, which means son of Guanábocon. His household included his servants and favorites, who are called naborías, and there were sixteen people altogether, all relatives, among whom there were five brothers. One of these died, and the other four received the holy baptismal water; and I believe they died as martyrs because of what was seen in their death and steadfastness. The first to be killed and to receive the holy baptismal water was an Indian named Guatícaba, who later took the name of Juan. He was the first Christian who suffered a cruel death, and I am certain he died a martyr.[14]

For Pané, God "was pleased to illumine with the light of the holy Catholic faith" – God acted. And an entire household was, passive voice, converted, all at once – it happened to them: They were illumined, they received baptismal water, they were killed.

In a later incident, Pané described a more detailed process, albeit in this instance, a failed effort:

> Consequently we were with that cacique Guarionex almost two years, always teaching him our holy faith and the custom of the Christians. In the beginning he showed us goodwill and gave us hope that he would do whatever we wished and that he wanted to be a Christian, saying that we should teach him the Pater Noster, the Ave Maria, and the Creed and all the other prayers and things that pertain to a Christian. And so he learned the Pater Noster and the Ave Maria and the Creed, and likewise many members of his household learned them; and every morning he would say his prayers and made those of his household say them twice. But afterwards he grew angry, and he abandoned his good intention.[15]

---

[14] Pané, *An Account of the Antiquities of the Indians*, p. 32.
[15] Pané, *An Account of the Antiquities of the Indians*, pp. 34–5.

Pané, along with many of the Dominicans and Franciscans who accompanied all the subsequent voyages, conceptualized conversion as a more complex process, involving the minds and spirits of persons. They pursued what was called gentle and we might call *gradual* conversion. In comparison with forced conversions, its pace was relatively slow. As those who pursued gradual conversion fanned out across the islands and then the mainland, they sought to introduce indigenous peoples to the Lord's Prayer, the Ave Maria, the Creed – all parts of medieval Christian worship – even as they were learning the languages of those people and translating the texts into indigenous languages.

In those early years, many Europeans, like More, assumed an immediate relationship between "innocence" and "conversion": "Innocent" persons would choose Christianity as the "religion" that was "natural" – most harmoniously in accord with their natures. Conversion, following such reasoning, involved foremost a willingness to teach Christian texts. Once those texts were known, then Christianity would follow. For those Europeans, conversion did not need to be forced: Everyone would become Christian in time.

Neither side held necessary to conversion the dense physical and sensual presence of European Christianity – incense and church bells; church structures and cloisters; clerical stoles, albs, chasubles; altar cloths, patens, chalices. In the Aztec and the Inka empires, Hernán Cortés and Francisco Pizarro sought to extirpate "idolatry" – the worship of false gods – by either destroying or translating to Christian use the material presences of indigenous religions. But the density of Christianity in Europe materially, temporally, and visually did not figure in the debates on conversion. Although Europeans did build churches, then cloisters, and import clerical robes and liturgical objects, as well as missals, breviaries, antiphonaries, psalters, and then catechisms, not until the Jesuits arrived in the mid-sixteenth century were images, music, the senses explicitly used to convey "Christianity" to the New World.

Debates on conversion revealed a range of different understandings of what it meant to "be a Christian." For some, forced baptism made of the peoples of the western hemisphere "Christians" – though they understood not a word of what was said, though their entire lives had been lived without Christian time or Christian landscapes. For others, simple statements, accepting the protection of Christ, made a person a "Christian." For Pané, a faith that was manifested as steadfastness was sufficient to make a person a "Christian." For still others, "Christian" was open-ended, a process with no specific end-point, marked by significant moments, such as the willing acceptance of baptism. For all, being "Christian" had become separable from places of worship and liturgical time.

As the strangeness of the New World came home to Europeans, debates on *how* to convert became inextricably intertwined with debates on human nature. Following those earliest evocations of Genesis, those who saw in the peoples of the New World prelapsarian humanity argued for the naturalness of Christianity – its essential affinity with innocence, the immediacy of Christianity's connection to the absence of the vices of Europe. By mid-century, those who defended gentle conversion found themselves actively and explicitly opposing enslavement. Those who argued in support of enslavement took as their predicate that there existed in the world peoples who, by their very nature, could never be Christian. The peoples of the western hemisphere did not simply not share the same nature as Europeans, they argued. Those peoples were essentially different, and that difference made it impossible for them to become Christians. By their nature, some people could be Christian. By their nature, some people could never be Christian. This argument had devastating consequences in both hemispheres.

Cannibals

> They learned by hearsay that not far from those islands [Hispaniola] are the islands of wild men who feed on human flesh. They mentioned afterwards that this was the reason that they had fled in such a panic at our arrival: they thought we were Cannibals. This, or Caribs, is the name they give to those savages. . . . The gentle natives complained that the Cannibals caused constant distress to their islands with their frequent raids for plunder, like hunters attacking and ambushing game as they pursue it through the woods. They castrate the boys they catch, in the way we do roosters or pigs, if we want to rear them to be fatter and more tender for the table; when as a consequence the boys have become large and fat, they eat them.[16]

The word "cannibalism" has its origins in that complex interaction between the western hemisphere and Europe. It did not exist before 1492. It arose between Arawak accounts of Carib anthropophagy and Columbus's hearing, and when Columbus recounted the description of the Arawaks' enemy, he named them "Cannibals." As the tale circulated in Europe, here as the Spanish court chaplain, Peter Martyr d'Anghiera, retold it, the name attached to the anthropophagy.

[16] "On Tainos," Symcox and Sullivan, p. 167.

Columbus heard about cannibalism and recounted what he heard, which was, in turn, told again and again in Europe in a number of different contexts. Cannibalism revealed the limit of analogy as a means for assimilating the New World to Europe: While nakedness could be a marker of innocence, for Europeans, cannibalism divided those who practiced it both culturally and materially – their bodies were different for having consumed other bodies, their persons not discrete from other human beings in the same way, their natures, therefore, not quite the same as that of others.

Cannibalism was among the first attributes offered as evidence for the essential difference of the peoples of the western hemisphere. That argument drew primarily on Aristotle's definition of "barbarians," which he developed in his argument for the justification of slavery based on differences in human nature. In the years after Columbus's first landing, Europeans' conception of "barbarism" accrued resonances, as new accounts told of peoples who practiced "cannibalism," "idolatry," and "superstition."

The concept of barbarism became embroiled in debates on conversion, as Europeans confronted the relationship between nature and Christianity, figuring in arguments for enslavement and against gentle conversion. The forced conversions of the western hemisphere had brought not peoples of ancient and familiar – if violently repudiated – "religions," Jews and Muslims, into Christianity. While Muslims and Jews were "not Christians," they nonetheless shared with Christians history, bodies of knowledge, and languages. The peoples of the New World were that – new in ways Europeans had not even imagined. As Jean de Léry reported of the Tupinamba in Brazil, some did not share writing, printing, or texts of any kind:

> They know nothing of writing, either sacred or secular; indeed, they have no kind of characters that signify anything at all. When I was first in their country, in order to learn their language I wrote a number of sentences which I then read aloud to them. Thinking that this was some kind of witchcraft, they said to each other, "Is it not a marvel that this fellow, who yesterday could not have said a single word in our language, can now be understood by us, by virtue of that paper he is holding and which makes him speak thus?"[17]

In the courts of Europe and in theological faculties, Christians argued about the relationship between "barbarism" and Christianity. If

---

[17] Jean de Léry, *History of a Voyage to the Land of Brazil*, translated by Janet Whatley (Berkeley: University of California Press, 1990), pp. 134–5.

"innocence" seemed to have a natural affinity with Christianity, for those Europeans who argued for enslavement, no "barbarian" could be "Christian," while for others, including many of those who forced conversions, Christianity was part of the process of extirpating barbarism. "Barbarism" in other words, posed deep-reaching questions about the relationship of Christianity to human nature. At Valladolid in 1550, Juan Gines Sepulveda, a Dominican theologian, argued that the peoples of the western hemisphere did not share a "nature" with European Christians. They were "barbarian," and, following Aristotle, because of their nature, could be enslaved. Las Casas, arguing directly against Sepulveda, did not challenge "barbarism" as a category of human nature, but rejected it as a category for the nature of the peoples of the western hemisphere – barbarism was a viable category for human nature, just not the appropriate category for the peoples of the west. Both accepted the premise that "barbarism" was an attribute of groups, not individuals. Both accepted the category, "barbarian," as essential – of the very nature of a person.

As Europeans made their way into what are modern-day Mexico, Brazil, and Peru, they found cannibalism practiced in a number of different contexts. While the cannibalism of the Tupi on the coast of Brazil occurred within the context of warfare – evoking Homeric associations – Aztec and Inka cannibalism occurred within the context of what Europeans saw as "idolatry" or "false worship"

> I have already described the nature of [Aztec] sacrifices. They strike open the wretched Indian's chest with flint knives and hastily tear out the palpitating heart which, with the blood, they present to the idols in whose name they have performed the sacrifice. Then they cut off the arms, thighs, and head, eating the arms and thighs at their ceremonial banquets.
>
> Bernal Díaz, *The Conquest of New Spain*[18]

The New World did not simply confound European categories of knowledge. For each category Europeans articulated, the New World presented them with a plethora of practices that resisted ready categorization of any kind. Was all cannibalism barbarous or only certain kinds? Were all those who ate the flesh of human beings barbarians?

> For each meal [Montezuma's] servants prepared him more than thirty dishes cooked in their native style, which they put over small earthenware braziers to prevent them from getting cold. They cooked more than three hundred plates of the food the great Montezuma was going to eat, and more

---

[18] Bernal Díaz, *The Conquest of New Spain*, translated by J. M. Cohen (Harmondsworth: Penguin, 1963), p. 229.

than a thousand more for the guard. I have heard they used to cook him
the flesh of the young boys. But as he had such a great variety of dishes,
made of so many different ingredients, we could not tell whether a dish was
of human flesh or anything else, since every day they cooked fowls, turkeys,
pheasants, local partridges, quail, tame and wild duck, venison, wild boar,
marsh birds, pidgeons, hares and rabbits, also many other kinds of birds
and beasts native to their country, so numerous that I cannot quickly name
them all. I know for certain, however, that after our Captain spoke against
the sacrifice of human beings and the eating of their flesh, Montezuma
ordered that it should no longer be served to him.

Bernal Díaz, *The Conquest of New Spain*[19]

Unlike "innocence," which remained on American soil, "barbarism,"
which had originated in Greek discussions of foreigners, returned to
sixteenth-century Europe, carrying with it its New World connotations –
idolatry, superstition, cannibalism.

I am not sorry that we notice the barbarous horror of such acts, but I am
heartily sorry that, judging their faults rightly, we should be so blind to our
own. I think there is more barbarity in eating a man alive than in eating
him dead; and in tearing by tortures and the rack a body still full of feeling,
in roasting a man bit by bit, in having him bitten and mangled by dogs and
swine (as we have not only read but seen within fresh memory, not among
ancient enemies, but among neighbors and fellow citizens, and what is
worse, on the pretext of piety and religion), than in roasting and eating him
after he is dead.

Michel de Montaigne, "On Cannibals" (1580)[20]

Debates on slavery and conversion carried back to Europe terms European in their origins, but now transformed by their New World connotations, translating them onto European soil. And the debates carried
those notions deeply into the heart of European Christianity. What did it
mean to be a Christian? What was the relationship between human nature
and Christianity? Did Christianity "civilize"? Could one be "barbaric" and
"Christian" at the same time?

Furthermore, if it comes to the brutal action of really (as one says) chewing
and devouring human flesh, have we not found people in these regions over
here, even among those who bear the name of Christian, both in Italy and
elsewhere, who, not content with having cruelly put to death their enemies,
have been unable to slake their bloodthirst except by eating their livers
and their hearts? I defer to the histories. And, without going further, what

---

[19] Díaz, *The Conquest of New Spain*, pp. 225–6.
[20] *The Complete Essays of Michel de Montaigne*, translated by Donald M. Frame (Stanford: Stanford University Press, 1976), p. 155.

of France? (I am French, and it grieves me to say it.) During the bloody
tragedy that began in Paris on the twenty-fourth of August 1572 – for which
I do not accuse those who are not responsible – among other acts horrible
to recount, which were perpetrated at that time throughout the kingdom,
the fat of human bodies (which, in ways more barbarous than those of the
savages, were butchered at Lyon after being pulled out of the Saône) – was
it not publicly sold to the highest bidder? The livers, the hearts, and other
parts of these bodies – were they not eaten by the furious murderers, of
whom Hell itself stands in horror? Likewise, after the wretched massacre
of one Coeur de Roy, who professed the Reformed Faith in the City of
Auxerre – did not those who committed this murder cut his heart to pieces,
display it for sale to those who hated him, and finally, after grilling it over
coals – glutting their rage like mastiffs – eat of it?

                    Jean de Léry, *History of a Voyage to the Land of Brazil*[21]

Debates on conversion brought a constellation of terms – "innocence,"
"barbarism," "cannibalism," and "idolatry" – into direct contact with
thinking about Christianity, linking images of the New World with
"Christians" in many different ways. As Europe erupted in its own violence
over questions of what true Christianity was, the New World permeated
the polemics. Protestants accused Catholics of being cannibals and practicing idolatry. Catholics characterized Protestant worship in terms of
absences, in the same way as the cultures of the western hemisphere.
These were not simple translations from one world to the other: The
accusation of cannibalism linked Catholics to the profound strangeness
of that "New World," linked their natures to "barbarians," and in so
doing severed them from Protestants, though those Protestants could be
their brothers, fathers, mothers, sisters, neighbors. Persons who had been
baptized "Christian" could, according to the polemic, be "barbarian" and
therefore not able, by their very nature, to be truly "Christian." Words
moved in their attachments: Tupi, according to Michel de Montaigne,
observing the violence of France during the Wars of Religion, were less
barbaric than the cannibals of Europe.

[21] Jean de Léry, *History of a Voyage to the Land of Brazil*, p. 132.

3

"The Word"

Printing

In 1454–55, Johannes Gensfleisch zur Laden zum Gutenberg printed a Latin Bible.[1] A goldsmith, he had developed an ink that enabled the use of metal fonts – technological innovations that made printing a viable medium for the mass production of texts. The implications of his choice of text – Bibles in numbers unimaginable before those two small changes in technology made it possible to put them in the hands of utterly new readerships of widely different experiences and social place – would only be taken up fifty years later, by Desiderius Erasmus. And yet, without the material products of the technology of print – those thousands of Bibles – "the Word of God" could not have become as intimate, as immediate, or as personal as it did for thousands of sixteenth-century Christians.

Gutenberg's ink seems to have been a combination of graphite, copper, lead, and titanium, providing a particularly clear black with surface glitter. It was not as susceptible to water or fading as the ink used in manuscripts, providing a more durable division of black from the cream-colored paper. And it held to metal, unlike earlier inks, producing a relatively even print. By 1470, other printers had refined Gutenberg's metal type to the process that would be used until the eighteenth century: a letter engraved into a hard metal punch, which was then used to produce multiple copies of that letter in softer metal, which made possible identical letters used simultaneously on the same page. Equally significant, as it turned out, moveable type facilitated the development of a Greek font within a decade, which mimicked manuscript Greek – 200 characters instead of

---

[1] On the Gutenberg Bible, see http://www.bl.uk/treasures/gutenberg/homepage.html.

the 24 letters of the Greek alphabet – but which also brought Greek texts into far broader circulation than before.

Printing altered both the production of texts and their reception. Each manuscript, as its name indicates, was and is a product of the hand. Before printing, a scribe was commissioned to copy a text. Typically, a scribe worked from beginning to end, from the first word to the last, copying word by word. Typically, a single book took one year of one person's labor to produce. Each manuscript was singular: not only the product of a human hand (or human hands), produced over a year's time, but also, all efforts to reduce error notwithstanding, different from every other text in its lettering, shape and cadence of the words, and in the errors of transcription.

That word, "typically," is a marker of the transformations both of the production of texts and of readerships. At its root lies what type printers perfected in the fifteenth century: each letter the same shape throughout a page – a constancy and a consistency even the best scribes could not duplicate. Moveable type fonts and printing did not simply enable the production of multiple texts, but of texts that were far more identical than any scribal production – a new uniformity whose potentialities publishers and authors would explore throughout the sixteenth century.

Moveable metal type and the printing press separate manuscript production from printing. Both required fundamentally different skills from those of the scribe, and each required skills different from the other: The person who set the moveable type needed to be literate, to be able to read the author's manuscript copy or the printed text to be copied, whereas the pressman needed foremost to be strong enough to handle a machine that pressed paper onto metal type evenly to produce the black markings of words, and no more.

Printing, moreover, required a single space for the entire process. Monastic scribes often worked together in scriptoria – the room specifically designated for the activity of copying – in their monasteries, and they might divide labor not simply between scribe and illuminator, but between scribes; scribes per se, however, did not need to work in the same space, and indeed, by the fifteenth century, lay scribes were working on commission in their own homes. Printing, in contrast, necessitated a workshop. The compositor set the type in a line, arranged the lines to form a page, set pages into a form, or frame, the size of a sheet of paper, which was then set into the press. In a typical workshop, another person inked the form – optimally, before printing, the type would once again be checked for errors – and then set a sheet of wet paper on it. The pressman worked the press, a machine designed to bring even pressure down onto the paper so that the inked letters left individual indentations which held that durable and sharp black ink.

At the center of the production of a printed text was the sheet of paper, of a relatively constant size. A compositor might work from the beginning of a text to the end, but that did not structure his thinking: The intended size of the book determined how many pages he needed to set, the arrangement of those pages in the form, and, therefore, the number of any individual letters he needed to set those pages. The smaller the book, the more pages were fit into the form, which remained a constant size; the more pages, the greater portion of the text needed to be set simultaneously for the press run. The first and last pages of a text could well be set and printed at the same time, while inner pages could be composed separately. The size of the book also determined the organization of the entire book at the end of the process, requiring the typesetter to provide markings for either the publisher or his customer to set the printed pages in their proper sequence.

By the sixteenth century, publishers deployed with marked efficacy different sizes for different ends. Broadsheets were printed on a full sheet of paper, on one side. While a broadsheet was the largest format, it was also a single sheet – easily folded, carried from place to place, then posted. Folio, the size of Gutenberg's Bible, was the next largest format. For folio-sized books, the compositor set a total of four pages for each sheet of paper – two front and two on the back side – and once printed, they were folded once, along the inside edge of the page, the pages arranged in their proper sequence, and then either the printer or the customer who bought the pages had them sewn together and, perhaps, bound. In the sixteenth century, publishers often printed in folio texts that were accorded singular authority – Erasmus's Greek New Testament and Commentaries, Luther's German Bible, the Missal and Catechism of the Council of Trent. Quarto, half the size of folio, involved four pages on each side of the sheet of paper and two folds. Perhaps the majority of polemical pamphlets were published in this format, which allowed a publisher to produce eight pages simultaneously and, thus, the pamphlet in a day. In this format appeared dialogues between peasants and clergy that might be performed, exhortations, explications of specific points of dispute in communities, and the first evangelical liturgical works. Octavo, in which eight pages were printed at the same time, and then, when the flip side had also been printed, four folds, was used for lengthier treatises, summae of doctrine, and the copies for scholars of such core texts as Erasmus's Greek New Testament. By mid-century, publishers were deploying smaller formats – one-sixth to one-twelfth the size of a folio – to place in the hands, predominantly of young men, portable handbooks and catechisms of divergent orthodoxies. The smallest possible text, 128 pages to a sheet of paper, was difficult to produce, from setting type to stitching so many tiny pages together, but served both to be so small that a child could carry it in her hand and, as the smaller formats did so well, to be hideable, increasingly to serve clandestinely communities who were persecuted, hunted down, and whose books were seized and burned.

In the middle of production, Gutenberg was able to make adjustments: He abandoned an older practice, of marking the beginning of each new segment of text with an elaborate letter – a holdover from manuscript production, in which a scribe began from such a letter – and he increased the number of lines per page from forty to forty-two, something the mechanics of moveable type made possible over many pages. Most significantly, when we come to consider reception and readerships, Gutenberg increased that very first print run – the number of copies he was producing at a single time. A scribe produced a single text in roughly a year's time. Gutenberg's first press run produced 180 copies of the same text. By the sixteenth century, presses were producing more than 2,000 copies in a run of texts that, like Luther's Bible, were expected to sell, or that, like the Twelve Articles, sought a wide readership in order to bring men and women to action. Within seventy years of Gutenberg's innovations, publishers and authors could envision reaching hundreds of readers, at the same time, who themselves might live miles apart, some in villages, most in towns, and have no other connection than the book in their hands.

Reading

Printing changed reading. In producing more copies of the same text, it fostered readerships that were linked through the reading of the same text. In the 1520s, for example, journeymen in their workshops and peasants in their villages were reading pamphlets that called for the world to be ordered according to the evangelical principle of brotherly love. Belonging far more to the marketplace, printing produced texts for people who could not afford manuscripts, which, being labor-intensive, were expensive in relation to print. It made texts available to new kinds of readers: journeymen, artisans, peasants, as well as merchants and innkeepers. Attentive to new markets, printers also produced texts for non-clerical and non-noble readers. Printers turned early to texts in vernacular languages, most famously Bibles in translation, as well as handbooks for household management, devotional works of various kinds, fables, poetry, and chronicles. Printing made available to many more readers, of different social groups, both new kinds of texts and multiple copies of the same text.

That said, the relationship between printing and "literacy" is neither causal nor direct. There is no way to measure "literacy" in the early modern world: There were no tests, no standardized measurements at all. There was no mandated education, and schools were not designed to provide either universal education or a consistent standard of education. The relationship between printing and reading is far more complex and more interesting. Manuscripts were produced in a world in which a tiny minority read and studied texts that traditionally had been overwhelmingly in Latin. Printing brought into circulation many more vernacular texts. But those texts were not construed as a thing apart from the spoken word as they are today. Orthographically and grammatically, those early texts reflect local pronouncement and usage. In 1500, there were no dictionaries. None. Not for Latin, whose spelling and usage was largely held to be set by classical texts as they had been transmitted. None for the spoken languages of marketplace, trade fair, and household. There was, in other words, no norm against which the spelling of any printed vernacular text might be judged. The same workshop, moreover, in the same text would print the same word with perhaps as many as a half dozen different spellings, no one of which was more correct. Indeed, most, perhaps all, early modern reading was aloud. We know that journeymen read pamphlets aloud to their co-workers, but even scholars alone in their studies might read aloud. The printed word and the spoken word were, for the journeymen setting the type, not so distant from one another as they have come to be.

In the same years as printing was developing the technology and labor practices that continued until the French Revolution, lay devotional groups, foremost the Devotio Moderna, were placing greater emphasis on reading as a devotional activity for lay men and women. The wives of merchants and masters might not be able to purchase an illuminated Book of Hours, but they could purchase a printed edition of *The Imitation of Christ*. Works such as *The Imitation* fostered an increasingly intimate relationship between reading and faith. Using that moveable type with its regularities and consistencies, all these works set before their readers' eyes words, in black on cream, that were consciously chosen not simply to set forth what Christ had said, but to evoke how Christ had looked, what his gestures looked like when reenacted, to inspire in the mind's eye of each reader a sense of Christ's physical immediacy. The most beloved of those texts, *The Imitation of Christ*, furthermore called upon its readers to imagine the person of Christ, to seek the mimesis of his person and works in their daily activities, and to hold Christ as a living and acting real presence in their minds.

In 1500, with no universal education, different groups had different reading practices. Universities continued to teach the practices of glossing and commenting on texts – two different modes of engagement with a text in which the reader responded directly to the text before him, sometimes explicating a word, sometimes exploring the interconnections between that text and others. Universities were still centers of Latin learning: University students studied Latin texts as they learned to write in complex Latin prose – they worked in a language no longer native to anyone but constituting a republic of letters across political and, in the sixteenth century, the growing religious divisions of Christendom. Within that republic of Latin letters was a smaller group who read Greek and an even smaller circle who were learning Hebrew from Jewish scholars and rabbis. Readers of Greek and readers of Hebrew grew in numbers over the course of the sixteenth century, as more Christians sought to read the languages of the New and Old Testaments, even as they ever more violently distanced themselves from Jewish scholars and rabbinical scholarship. By the end of the fifteenth century, towns had Latin schools for boys, some of whom were destined for the clergy, some to serve various sovereigns as secretaries. Yet another group were those lay men and women who read Books of Hours and Psalters, both of which continued to be produced by hand in beautiful illuminated volumes. Normally in Latin, these texts were read within the rhythms of the liturgical year: not sentence by sentence from the first page to the last, but day by day. If Books of Hours helped make devotional reading an intimate and domestic activity, the Devotio Moderna fostered within a group of lay men and women who could not afford the beautifully handmade Books of Hours an analogous sense that reading could have spiritual meaning.

Reading the Bible

In hindsight, Gutenberg's choice of text seems obvious: *Bibla* derives from the Greek word for book; "the Bible" meant "the book." And yet, he chose to produce as a codex, a text arranged sequentially between two covers, a work most European Christians at that time neither owned nor read. He chose to produce in a medium financially affordable for lay men and women whose wealth was urban, commercial or artisanal, a book in a language increasingly removed from the marketplace and the hearth: Latin. In 1450, those Europeans who read the Bible were a relatively small number: those who read Latin, who studied the Bible as a part of, usually, the study of theology – university students and faculty, members of religious orders whose house owned one or more Bibles. The great majority of Christians might well see a great bible – beautifully illuminated, on parchment, in folio – in their churches. On the walls of their churches, they might find scenes from the Old Testament, or, far more frequently, scenes from the Gospel narratives of Jesus' life. Insofar as Christians attended Mass, they had heard the Bible, but in fragments that were determined by the liturgy. They heard Psalms, lessons from the Gospels and the Epistles. But the great majority of European Christians did not know the Bible as a single text, to be read from one cover to the other. The devotional works they read – Books of Hours, Psalters, *The Imitation of Christ* – excerpted from the Bible, but did not seek to teach their readers to conceive of it as "the Book," comprising a range of different genres, from poetry to letters, that might itself be read as a devotional text.

We do not know who Gutenberg imagined the market for printed Bibles would be. At the moment when he printed his folio Bible, there was certainly a demand for multiple copies of the Bible, but it was almost exclusively ecclesiastical: parish churches, which often had a Bible on display; cloisters, who owned Bibles for study. University students and faculty owned Bibles, but most preferred a more portable format, octavo, roughly a quarter of the size of Gutenberg's Bible, and used manuscript copies, handed down. When Gutenberg chose to put the Bible into print, there was no exceptional demand, no increase in interest that preceded it, so far as we know – he printed it on speculation that so many copies would find a market.

Whatever Gutenberg's thinking may have been, his Bible electrified contemporaries. Aeneas Silvias, who would become Pope Pius II in 1458, wrote an exultant letter to a Spanish cardinal, commending especially the legibility of the type, which he could read without glasses. Although printing had been available for a long time, without a viable ink and moveable type, it had not been a viable medium for producing works of the length and textual complexity of the Bible. With his Bible, Gutenberg did not simply advertise his innovations. He opened horizons: for new ways of formatting the text that took full advantage of printing's potentialities; for new readerships; and, as Erasmus saw so clearly in the sixteenth century, for the possibility that scholars might all read the same text and ground a shared scholarly enterprise in it.

Between Gutenberg's Bible and the early sixteenth century, Bible production simply took off in numbers, languages, and formats. A book the size of the Bible would take a single scribe more than a year to produce by hand. Given both the potential for error inhering in manuscript production and the relative isolation of medieval scribes from one another, by the thirteenth century, there were many different versions of the *Vulgate* – the Latin translation of the Bible Jerome largely completed in the fourth century. Those variations ranged from a difference in a word through the divisions of each book – no Bible in this period was divided into verse, and chapter divisions were not consistent – to the books included in "The Bible." Jerome had set the books of the Old Testament, the number and order of the Gospels in the New Testament, and the order of the books of the New Testament, but by 1450, his great effort at organization and stabilization of the late antique texts was obscured among all the variant copies, and "the Bible" was not one text, but many, nearly as many as there were copies. In a single town, Mainz, for example, in the same years, 1452–54, a manuscript version of the Vulgate, written on paper from the same supply as the Gutenberg Bible, did not include the apocryphal fourth book of Ezra, as Gutenberg had done – even in the same town, at the same time, different versions of the Vulgate were being produced. "God's Word" was not singular.

Between 1450 and 1500, printers produced eighty-one "plain-text" versions of the Vulgate, that is, versions without any commentary on the page, and thirteen more with some kind of commentary. Most looked to the Gutenberg text, the beginning of a kind of standardization that had not been possible with medieval manuscripts. Even as they published Vulgate Bibles, printers commissioned and printed translations: beginning in 1466, with a complete Bible in German; one in Italian in 1471; the New Testament in French in 1474 and complete Bible in 1478; and Jan Hus's Czech translation of the New Testament in 1475 and the complete Bible in 1488. By 1500, there were some thirty different translations of the Bible into German. Printers developed new fonts as well as new formats for the printed page: in 1482, a Hebrew font; throughout the period, fonts to improve legibility. So, too, in competition for markets, publishers introduced new textual aids: A folio Bible of 1479 divided all the chapters of the New Testament into four to seven sections; the

Bible the Basel printer Johann Froben published in 1491 extended the practice of dividing to the Old Testament as well. Perhaps most important, however, was the production of portable Bibles. The earliest printed Bibles, like the best-known manuscript Bibles, were the largest size, ranging in height from twelve to sixteen inches, depending on the paper. Froben's 1491 Bible was the first printed Bible in octavo format, a Bible that could be carried. While thirteenth-century university students had had a comparably small manuscript Bible, this Bible nonetheless electrified: making physically explicit the possibility that Bibles could be freed from the lectern or the study table and carried freely, not simply by impoverished university students, but by those who could now afford such a small-format and relatively humble Bible.

By 1500, lay men and women were buying Bibles, some to read, some to donate to their churches, some simply to own. More Europeans could purchase Bibles in the language of their home and in every size in which manuscript Bibles had been produced, from small portable editions to grand, hand-colored folios. The competition for readerships had also fostered a dizzying proliferation of commentaries and other textual aids combined with the Bibles. By 1500, lay men and women were reading their Bibles privately – away from the university, the cloister, or even the parish church. And many were changing how they were reading their Bibles.

Reading "The Word of God"

An event and a new method transformed how Europeans viewed and read their Bibles. In 1453, the capital of the Byzantine Empire, Constantinople, fell to the Ottoman Empire. At the time, Pope Pius II and Philip the Good, Duke of Burgundy, decried the loss of one of the ancient centers of Christianity to Muslim conquerors – a loss in the battle between Christianity and Islam. And yet, the fall of Constantinople is inseparably intertwined with the efflorescence of Greek scholarship in the west that culminated in the publication of Erasmus's Greek New Testament. The fall of their capital drove Byzantine scholars to carry their libraries west. Individual Byzantine scholars had traveled west before: The Medici and Popes had invited them to Florence and Rome to teach Greek to the humanists in their courts. So, too, Arab scholars had transmitted to the west individual texts and fragments of works by Greek philosophers, mathematicians, and natural scientists. But those earlier scholars had not been driven. They had not feared the loss of treasured texts, ancient manuscripts preserved for a millennium and more. In the mid-fifteenth century, Byzantine scholars carried to the west the entire corpus of the works of Plato and Aristotle, works of the Greek Church Fathers, such as John Chrysostom. For the first time since at least the fifth century, to take but one example, western Europeans could read Plato's *Republic*, a work that would inspire Thomas More, and others, to imagine a world in which the state did not simply dictate morals, but shaped ethics.

Even as new texts migrated west, a new method was captivating those who studied the texts: philology. Philology approaches language as itself deeply historical: Words are not universal abstracts, constant in their meaning over generations, but used by specific individuals, in particular moments in history, in ways that are determined by that individual and that moment. In 1440, a Florentine humanist, Lorenzo Valla, drew on the method of philology – the study of the precise use of any word in time – in demonstrating that a document was a forgery. Both the notion of forgery and the particular document captured attention. The document, known as the Donation of Constantine, had been the foundation, over hundreds of years, for papal claims to sovereignty over lands far beyond the Papal States. Valla effectively undermined those claims, using what had seemed the obscure method of the scholar: the close study of the use of Latin words, particular grammatical and syntactical constructions, at particular moments in time. Valla then turned to the text of the Vulgate, which was used for the liturgy and which was the foundation for most of the Bibles then in circulation. From his study of Greek, he wrote his first Collations on the New Testament in 1442 and began circulating a draft in 1443. In 1453, Valla returned to Rome, where he met Byzantine refugees, one of whom in particular, Cardinal Bessarion, aided Valla's study of the Greek text of the New Testament. Until his death in 1457, Valla revised and altered his earlier notes, engaging more explicitly with what he found to be problems in Jerome's choice of words, as well as the resonances of the Greek that had been lost in translation. Valla did not publish his collations. He did not seek to bring his reflections on the Greek text of the New Testament and its Latin translation to unknown readers. His collations, therefore, nearly disappeared.

Almost fifty years later, while searching through manuscripts at the Abbey of Parc near Louvain, Erasmus discovered Valla's second collation. Erasmus's encounter with Valla's collations worked both immediate effects – to publish them as Lorenzo Valla's *Annotations* to the New Testament, in 1505 – and deep and long-term changes. It is not that Erasmus found a new method there – he had already found deep pleasure and intellectual value in the study of ancient languages as living, inseparable from the lives that gave breath to words. And Erasmus already knew and admired Valla as a brilliant Latin stylist. Nor did Valla introduce Erasmus to the study of the Greek New Testament – Erasmus had been studying the Pauline Epistles in the circle of John Colet in England. No, it was as though two wires crossed: the lessons of the Devotio Moderna – the spiritual value of reading and the Gospels as the vital source for Christian life – and Valla's emphasis upon the living Greek. In that particular mix of experience and reading, we find the catalyst for his edition of the Greek New Testament.

When he discovered Valla's notes, Erasmus already found troubling the plurality of versions of the Latin Bible. That plurality represented exactly the kind of sloppiness – of copying, of attention to individual words as well as syntax and style – that he fought his entire life. Though Parisian theologians had sought in the thirteenth century to stabilize the text of the Bible, to foster a single text – without variations in word choice, syntax, or divisions of text – the numbers of manuscript and printed versions of the Latin Bible in the fifteenth century testify to the failure of that effort at standardization. Crippling to those efforts had been the absence of a clear principle by which one might choose this text over that, this word over that – the copying of manuscripts had produced a cornucopia of textual variations, as well as immediately recognizable errors. In Valla's sense, that words exist within human time and are used in specific ways by communities that are historically discrete, Erasmus found the method by which he might approach all those variant versions of the Bible. When complete, his Latin translation of the Greek New Testament diverged 52,000 words from some 125,000 words in the Vulgate, translating differently roughly 40 percent of Jerome's text.

And it is here that Erasmus marks a watershed: Like Valla, and others, he thought of language as a living thing, existing in human time, and used by distinctive individuals. Far more than Valla, he saw the various books of Scripture in terms of distinctive authors, in terms of discrete voices. As Erasmus made explicit in his own Latin translation of the Greek, in the beginning was not "verbum" – the written word – but "sermo," the spoken word. For him, and for thousands of Christians in the sixteenth century, between the two covers of that printed thing, of that codex, were to be found "the Word of God," not dry traces on vellum or paper, but the spoken words of a living God.

Without the fusion of a deep feel for language as living and vital with the capacity of the technology of print to put into the hands of thousands the

Word of God, there could have been no Reformation. Without print, the lessons of philology would not have had their power to move thousands to change their lives. Without philology, the printed page would have been but fixed black marks on paper.

The foundation of the study of the Word of God, Erasmus held, was an authoritative edition of the Bible, beginning with the New Testament. Like Valla and Colet, Erasmus found exhilarating the study of Greek manuscripts of the New Testament – they revealed dimensions of meaning obscured in Jerome's translation. Erasmus collected four different manuscripts in Greek in order to cross check and establish the most reliable version – governed by the principles of philology. Judged by modern standards, Erasmus's edition has long been found wanting: It was not the product of an exhaustive search for the oldest available manuscripts. But that very principle is what Erasmus's Greek New Testament put into motion: to find the text closest to the living spoken word.

Erasmus also recognized the potential of the printing press to produce an authoritative version of a text. Each manuscript had errors: No text was perfect. Each was therefore read not as an archetype, but as a human – and therefore, imperfect – record of what the author had said, in the great majority of cases, in Latin, the language of the scriptoria. From the earliest editions of his popular *Adages*, Erasmus had worked closely with Froben to produce texts of consistent spelling and grammar, determined through careful collation of use and determination of correct usage. Erasmus recognized that the errors in printing could be reduced dramatically, precisely because of the process of production, in which the typesetting could be checked before a single page was printed, and future productions of a page could be corrected.

Frustratingly for Erasmus, his very first edition of the Greek New Testament was rushed: printed in 1516 to appear in advance of another edition. His intent, however, was to print an edition that would provide scholars with a carefully compiled, precise, carefully corrected, uniform, and stable – authoritative, according to Erasmus – text. That text, he hoped, could then serve as the solid foundation for the study of God's words; for translations; and thereby, for the reading of the Bible Erasmus envisioned for all pious Christians.

As he wrote in the Paraclesis, which prefaced that first printed edition of the Greek New Testament:

> Indeed, I disagree very much with those who are unwilling that Holy Scripture, translated into the vulgar tongue, be read by the uneducated, as if

ΕΥΑΓΓΈΛΙΟΝ ΚΑΤΑ
ΙΩΑΝΝΗΝ.

EVANGELIVM SECVNDVM
IOANNEM.

Ἐν ἀρχῇ ἦν ὁ λόγος, καὶ ὁ λόγος ἦν πρὸς τὸν θεόν, καὶ θεὸς ἦν ὁ λόγος. οὗτος ἦν ἐν ἀρχῇ πρὸς τὸν θεόν. πάντα δι' αὐτοῦ ἐγένετο, καὶ χωρὶς αὐτοῦ ἐγένετο οὐδὲ ἕν, ὃ γέγονεν. ἐν αὐτῷ ζωὴ ἦν, καὶ ἡ ζωὴ ἦν τὸ φῶς τῶν ἀνθρώπων, καὶ τὸ φῶς ἐν τῇ σκοτίᾳ φαίνει, καὶ ἡ σκοτία αὐτὸ οὐ κατέλαβεν. ἐγένετο ἄνθρωπος ἀπεσταλμένος παρὰ θεοῦ, ὄνομα αὐτῷ Ἰωάννης. οὗτος ἦλθεν εἰς μαρτυρίαν, ἵνα μαρτυρήσῃ περὶ τοῦ φωτός, ἵνα πάντες πιστεύσωσι δι' αὐτοῦ. οὐκ ἦν ἐκεῖνος τὸ φῶς, ἀλλ' ἵνα μαρτυρήσῃ περὶ τοῦ φωτός. ἦν τὸ φῶς τὸ ἀληθινόν, ὃ φωτίζει πάντα ἄνθρωπον ἐρχόμενον εἰς τὸν κόσμον. ἐν τῷ κόσμῳ ἦν, καὶ ὁ κόσμος δι' αὐτοῦ ἐγένετο, καὶ ὁ κόσμος αὐτὸν οὐκ ἔγνω. εἰς τὰ ἴδια ἦλθεν, καὶ οἱ ἴδιοι αὐτὸν οὐ παρέλαβον. ὅσοι δὲ ἔλαβον αὐτόν, ἔδωκεν αὐτοῖς ἐξουσίαν τέκνα θεοῦ γενέσθαι τοῖς πιστεύουσιν εἰς τὸ ὄνομα αὐτοῦ, οἳ οὐκ ἐξ αἱμάτων, οὐδὲ ἐκ θελήματος σαρκός, οὐδὲ ἐκ θελήματος ἀνδρός, ἀλλ' ἐκ θεοῦ ἐγεννήθησαν. καὶ ὁ λόγος σὰρξ ἐγένετο, καὶ ἐσκήνωσεν ἐν ἡμῖν, καὶ ἐθεασάμεθα τὴν δόξαν αὐτοῦ, δόξαν ὡς μονογενοῦς παρὰ πατρός, πλήρης χάριτος καὶ ἀληθείας. Ἰωάννης μαρτυρεῖ περὶ αὐτοῦ, καὶ κέκραγεν λέγων, οὗτος ἦν ὃν εἶπον, ὁ ὀπίσω μου ἐρχόμενος ἔμπροσθέν μου γέγονεν, ὅτι πρῶτός μου ἦν.

IN principio erat uerbum, & uerbum erat apud deũ, & deus erat uerbum. Hoc erat in principio apud deum. Omnia per ipsum facta sunt, & sine ipso factum est nihil, quod factum est. In ipso uita erat, & uita erat lux hominum, & lux in tenebris lucet, & tenebræ eam non comphenderunt. Fuit homo missus a deo, cui nomen erat Ioannes. Hic uenit in testimonium, ut testimonium perhiberet de lumine, ut oẽs crederent per illũ. Non erat ille lux, sed ut testimonium perhiberet de lumine. Erat lux uera, quæ illuminat oẽm hominem uenientem in hunc mundũ. In mundo erat, & mundus per ipsum factus est, & mundus eũ nó cognouit. In propria uenit, & sui eum nó receperũt. Quotquot aũt receperunt eũ, dedit eis potestatẽ filios dei fieri his qui credũt in nomine eius. Qui non ex sanguinibus, neq3 ex uoluntate carnis, neq3 ex uoluntate uiri, sed ex deo nati sunt. Et uerbum caro factũ est, & habitauit in nobis, & uidimus gloriã eius gloriã uelut unigeniti a patre, plenum gratiæ & ueritatis. Ioannes testimonium perhibet de ipso, & clamauit dicẽs. Hic erat de quo dicebã, qui post me uenturus est, prior me cœpit esse, quia prior me erat.

FIGURE 3.1. First page of Gospel of John, *Novum Instrumentum*, Erasmus of Rotterdam, editor. Basel: Johannes Froben, 1516, p. 192. Bridwell Library, Perkins School of Theology, Southern Methodist University.

Christ taught such intricate doctrines that they could scarcely be understood by very few theologians, or as if the strength of the Christian religion consisted in men's ignorance of it. The mysteries of a king, perhaps, are better concealed, but Christ wishes his mysteries published as openly as possible. I would that even the lowliest women read the Gospels and the Pauline Epistles. And I would that they were translated into all languages, so that they could be read and understood not only by Scots and Irish but also by Turks and Saracens.... Would that, as a result, the farmer sing some portion of them at the plow, the weaver hum some parts of them to the movement of his shuttle, the traveler lighten the weariness of the journey with stories of this kind! Let all the conversations of every Christian be drawn from this source.

... Only a very few can be learned, but all can be Christian, all can be devout, and – I shall boldly add – all can be theologians.[2]

Erasmus's Paraclesis was taken up immediately, published in translation in dozens of pirated versions. Its central vision of the New Testament, as the source for the philosophia Christi, the living of a Christian life, resonated powerfully for thousands of European Christians.

With Erasmus's publication of the Greek New Testament, "God's Word" was no longer something of the universities and the clergy, but spoken at particular times and in particular places – concrete and lived, though, in the Greek, in the past. In this, Erasmus's Greek New Testament contrasts with the contemporary project of that same Cardinal Francisco Ximenes de Cisneros who had led the forced conversion of Muslims: the first polyglot Bible, or, as it was called, after the town in which it was produced, the Complutensian Bible. The scholars working under Cisnero's direction had compiled a Greek New Testament by 1514 – hence Erasmus's rush to publication – but they did not print it until 1522, after Erasmus's edition had appeared. They waited for papal approval. And they situated their text in a different relationship to the Vulgate. In the arrangement of the pages of the Old and New Testaments, the Complutensian scholars affirmed the Vulgate's authority. The Old Testament text presented a Hebrew text to one side; the Vulgate text in the center; and on the other side, the Greek Septuagint – an early translation of the Hebrew Bible into Greek. The New Testament used a different Greek font, an especially legible font developed from eleventh- and twelfth-century manuscripts of Greek texts, to present the Greek text, still linked on the plane of the page to the Vulgate.

---

[2] *Christian Humanism and the Reformation: Selected Writings of Erasmus*, edited by John Olin (New York: Fordham University Press, 1965 [1980]), pp. 96–97, 100.

FIGURE 3.2. Bible, Polyglot (Complutensian). Arhald Guillen de Brocar, vol. I, folio y6 verso. Alcala de Henares, 1514–1517. The Pierpont Morgan Library. Photo credit: The Pierpont Morgan Library / Art Resource, New York.

In both the Old and New Testaments, the spatial organization of each page followed the manuscript tradition, in which commentary or texts in some other way derivative appear on either side, and the authoritative or "original" text appears in the middle. The Complutensian Bible sought to affirm the Vulgate text as the core text. In contrast, Erasmus emphasized the Greek New Testament as more "original" – closer to the words Jesus spoke or Paul wrote – and questioned the transparency and vitality of Jerome's translation, himself undertaking a translation which restored to the Gospels their living language.

Translations of the Bible into vernacular languages were not new to the sixteenth century. As we have seen, publishers were producing Bibles in German, Italian, and French by the late 1470s. But the vernacular Bibles that followed upon Erasmus's Greek New Testament not only shared his desire to restore to the Word of God its vitality, its life, its immediacy – they extended that principle, to translate the Word of God into the daily speech of common Europeans. In translating the New Testament into German, in 1521–22, Martin Luther (1483–1546) periodically left the Warburg, where he was hiding from imperial arrest, to listen to people speaking in the squares and markets of local towns. His translation, immediately taken up by the laity for whom it was done, rendered the words of the ancient texts in the expressions of everyday life. In 1534, Luther, in collaboration with a number of scholars in Wittenberg, published a complete Bible in German, which also included woodcut illustrations by the Wittenberg artist, Lucas Cranach – yet another step in a process of translating the Bible for all Christians.

William Tyndale, inspired by Luther's German New Testament and working from Erasmus's edition of the Greek text as well as his Latin translation and Luther's German, and often working physically close to Luther, completed a translation of the New Testament into English in 1525 – though he could find no publisher for it until 1526, and then, not in England, where his efforts had been banned, but in Worms. Luther's was the first of the evangelical Bibles – Bibles that sought to make the Word of God the Living Word. Tyndale's Bible would serve as the foundation for the Geneva Bible – the English Bible that Shakespeare, Donne, and the Puritans read – completed in 1560 and first published in England in 1575. Like Luther's and Tyndale's translations, the Geneva Bible sought contemporary usage in order to link the world of the Gospels to sixteenth-century English men and women, and in Shakespeare, in particular, it crossed into colloquial speech, itself becoming the substance of commonplaces of everyday expression.

FIGURE 3.3. Saint Paul, Letter to the Romans, New Testament, Martin Luther, translator. Photo credit: Bildarchiv Preussischer Kulturbesitz / Art Resource, New York.

In 1530, Jacques Lefèvre d'Étaples, or Jacobus Faber Stapulensis, as he was known in Latin, completed the first translation of the Bible from the Hebrew and Greek texts into French. He relied on Erasmus's edition of the Greek text for his translation of the New Testament. Unlike other evangelicals, he translated the Old Testament first, a different sense of the Bible. Yet another sense of the Bible may be glimpsed in the extraordinary popularity of his separate French editions of the Psalms and the Pauline Epistles – texts that were often read in private, away from public scrutiny, and which speak of a life of faith under duress.

Even as they echoed Erasmus's sense of the living word, Luther's and Tyndale's translations reflected choices with which Erasmus was not in agreement. Luther added "alone" to his translation of Paul's Letter to the Romans: "thus, we hold, then, that man is justified without the works of the law to do, *alone* through faith" (3:28) – a decision that arises not from the text itself, but from his understanding of Paul's intended meaning. Thomas More, Erasmus's close friend, and, like Tyndale, a native English speaker, accused Tyndale of corrupting meaning when he chose for specific Greek words, "congregation" instead of "church"; "senior" and then "elder" instead of "priest"; "repent" instead of "do penance"; and "love" instead of "charity." As these translations spread, and lay men and women read these texts, they were no longer hearing or reading the same words Erasmus had so carefully chosen, but other resonances, other associations.

Preaching the Word of God

We do not know if the Swiss preacher, Huldrych Zwingli (1484–1531), had Erasmus's Greek New Testament before him on January 1, 1519, when he mounted for the first time the pulpit in the Great Minster in Zurich. We know that he had anxiously awaited its publication, studying Greek, and then Hebrew, in order, following Erasmus's principle, to read the most authentic version of the biblical texts. We know, from contemporaries, that he riveted his audience, who had come to hear the people's priest just hired by the City Council. He was hired for his gifts as a preacher. But on that January day, Zwingli startled the entire congregation, deeply shocking some of its members, including some who had been responsible for his hiring. He did not preach in the traditional manner, drawing on Scripture as, say, Johann Geiler von Kaisersberg had done so famously in Strasbourg, to illustrate moral lessons. He opened with the text of the first Gospel, Matthew, and preached from that text. His next sermon took up the next section of the Gospel, and so he worked through the entire Gospel of Matthew over the course of weeks. From there he moved to the Acts of the Apostles, working chapter by chapter through it, then Paul's Letters, and then the Old Testament.

FIGURE 3.4. Georg Pencz, "The Contradicting Sermons." Woodcut with text by Hans Sachs, Nuremberg, 1529. Kupferstichkabinett, Staatliche Museen, Berlin, Germany. Photo credit: Bildarchiv Preussischer Kulturbesitz / Art Resource, New York.

The practice, known as continuous reading, transformed the relationship between sermon and Scripture. While medieval homilies – the most common form of sermon – took up a text from scripture, the scriptural text was determined according to the dictates of liturgical season. Scripture, in other words, was subsumed to liturgy, broken into fragments to illumine and anchor moral lessons. Zwingli inverted priorities, according Scripture primacy in the structuring of the sermon, and thereby also altered the relationship between sacred text and the voice of the preacher. Scripture was no longer anecdotal, but the focus, and the preacher was no longer drawing on it for external reasons, but giving living human voice to it as he read it aloud to his congregation.

That voice was, in the sixteenth century and afterwards, predominantly male. Only among the Anabaptists, who were persecuted across Europe, do we find women preaching. For most groups of evangelicals, the Word of God was masculine in timbre. And in giving sound to the Word of God, preachers' persons were physically, through that sound, linked to

God the Father, their very giving sound the source of their authority. So many accounts from those who went to hear one preacher rather than another testify that they believed they were "hearing the pure Word of God."

Zwingli seems to have been the first to preach according to the principle of continuous reading. But he was alone neither in the voice he gave to Scripture in his preaching nor in his emphasis on Scripture as the preeminent authority. By 1500, preaching had become pervasive across Europe. The great medieval preaching orders, the Dominicans and Franciscans, had established houses in major towns, as well as in many smaller towns. Across Europe, in town after town, lay men and women had endowed positions, which might be attached to their parish church or to the Cathedral, for clergy to preach specifically to the laity. Rural villages might hear a rare homily from their parish priest, but so, too, they might be visited by itinerant preachers.

If preaching had become pervasive by 1500, the sixteenth century was the age of preachers. There had been great preachers before: Bernardino of Siena, Geiler von Kaisersberg, Girolamo Savonarola. Never before, however, had there been so many at the same time who inspired, provoked, challenged, moved their audiences to change the conduct of their lives in one way or another. In part, the power of so much preaching in the sixteenth century was inseparable from the mixing of the preachers' voices with the Gospel: In preaching directly from the biblical texts, they gave breath and sound to that text they were calling all Christians to read, to hear, to look to, for the living of their lives. In the early 1520s, in town after town, preacher after preacher declared himself, like Zwingli, "evangelical" – his understanding of "true Christianity" and "true Christian worship" was determined by the Word of God. They did not call themselves either "reformers" – though many did indeed call explicitly for the reforming of the lives of Europeans to accord more closely with their understanding of the Bible – or "Protestants," a name given to some of them in 1529. In town squares, in marketplaces, in parish churches, in cathedrals, in the great medieval halls built for preaching, individuals of widely varying education and experience called their audiences to conform their lives to the Word of God. Their particular linking of voice and Gospel may also explain why it is difficult to find great preachers loyal to Rome in the first decades of the century: While Johann Eck (1486–1543) was an effective polemicist in print, and the Franciscan Thomas Murner (1475–1536/7) a brilliant satirist, not until Peter Canisius (1521–1597) do we find a figure in the pulpit who proved as effective in moving people to change their lives.

The sixteenth century also witnessed an exceptional number of gifted preachers. A number of his contemporaries sought to capture in words Martin Luther's power as a preacher: his ability to render theology in familiar metaphors, to translate the worlds of Latin learning into everyday speech and make theology come alive, his passion. John Calvin (1509–1564) had neither Zwingli's musically trained voice nor Luther's feel for colloquialisms, yet his preaching drew such numbers in Geneva that the church could not hold them all. Printed editions of his sermons capture his lucidity and his deep engagement with the text of Scripture, but lack the living voice of the man. Johannes Schilling in Augsburg is otherwise unknown except for the crowd of 2000 who appeared before the City Council to defend him. William Farel (1489–1565) so provoked some that they expelled him from Geneva, and so inspired others that they brought him back. Many divided communities, but others became beloved for leading their communities to articulate a "Reformation" of doctrine and worship that preserved communal relations: the Dominican Martin Bucer (1491–1551) in Strasbourg; the Franciscan Michael Keller in Augsburg; Andreas Osiander (1498–1552) in Nuremberg. One, Johannes Bugenhagen (1485–1558), while preacher in Wittenberg, worked with the towns of Hildesheim, Hamburg, and Lübeck, the principalities of Pomerania, Schleswig-Holstein, Braunschweig, and Braunschweig-Wolfenbüttel, and the Kingdom of Denmark to formulate forms of worship that both adhered to Luther's liturgical principles and attended to the distinctive devotional life of each place – offering a model for a "Church" that was at once deeply familiar and translocal.

While some built communities of faith, many others were driven onto the roads, traveling from place to place, preaching their particular vision of true Christianity. They remind us at once of the costs of those visions and their mobility, as they were carried from audience to audience, finding reception in some places, expulsion in others. Bernard Ochino (1487–1564), born in Siena, fled arrest in Italy, found refuge in Geneva, preached to the immigrant Italian community in Augsburg, and then, driven out by the Emperor, settled in England. Peter Martyr Vermigli (1499–1562), born in Florence, preached in Brescia, Pisa, Venice, Rome, and Lucca before fleeing, first to Zurich, then Basel, then Strasbourg, whence Thomas Cranmer (1489–1556) invited him to England in 1547, where, once again, the shifting waters of religion led him to return to Strasbourg in 1555, then, because of frictions with the evangelicals in Strasbourg, to move to Zurich, where he remained to his death. Dozens, such as the preachers Balthasar Hubmaier (c. 1480–1528), born near Augsburg, who preached in and around Zurich, or Thomas Müntzer (1488–1525), who preached in Zwickau, Prague, Allstedt in Saxony, and Mühlhausen, were executed for their understandings of evangelical Christianity and its import for the ordering of the world.

No one experience, education, or category united them all. They came from large towns and villages. They had grown up speaking German, French, English, Italian, Dutch, Spanish, Danish, Polish, or one of dozens of dialects. Most – but not all – had learned Latin. Some, such as Bucer, were Dominican; others, such as Schilling, were Franciscan. Some were Carmelite, some, such as Luther, Augustinian monks, some Augustinian canons. Some, such as Thomas Cranmer or Philipp Melanchthon (1497–1560), had not joined any order. Some, such as Conrad Grebel (1498–1526), were the children of wealth. Many more were neither rich nor poor, from families who hoped their sons might have prosperous careers as lawyers (Luther) or priests (Cranmer).

They called themselves evangelicals and spoke of "the Word of God." They did not speak of "the Words of God," allowing for plurality, even in the sense of discrete words. Their close and dedicated readings brought them to diverse and divergent understandings of what God commanded, what was true, what each Christian ought to do. As they discovered in the decade following the publication of Erasmus's Greek New Testament, even with that first attempt at a single, uniform, constant authoritative text, their readings – of Genesis and the Ten Commandments, the four Gospels, Paul's Letters, Revelation – differed in the small and the large.

And whatever form of sermon a preacher chose – continuous reading, a homily, exegesis, or explicatio – none simply involved reading the scriptural text aloud. Each also involved offering a commentary or gloss on that text: interpretation. In that moment when Zwingli preached his understanding of Scripture to his congregation, he diverged from Erasmus's original intent in printing the Bible. It was also almost immediately apparent that the text of Scripture was open to more than one interpretation. While Zwingli's understanding of Christian ethics had much in common with Erasmus's, his understanding of the meaning of the Last Supper, the last meal Jesus shared with his apostles before his arrest, trial, and crucifixion, diverged so deeply that the two no longer saw themselves as belonging to the same Christianity. In the 1520s, readings of the

Bible, and particularly of texts that many found core to their understanding of the whole – the Gospels, Paul's Letters – splintered at a frightening rate, proliferating as one local preacher after another took up the text of Scripture and read it aloud to congregations of different languages, local devotional practices, saints, holy days, images, architecture.

As their readings diverged, the visions of "true Christianity" and "true worship" articulated in sermon, pamphlet, and protest splintered from one another. Even as Bucer in Strasbourg and Zwingli in Zurich emphasized Christian brotherly love as the foundation for a shared Christian life, their understandings of how one worshiped God diverged: Bucer wrote of the mystery at the center of the liturgy; Zwingli argued for a carefully inculcated experience of commemoration. Johannes Brenz (1499–1570), who had studied with Johannes Oecolampadius (1482–1531) in Heidelberg, broke decisively with him concerning the moment of communion at the center of the eucharist.

Even as preachers splintered from one another, in the same town as well as from town to town, principality to principality, individuals in their audiences also splintered from one another. Some became loyal listeners to a figure they held to preach "the pure Word of God," even as others protested to ecclesiastical and civil authorities the false teaching that endangered the souls of listeners. Some challenged the authority of the preachers on the basis of their own understanding of "true Christianity" and "true Christian worship." In Augsburg, for example, three women questioned Urbanus Rhegius's celebration of the eucharist, which drew heavily on Luther's understanding, because he was not living celibately, which, for them, was inseparable from the ritual.

In the 1520s and 1530s, as we shall see more fully, peasant communes and princes instituted different forms of worship and articulated differing understandings of the relationship between conduct and Christian piety. All, however, anchored in Scripture their claim to the authority to alter ancient traditions of worship and ancient mores. City councils, princes, and kings legislated "Reformation" – the reforming of Christian doctrine, what was taught; Christian ethics, what one did; and Christian worship, how one honored God. As each extended its jurisdiction over areas that had traditionally been the purview of Pope and bishop, each grounded that extension in the authority of Scripture, which, as Zwingli had said, preceded all other authority. In 1524–25, peasants and artisans also grounded their vision of a social and political order in the Bible, making explicit for all the revolutionary potential of the Gospels and the Acts of Apostles.

At the center, for all, was a text that, like late medieval devotional literature, spoke to each person intimately, personally, and absolutely. If late medieval lay devotional movements, such as the Devotio Moderna, had taught an intimacy of reading, the close identification of reader with sacred text, sixteenth-century Bibles' pursuit of immediacy of language invited an even greater intimacy, blurring even more the temporal distance between Jesus' speaking and sixteenth-century Christian. These texts, made ever more accessible, seized the imaginations of devout readers. These texts, given sound and breath, reached audiences who could neither read nor purchase a Bible of their own. And they reached Christians whose experience and education Erasmus had not envisioned when he published that first edition of the Greek New Testament. The preachers knew their audiences better – their efficacy depended directly on their ability to reach carpenters, apprentices, serving women, day laborers, as well as merchants and town councilors – and yet, even they were surprised by the power of the Word of God to seize their audiences and move them to action. No one, not Erasmus, not Luther, not Zwingli, nor any of the other preachers and pamphleteers, foresaw what Augustine had intimated twelve centuries earlier: The text of the Bible only seems simple and rudimentary.

No one was prepared for the speed of change. And no one, foremost the deeply pacifist Erasmus, envisioned how that one text would tear asunder the very fabric of Europe: not simply politically, state from state, but echoing the expulsions, forced conversions, and executions of the Reconquista, neighbor from neighbor, husband from wife, mother from son.

PART II

FRAGMENTATION

4

The Word of God and the Ordering of the World

To the Christian reader, the peace and grace of God through Jesus Christ.

There are many antichrists who, now that the peasants are assembled together, seize the chance to mock the gospel, saying, "Is this the fruit of the new gospel: to band together in great numbers and plot conspiracies to reform and even topple the spiritual and temporal powers – yes, even to murder them?" The following articles answer all these godless, blasphemous critics. We want two things: first, to make them stop mocking the word of God; and second, to establish the Christian justice of the current disobedience and rebellion of all the peasants.

The Twelve Articles[1]

In 1525, rural and urban laborers, shopkeepers, and even some nobles called for the world to be ordered according to the teachings of Christ. For them, the Bible was not – as Erasmus had envisioned – a private text for personal devotion. Nor was it – as Luther had envisioned – a guide for each person to live his or her life within traditional society. For them, the Bible articulated a vision of a true and just society, and that society looked nothing like the world in which they lived.

We cannot claim, as Erasmus and Luther did, that the men and women who called for a new ordering of society "misunderstood" or "misread" the Bible. We are, all of us, heirs to the proliferation of readings of that text, sacred to millions. As different Christians found different visions in that text – of the true Christian life, of true Christian society, of a Christian state, of true worship and true morals – the world Europeans had known was torn asunder. By the end of the sixteenth century, European life was

---

[1] The text of the Twelve Articles is provided in Appendix I, Peter Blickle, *The Revolution of 1525: The German Peasants' War from a New Perspective*, translated by Thomas A. Brady, Jr., and H.C. Erik Midelfort (Baltimore and London: The Johns Hopkins University Press, 1981), p. 195.

altered: whether it was the wife who sought asylum among strangers who shared her understanding of true Christianity; or the monarch whose subjects challenged his or her authority on the basis of Scripture, which they held to be of greater authority than any he or she might possess by royal blood, ancient practice, or even popular acclaim; or the artisan forced to flee because he would not worship as his ruler dictated. Even the indifferent found their world altered as others in their villages, towns, principalities, or domains sought to order the world according to their understanding of Scripture.

No one was prepared for the proliferation of readings, and few in that first generation allowed for the possibility of multiple true readings. Each reading was, for that person and his followers, "true," exclusively and absolutely true. Itinerant preachers carried their vision of true Christianity from town to town, rural village to rural village, household to household. In workshops in cities, a single literate artisan might read aloud books of the Bible as his fellow printers or weavers or tanners listened while they worked. And different readers found different Christianities; different listeners heard different morals. The prodigal son resonated differently among younger sons of noble households than he did among artisanal families, where young hands were needed for the survival of the family.

Evangelicals: The Authority of Scripture

The first and fullest revelation of the Bible's revolutionary potential in the sixteenth century occurred in 1525–26, when, in the words of the historian Peter Blickle,

> The Holy Roman Empire of the German Nation lay helpless as castles, palaces, princely residences, and monasteries were put to the torch, from Thuringia to Tyrol, and from Alsace to the territory of Salzburg. Noble and ecclesiastical lords were forced to flee before their peasants, and the imperial ruling powers had to struggle for survival. Later, it was the villages that lay helpless while peasants were beaten, butchered, and executed by the princes' mercenary troops. As villages and farms went up in flames, hopes and yearnings for a better, Christian world of brotherhood and neighborly love went with them.[2]

Scholars have delineated many causes for what Blickle has called "The Revolution of 1525," such as social and political grievances or the

[2] Blickle, *The Revolution of 1525*, p. 18.

intensifying tensions between landlords and peasants in the long-term shift from feudal agriculture to global capitalism. But unlike earlier medieval agrarian and urban revolts, in 1525, the peasants published a pamphlet, *The Twelve Articles*, in which their first demand was not economic redress, but the right of parishes to call and remove their own pastors, "for only thus could they assure the pure teaching of the gospel without the interpretation and tradition of the old church."[3]

The "revolution" lay not in revolt against lords ecclesiastical and secular. Others, most famously Emperor Henry IV in the eleventh century or King Phillip IV of France in the fourteenth, had certainly challenged popes. Others, from popes to peasants, had certainly challenged secular rulers. The amplitude of conflicts from late antiquity to the sixteenth century testifies to the absence of any abiding consensus on the jurisdiction accorded either secular or ecclesiastical lords. Indeed conflicts over who had which authority over what were the norm, not the exception. But those had been *jurisdictional* challenges: whether secular rulers had authority over priests; whether the pope had authority over bishops within the domains of secular monarchs; whether lords secular or ecclesiastical had the right to collect the various incomes – taxes, tithes, dues – that they sought to impose on their "subjects."

European Christians had largely accepted the premise John of Salisbury articulated in the twelfth century:

> the prince is the public power and a certain image on earth of the divine majesty. Beyond doubt the greatest part of the divine virtue is revealed to belong to the prince, insofar as at his nod men bow their heads and generally offer their necks to the axe in sacrifice, and by divine impulse everyone fears him who is fear itself. I do not believe that this could have happened unless it happened at the divine command. For all power is from the Lord God, and is with Him always, and is His forever. Whatever the prince can do, therefore, is from God, so that power does not depart from God, but it is used as a substitute for His hand, making all things learn His justice and mercy.[4]

That conceptualization, much discussed and debated over the intervening four centuries, located ultimate power with the Christian God; constructed a hierarchy the "higher" one went, the "closer" to divine power

[3] Blickle, *The Revolution of 1525*, p. 19.

[4] John of Salisbury, *Policraticus: Of the Frivolities of Courtiers and the Footprints of Philosophers*, edited and translated by Cary J. Nederman (Cambridge: Cambridge University Press, 1990), p. 28.

one came; and construed power as descending from God through an ordered hierarchy, from top to bottom, power diffusing as it descended.

Seven centuries older than John of Salisbury's conceptualization of the origin of power and the ultimate grounding of all authority was the doctrine of the two swords, first articulated by Pope Gelasius I in the fifth century, which distinguished two kinds of rule, "sacerdotium" – the rule of priests – and regnum, the rule of kings, both of which governed a single Christendom, though differently. Over time, medieval theorists struggled to delineate more precisely the jurisdictions of two hierarchies, the one "spiritual," the ecclesiastical hierarchy, the other "temporal," of this world, "secular," each of whose authority, they held, derived directly from God. In the fourteenth century, Marsilius of Padua had sought, unsuccessfully, to make the case for locating authority in the body of all Christians. In 1500, pope and monarch still fought over jurisdiction; no other authority was widely recognized to be both divine in origin and greater than either.

The revolution lay in setting Scripture above both pope and monarch. Putting the Bible in the hands of "subjects," as it turned out, placed in the hands of thousands an authority that, when read with that fierce intimacy, when breath gave sound to words, linked the persons of peasants, journeymen, monks, parish priests, wives and daughters to a God they held to be both immediate and omnipotent. "The Word of God" was not simply the touchstone for preaching and pamphlets. Nor was it simply the wellspring for visions of a Christian utopia – though it proved to be that powerfully as well. No, for those who called themselves "evangelicals" in the 1520s, the Word of God possessed an authority greater than the one that had been accorded popes and princes for centuries – God's will not mediated through human will or human frailty, but immediate, audible, direct. Those who had been at the bottom of a hierarchy of political power and social status quoted Jesus's words, their bodies a vehicle for giving sound to the Gospels – themselves a medium for the Word of God and with it, God's will and God's providence. That object, the printed Bible, in a hand was the locus, the site, for authority that trumped prince and pope.

The Twelve Articles placed the preached and printed Word of God absolutely, unconditionally, above all other authority. In keeping with that ranking, peasants and commoners across a swath of Europe put all ecclesiastical and political practices – tithing, taxing, restricted access to wood for heating and animals for meat – to the test of Scripture and found none in accord with God's will as they found it articulated. They found in the commandment to love one's neighbor as oneself, a notion of "brotherhood" which opposed directly, they held, the traditional social, ecclesiastical, and political hierarchies. And for a little more than a year, they sought to bring the world into accord with their understanding of the Word of God. In the light of modern socialist revolutions, their visions do not seem so radical, not the redistribution of rights and privileges according to the ideal of Christian brotherly love, not the notion of the community of goods. But in the sixteenth century, their vision was terrifying. Most immediately, it provoked an even more violent repression. The pikes were broken, the voices silenced. But no one forgot the protean and volatile power of the printed Word of God.

The Revolution of 1525 made explicit the tension that would run through the sixteenth century. On the one hand, thousands of European Christians found in the Word of God an authority for the ordering of politics and society they held to be higher, truer, more trustworthy. "Subjects," first, of the Emperor in central Europe, then, of the kings of France, England, and Scotland, in the thousands rejected lineage, custom, tradition, and called for the ordering of the world according to God's Word. They did not simply hold their rulers to the ethics they found in God's Word, though the lives of princes, popes, bishops, and priests were held to the test of Scripture for their uprightness, their probity, their propriety. Evangelicals rejected fundamentally that those rulers possessed any authority exceeding the Word of God they heard from their preachers and held in their hands.

If the revolutionaries articulated visions of Christian utopias, in which the meek walked shoulder to shoulder with the powerful and all shared the goods of the earth, other evangelicals saw in the Revolution of 1525 the specter of the abyss: a world without order, sense, familiarity. The Revolution had peeled away what the world might look like if all European Christians sought to make it conform to their readings of the Bible. It was not simply the violence: the mobs armed with pikes, staffs, scythes, and anything else they might seize. Many of the readings horrified the same Europeans who held Scripture to be the highest authority. It was, as contemporaries put it, "a world turned upside down." What, then, was to be the balance between the world as it was in 1500 and Scripture? Was Scripture to be the template for the world? If so, how? If Scripture was not to be the template for the world, what was its relationship to the world to be?

European Christians articulated a range of answers to those questions. There was not one "evangelical" position. Nor was there any simple progression, either from the vision of the revolutionaries to a more moderate ideal of change, or from generation to generation. It was not that sons became "evangelical," or later, "Protestants," and fathers remained Catholic: The century is filled with stories like that of the Hotman family, in which the father, François, a French Protestant, disowned his son, Daniel, for being a Catholic. Christians simply fragmented, one from another, along no predictable or, indeed, even now, visible lines. Different Christians found in their reading of their Bibles and in listening to the preachers they trusted (as opposed to the preachers they did not) different answers to the question of the relationship of the Bible to the world.

Differing conceptualizations of the relationship between the printed and preached Word of God and the ordering of the world splintered medieval Christendom, dividing European Christian from European Christian. Sixteenth-century polemics cast those conceptualizations, as we shall see, in terms of stark oppositions, but those polemics obscured the sheer variety of conceptualizations and their range. Far more helpful as a conceptual model is a spectrum. There were not in the sixteenth century, just two – "Protestant" and "Catholic" – or three, "radical" and "magisterial Protestant" and "Catholic," but a range of different understandings of the import of the Word of God for life as it was to be lived. The revolutionaries found in the command to love one's neighbor the foundation. Others found in Matthew 22:15–22 the key:

> Then the Pharisees went and plotted to entrap him in what he said. So they sent their disciples to him, along with the Herodians, saying, "...Tell us then, what you think. Is it lawful to pay taxes to the emperor or not?" But Jesus, aware of their malice, said, "...Show me the coin used for the tax." And they brought him a denarius. Then he said to them, "Whose head is this, and whose title?" They answered, "The emperor's." Then he said to them, "Give therefore to the emperor the things that are the emperor's, and to God the things that are God's."

Still others looked to the Letters of Paul or the Gospel of John – the "Word of God" spoke variously, offering different ways to live in the world, depending on where one looked and who was looking.

Sixteenth-century Christians fragmented on the relationship of the Word of God to their lives and on the question of the pace of change. At one end of the spectrum were the revolutionaries of 1525, who sought to bring the world immediately, through violence if necessary, into conformity with their particular reading of the Gospels, with its emphasis on brotherly love and a community of goods. At the other end of the spectrum were those who would come to be called "Catholics," those whose readings of Scripture were governed by a notion of "tradition." Between the two ends of the spectrum were those evangelicals who accorded God's Word supreme authority, but stepped back in horror from a world turned upside down. Closer to the revolutionaries on that spectrum, at times overlapping with them, were the Anabaptists, some of whom took up violence, most of whom eschewed violence, who sought to bring sixteenth-century lives most literally into accord with what they found in the Gospels. We begin with them.

A Spectrum of Christians: Anabaptists

In hindsight, the revolutionaries and the Anabaptists have been called "radical," linked in the scholarship by that name to the student radicals of the 1960s. There is no consensus as to the extent of overlap between the revolutionaries and Anabaptists, but all shared the conviction that life in sixteenth-century Europe could be brought into alignment with the life described in the Gospels and the Acts of the Apostles. No one else in the sixteenth century sought so dramatic a realignment.

It speaks to that intimate power of the Word of God that Anabaptists may have been the single largest group of evangelicals in the sixteenth century: They were found from Spain to Poland, from London to the countryside in Italy. We cannot know their total numbers, but the hundreds of Anabaptists arrested, interrogated, and executed throughout Europe attest to the geographic breadth and the demographic popularity of that particular understanding of "true Christianity."

Who were the Anabaptists? After the dramatic and violent attempt at making the world conform to an Anabaptist reading of Scripture in the Anabaptist Kingdom of Münster in 1535, surviving Anabaptists – many of whom did not agree with the violence of Münster – were viewed with ever greater wariness, and persecutions drove many groups underground. What bound them together? Surviving sources offer us a glimpse into a world markedly different from the "Churches" that would come to be organized and institutionalized by the end of the century. In most of Europe, Anabaptists had no access to church buildings where they might gather to worship. They therefore usually did not meet in any public spaces. They met in homes: the homes of those who were interested, but not yet members, as well as those who were members. Their places of gathering shifted with persecutions and the changing membership:

gardens for larger gatherings, the hearth of a peasant hovel in the winter, a workshop. Their membership was without spatial boundaries: no church walls, no pews, no apse, no nave.

Their membership was marked foremost by a single moment: baptism. Anabaptists accorded definitive weight to the Gospel narrative, in which Jesus asks John the Baptist to baptize him: Jesus, as they pointed out, was an adult and he asked to be baptized. Thus, the earliest Anabaptists were baptized a second time, as adults – hence "Anabaptists," those who are rebaptized. For all other Christians, that second baptism was anathema, a mortal sin, a transgression of the very first order. Attending closely to Jesus's age and words, Anabaptists reconceived baptism. For them, it was not an initiation of infants into a community into which they would grow, but the culmination of a process of reflection and conversion. For Anabaptists, baptism was the entry into membership of self-conscious, reflective, and scripturally literate adults. Children – from infants through adolescents – could live among Christians, but to be fully Christian, one had to be an adult and to choose to be baptized into the community of believers.

For them, the Acts of the Apostles offered a way of thinking about the relationship of the Bible to the world. A few bloody episodes such as Münster aside, most Anabaptists did not seek to change political or social hierarchies. Like the apostles in the Acts, many Anabaptist preachers were itinerant, their listeners gathering in "conventicles," in homes and gardens, away from public surveillance. Women as well as men read Bibles aloud in their gatherings, preaching a vision of Christian life lived apart from the world of princes and popes. A significant number of Anabaptists also refused to take any oaths – if one accorded Scripture highest authority, one could not bind oneself to any lesser authority, on the chance that the lesser authority asked one to do what the Bible forbade: killing one's neighbor, foremost.

Away from public scrutiny, guided by their own readings of the Gospels and the Acts, different conventicles took up different aspects of the lives of the apostles. Many sought to practice the community of goods – exceedingly difficult in a world increasingly capitalist. Many seem to have practiced polygamy, though the numbers are difficult to determine. Perhaps the great majority – again numbers are difficult to estimate – differentiated themselves primarily by two marks: adult baptism and the refusal to take oaths. Those, certainly, were the two acts of Anabaptists that provoked the most reaction on the part of other evangelicals, as well as of both papal and secular authorities. Over the course of the sixteenth century, Anabaptists were interrogated before Inquisitorial courts and prosecuted in courts local and royal. Hundreds were executed: drowned, hanged, burned at the stake, their mutilated bodies intended as a testimony to the power of the authorities they themselves sought to ignore.

A Spectrum of Christians: Lutherans

The Revolution of 1525 was a watershed and Anabaptists radicalized all other evangelicals. In the wake of the Revolution, other evangelicals called for a very different process of change. While they agreed that the world should be governed by the Word of God, they disagreed profoundly with the violence of the revolutionaries and the suddenness of the change they sought to enact. And the Anabaptists led to a direct confrontation with the relationship between practices long familiar, traditional to the lives of every Christian, such as infant baptism and the taking of civil oaths, and the Gospels. Were the Gospels or the Acts of the Apostles to be the model for sixteenth-century Christian life? Were Jesus's specific acts and commands to define the conduct and behavior of sixteenth-century Christians?

Those evangelicals who succeeded in founding publicly and legally recognized "Churches," foremost, those who came to be called Lutherans and Reformed Christians, envisioned a different relationship between the Bible and traditional life. For them, the Word of God was that which each and every Christian should hear and read, day in, day out. In that daily, intimate encounter, the Word of God would work change, a change that, these evangelicals held, might not even be visible to others. The change they pursued, therefore, centered on protecting and promulgating the Word of God.

These evangelicals appropriated the language of the "two swords," each transforming according to his own understanding of Scripture the relationship of temporal authority to God's ordering of the world. Even as their understandings of the Word of God placed all evangelicals at odds with certain political authorities, none of these evangelicals called for the overthrow of the traditional ordering of the world, political, economic, or social. In this way, they occupy the middle range of the spectrum: sharing with revolutionaries and Anabaptists the conviction that the Word of God was the highest authority and yet rejecting, with those who came to be called Catholics, a world modeled directly on the lives of the apostles, a world of goods in common, without hierarchies of authority.

Many of these evangelicals oriented themselves towards one of two figures, Martin Luther or John Calvin. They found one or the other's reading of Scripture singularly inspired, trustworthy – in their words, illumined by the Holy Spirit. While many evangelicals forged local Churches – Martin Bucer in Strasbourg, Johannes Brenz in Wurttemberg, groups of evangelicals in the Free Imperial Cities of Ulm and Augsburg – these local churches ultimately came to join the transnational Churches that Luther and Calvin were articulating. While Luther and Calvin each worked in a circle of trusted associates, their voices come forward from the sixteenth century as singular, quoted and requoted, the force of their leadership of different groups of evangelicals imprinted on the Churches whose organization they formed directly (and, in Luther's case, to which he gave his name), whose practices they articulated in dialogue with their different understandings of Scripture, and whose ethics they sought to instill in generations to come.

Even as he was working on the German translation of the Bible, Martin Luther was engaged with the question of the relationship of the Bible to the ordering of the world:

> But you ask further, whether the beadles, hangmen, jurists, advocates, and their ilk, can also be Christians and in a state of salvation. I answer: If the State and its sword are a divine service, as was proved above, that which the State needs in order to wield the sword must also be a divine service. There must be those who arrest, accuse, slay and destroy the wicked, and protect, acquit, defend and save the good. Therefore, when such duties are performed, not with the intention of seeking one's own ends, but only of helping to maintain the laws and the State, so that the wicked may be restrained, there is no peril in them and they may be followed like any other pursuit and be used as one's means of support. For, as was said, love of neighbor seeks not its own, considers not how great or how small, but how profitable and how needful for neighbor or community the works are.
>
> *Secular Authority: To What Extent It Should Be Obeyed* (1523)[5]

In the years leading up to the Revolution of 1525, Luther invoked the ideal of Christian brotherly love as that which should guide the Emperor, princes, and city councils. But Luther did not share the peasants' optimism about human nature: As he wrote in the same treatise, true Christians do not need the secular sword, but, because there are so very few true Christians in the world, and so much wickedness, the State and its sword are necessary.

When the Revolutionaries looked to Luther to support their cause, he first called on them to honor God's ordering of the world – to be

---

[5] Martin Luther, "Secular Authority: To What Extent It Should Be Obeyed," *Martin Luther: Selections from His Writings*, edited by John Dillenberger (Garden City, NY: Anchor Books, 1961), p. 381.

obedient to established authority – and then, when they did not acquiesce, he broke with them, in one of the deep fissures of the early years of the evangelical movement. He preserved the medieval division of "two swords" while changing the character of each and the worlds they governed. Like medieval theorists, he posited a division of human experience, but he divided human experience differently, rejecting, most importantly, that the clergy lived separately from "this world."

In understanding Luther's thinking about the relationship between the Bible and the world, it is useful to distinguish in his writings between the pastor and the polemicist. The polemicist, it must be said, never called for the world as it was to be ordered according to the Bible – Luther consistently envisioned God's Word working through human understanding to change human arrangements of politics, economy, and society. But the polemicist wrote in bipolarities, dividing, for instance, the world between Christians and non-Christians, calling for the state to govern with its sword non-Christians and calling for Christians to be obedient to the state as the sword God had ordered in the world. The polemicist broke with the revolutionaries over his understanding of Christian obedience. From his earliest writings on politics, Luther accorded political authority all those rights the Revolutionaries had contested: to collect taxes, to regulate all things commercial, to conduct war, to prosecute and execute secular justice. For him, the jurisdiction of the temporal sword encompassed "life and goods," but not "books" or faith. As Luther said so dramatically before the real "Caesar" of the sixteenth century, the Holy Roman Emperor Charles V, his conscience was captive to the Word of God. For Luther, a Christian should live in a hierarchy of obedience: obedience to God, as God revealed himself in Scripture, absolute and supreme; obedience to human authority, which God had ordered in the world, but only when that human authority did not seek to sever the intimate relationship between Christian and Bible. Should that authority seek to sever that intimate connection, "in this case, you are a tyrant and overreach yourself."[6]

The pastor divided human experience differently, for he was solely concerned with "Christians." Those Christians, the pastor recognized, worked, inflicted and suffered pain, hungered and went hungry, longed for salvation and sinned – they were, in Luther's abiding phrase, *simul justus et peccator*, at once righteous, a passive condition, and sinners, actively every day. Christians, as he made explicit in sermons and his catechisms,

---

[6] "Secular Authority," p. 388.

needed a very different kind of "sword," no longer of coercion, but of enforcement and protection.

For Luther, the most important relationship was not "in the world" at all, but the one that could exist anywhere: that between a Christian and God, as God revealed himself in the text of Scripture. God's Word, not human beings, effected change – in the heart of each individual Christian and then across the surface of the globe. Over the course of his lifetime, Luther challenged, first the pope, then the Emperor, but on the narrower question of each individual Christian's right to live subservient to the Word of God.

For that reason, he reconceived fundamentally "the spiritual sword." He rejected the office of Pope: The very definition of the office placed one human being in authority over God's Word. Lutheran churches were to be led by ministers, whose authority derived solely from their knowledge of the Word of God. Even as he called for a learned leadership for the Church he was building, emphasizing the importance of biblical scholarship ever more forcefully in the wake of the Revolution of 1525, he rejected the office of the priesthood, for which he found no scriptural basis. The true Church was "the priesthood of all believers," in which "ministers" or "servants of the Word" would "administer" or "offer" sacraments and lessons from Scripture. Even as he placed both Scripture and faith above all other authorities and rejected many different understandings of "true Christianity," "true worship," and "the true Christian life," he allowed for local variation in dialogue with political authorities and local preachers. For Luther, the greater one's authority over the lives of Christians, the greater one's knowledge of the Bible should be. For Martin Luther, the world was ordered along two axes: spiritual – political, and learned – "simple folk."

Luther along with Phillip Melanchthon and Johannes Bugenhagen were among the first evangelicals to articulate a new conception of "Church" and to seek to build it. That conception evolved in the context of the Empire in the 1520s and 1530s, with its fragmented jurisdictions and the Emperor's dream of universal Christendom. In 1529, at the Second Imperial Diet of Speyer, the hope that the Emperor might reform the medieval Church from the top down died, as his brother Ferdinand denied the Emperor's subjects the right to reform Christianity within their lands. Evangelicals filed a formal protest against the decree, acquiring with it the name, "*Protestants.*" In 1530, in the Free Imperial City of Augsburg, a group of princes including the Elector of Saxony, as well as the City Councils of Nuremberg and Reutlingen presented the Emperor with their "Confession of Faith." Drafted by Melanchthon, the Augsburg Confession, as it became known, was a statement of the core beliefs of a group, ranging from the nature of God and original sin, through the number of sacraments and their meaning, to the nature of ecclesiastical power.[7] It was the first sixteenth-century Confession to receive legal status, and it was presented in a political context: the Diet of the Imperial Court. Though it did not succeed in its express purpose – to bring the Emperor to support their vision of true Christianity – it became a manifesto: at once a series of statements that those who would become "Lutheran" held as true, and a definition of "the Church." "The Church," according to the Augsburg Confession, "is the congregation of saints, in which the Gospel is rightly taught and the sacraments are rightly administered."

The Augsburg Confession severed "the Church" from the papal hierarchy. "The Church" rested on three, and only three, components: membership or the community of saints, the Gospel, and sacraments. Gone were priests and pope, and with them the sacerdotal hierarchy of the medieval Church. In its stead, the Kingdoms of Denmark and Sweden, the Duchy of Saxony, the Landgravate of Hesse, the Mark Brandenburg, as well as dozens of city councils from Strasbourg to Nuremberg, following Luther's advice and the advice of those closest to him – foremost, Bugenhagen – legislated "Reformation," in which the temporal sword extended its jurisdiction to institute a "Church" whose physical boundaries corresponded with the boundaries of that particular temporal authority: city, duchy, principality kingdom. This "Church" was not the same as the Church of the Augsburg Confession, but a temporal institution, whose purpose was to teach the Gospel rightly and administer the sacraments rightly – under the governance of those temporal authorities whose sword served God.

The Lutheran Church differed in details from place to place. All, however, agreed to certain practices. Foremost, that Church was to have not priests, but "ministers" – men learned in the biblical languages, who studied the Bible and could therefore guide their congregations on specific questions of the Christian life. Lutherans were to be baptized as infants, to grow up within a community that both at home and within the structure of the church taught Christian doctrine. Fathers as well as ministers were to catechize, to teach through rote memorization, the core tenets of Lutheran doctrine. Fathers were to read the Bible aloud within their

---

[7] For the text of the Augsburg Confession, see http://www.bookofconcord.org/augsburg confession.php.

homes, if a family could afford a Bible. Children were to undergo a formal education, catechism, in the tenets of Lutheranism, learning by heart a formal statement of belief, the Apostles' Creed; the proper form of prayer, the Lord's Prayer; a moral code, the Ten Commandments; and the precise meaning of the sacraments each Church would offer: baptism and the eucharist, which Luther came to call the Lord's Supper. The Augsburg Confession included among the sacraments "Absolution," but when Luther wrote his *Large Catechism* in 1529, he no longer included Confession among the sacraments. In 1577, Lutherans agreed to a series of statements concerning the Supper but left to congregations the determination of their own "ecclesiastical practices."

The fragmented character of the Empire was the ground in which the Lutheran Church first took root. The Lutheran Church was built sovereignty by sovereignty, along a north-south axis, Sweden to Nuremberg. It did not take root in political landscapes to the west or the south. And the Churches instituted in the first half of the century found, with Luther's death, that his vision of true Christianity had formed their center; without him, Lutherans splintered. The Augsburg Confession alone could not hold them together, and in 1580, thirty-four years after Luther's death, German princes called for a single Book of Concord, to which those dispersed Churches of Nuremberg, Saxony, Hesse, Denmark, Pomerania, and Augsburg would agree, in order to form a single unified Lutheran Church that might stand against the universal Church the Emperor ever more forcibly promulgated. With the Book of Concord, published in 1580, Lutherans established those texts which would henceforth serve as the touchstone for the Lutheran Church: the Apostles', Nicene, and Athanasian Creeds; the Augsburg Confession; Luther's Small and Large Catechisms; as well as the Formula of Concord itself. The Book of Concord provided a core set of commonly accepted texts to which all Lutherans might turn to answer questions of doctrine and practice, to stipulate the limits of accommodation in a world of persecution and shifting political support.

A Spectrum of Christians: John Calvin and Reformed Christianity

But in that obedience which we have shown to be due the authority of rulers, we are always to make this exception, indeed, to observe it as primary, that such obedience is never to lead us away from obedience to him, to whose will the desires of all kings ought to be subject, to whose decrees all their commands ought to yield, to whose majesty their scepters ought to be submitted.

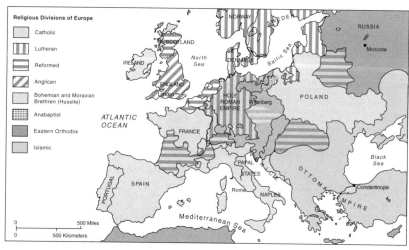

MAP 4.1. Churches in Europe.

... But since this edict has been proclaimed by the heavenly herald, Peter – "We must obey God rather than men" – let us comfort ourselves with the thought that we are rendering that obedience which the Lord requires when we suffer anything rather than turn aside from piety. And that our courage may not grow faint, Paul pricks us with another goad: That we have been redeemed by Christ at so great a price as our redemption cost him, so that we should not enslave ourselves to the wicked desires of men – much less be subject to their impiety.

John Calvin, *Institutes of the Christian Religion*, Book IV, Chapter XX, §32[8]

John Calvin's ordering of the world was forged in the aftermath of those first efforts, the Revolutionaries, the Anabaptists, and the Lutherans. Even as Calvin was dedicating his most widely disseminated work, *The Institutes of the Christian Religion*, to the King of France, evangelicals across Europe were facing persecution, prosecution, the seizure of their property, and the loss of their lives from their secular rulers. The group of evangelicals we have come to call "Reformed," those who looked to Calvin and Geneva for their leadership, articulated their understanding of the relationship between the Bible and the world in a landscape of splintered Christianity and political persecution.

On the spectrum, Reformed Christianity lies between Lutherans and Anabaptists, closer to the Anabaptists in many ways than to Luther. Like all evangelicals, Reformed Christians shared the conviction that the

---

[8] *Calvin: Institutes of the Christian Religion*, edited by John T. McNeill, translated by Ford Lewis Battles, vol. 2 (Philadelphia: The Westminster Press, 1960), 1520–21.

Word of God was the highest authority in the ordering of the world. Calvin
had learned, however, two lessons of the 1520s and 1530s, that shaped
the conceptualization of the relationship of the Bible to the world that he
articulated in letters and printed works. First, Calvin saw how dozens of
different readings had proliferated in the first years after the publication
of Erasmus's edition of the New Testament and Luther's translations of
the New and Old Testaments. Calvin's *Institutes* was, foremost, an effort
to provide the foundation for a common reading that would, in turn,
form the basis for building communities of Christians across Europe and
the Americas. Second, the political landscape of Europe had become far
more dangerous, as competing claims to true Christianity led increasingly
to violence, persecutions, and expulsions.

If those who looked to Luther ultimately accepted the name, Lutherans, in recognition of the centrality of his voice in defining what they
understood true Christianity to be, Calvin articulated a very different
vision of true Christianity – one of no center, no single head, of any kind,
other than Scripture itself, which, as printed object and preached word,
could be in all places at the same time. And if Luther turned to print
to disseminate his understanding of Scripture, Calvin turned to print to
forge a "Church" over distance and isolation. The physical properties of
books lent them directly to a world of political persecution. Portable,
they could travel to places such as Les Baux in Provence or Antwerp or
the Highlands in Scotland. Small, they could be hidden. Printed pages
provided the same text to dispersed communities that, in reading it, constituted a "Church" – not through administration, nor even through the
same practices, but through their orientation to a single text, uniform
over distance. With the *Institutes*, Calvin sought to provide both a reliable guide to finding the correct reading of Scripture and a foundation
for discerning God's presence in the wider world, no matter where one
might find oneself.

Reformed Christians looked not to Matthew 22 or to the Acts of the
Apostles, both of which presumed the possibility of political indiffer-
ence, but to the world of the Pauline Epistles: scattered groups that,
like the Corinthians or Thessalonians or Ephesians, lived "under the
cross," that is, at risk of persecution from a hostile state. They were to be
found in France, Scotland, the Netherlands, briefly Brazil, and ultimately
the northern coast of the Americas. In France, some communities built
"temples" – round or hexagonal structures without naves or apses, to
reflect that more horizontal vision of churches – which were destroyed

in the seventeenth century. In the Netherlands, many more communities became the political majority and therefore took over medieval churches, whitewashing their walls, removing the density of medieval altarpieces, tapestries, panel paintings, and carvings. But, like the Anabaptists, they did not need a structure in order to be a "Church."

In Geneva, Calvin and the other Reformed pastors were able to institute structures and practices that other communities took as their model, even when they could not realize them in day-to-day practices. In Geneva, Calvin argued for infant baptism, preserving the sense of the ritual as the initiation into a community that would foster the child's faith and Christian understanding, even as he rejected the medieval understanding of human nature, and with it the understanding of baptism as washing away sin. Christ had been baptized; therefore, baptism was necessary. Christ, however, was perfect and required no washing away; human beings were, by their nature, flawed, and no washing away could rid them of essential sinfulness. In his letters, Calvin supported infant baptism, but recognized that it might not always be possible to baptize in a font, to baptize in a church, to baptize among all the adult members of a community, to baptize in the first days of life. In Geneva, Calvin radically rethought the central ritual of collective worship, which he called "the Supper"; in his letters, he urged those who did not have a building or a collective space, who had not yet had the opportunity to teach the true meaning of the ritual, to postpone celebrating it until they did.

Departing radically from the medieval conceptualization, Calvin articulated a sense of "the Church" that had no center – though Geneva remained the model – no hierarchy: not simply no pope, but no bishops and no central place of decision making. In the early seventeenth century, when theological difference threatened to become ecclesiological division, Reformed Christians convened a "synod," at Dort, in the Netherlands, but no one person, not even Calvin, was accorded the authority to determine for all what was true doctrine or true worship. For Calvin, Scripture alone possessed exclusive and singular authority. Each Christian community was pendant solely upon the Word of God, wherever they might find themselves on the face of the earth.

Calvin preserved the language of two swords, but reconceived their nature and their jurisdiction. For Calvin, God was exclusively omnipotent – no human being could represent God's absolute power on earth because no human being possessed God's perfection, and all human beings, in direct contrast to God, were circumscribed, limited, bounded.

Thus, all forms of human authority were not simply subservient to the Word of God, but, by the humanity of their agents, imperfect, limited, bounded.

For Calvin, as well, the world was uniformly under God's jurisdiction – God's jurisdiction was not divided, and the human experience of that jurisdiction was not divided in the ways it had been. If Luther divided human experience between the political, economic, and social on the one hand and the religious and spiritual on the other, for Calvin, "the spiritual" was lived in the world. All human activity fell within the purview of the church: marriage, the sexual relations between adults, the rearing of children, how one dressed, how one spoke, how one carried oneself not simply in the public spaces of street, marketplace, or church, but within the confines of one's home. If Luther looked to God in an intimate relation of one faithful individual to his Creator, Calvin spoke both of God looking at all humankind, watching, observing, and of God's visibility throughout the world. Reformed Christians lived in God's sight, no matter where they were.

The Church in Geneva, the product of negotiations among Calvin, other pastors, and the City Council, was laid out in the Ecclesiastical Ordinances of 1541. It was to have four different kinds of office, drawn from the early Church as found in the Pauline epistles:

> *pastors*: "their office is to proclaim the Word of God, to instruct, to admonish, exhort and censure, both in public and in private, to administer the sacraments and to enjoin brotherly corrections along with the elders and colleagues."

> *doctors*: "The office proper to doctors is the instruction of the faithful in true doctrine, in order that the purity of the Gospel be not corrupted either by ignorance or by evil opinions."

> *elders*: "Their office is to have oversight of the life of everyone, to admonish amicably those whom they see to be erring or to be living a disordered life, and where it is required, to enjoin fraternal corrections themselves and along with others."

> *deacons*: "There were always two kinds in the ancient Church, the one deputed to receive, dispense and hold goods for the poor, not only daily alms, but also possessions, rents and pensions; the other to tend and care for the sick and administer allowances to the poor."[9]

---

9 *Calvin: Theological Treatises*, translated by J.K.S. Reid (Philadelphia: The Westminster Press, 1954), at pp. 58, 62, 63, 64.

As individual congregations looked to Geneva for their model, each Reformed church had all four offices. Each was to be, in the rhythms of daily life, autonomous: able to preach, to administer sacraments, to teach, to correct, and to care for the poor and sick. Each was instituted by its members – the authority to organize each "Church" lay with its members, not in any centralized hierarchy. And, following Calvin's reconceptualization, the life of the church was not to be a thing apart from daily life, but, depending on one's perspective, either integrated or intruding into that life.

Luther's articulation of the temporal and the spiritual placed politics and economics under the temporal sword and the preaching and teaching of the Word under the spiritual sword. For Luther, Christian brotherly love was the fundamental ethical principle: As such, it both enjoined the care of those poor who lived upright Christian lives and constrained the making of profit – usury – at the expense of one's fellow Christians. For Calvin, no Christian was flawless in his or her belief and conduct, and anyone could become a Christian, because Christianity was not a product of childhood education, nor anchored to a place, nor reserved to one people, but that which God, in his inscrutable design, gave freely to some and not to others. Calvin's conceptualization laid the foundation for congregations to settle in what they held to be the "wilderness" of the North American continent, for communities of various sizes and shapes to enforce codes of dress and conduct, and for common Christians to judge monarchs.

At center was a fundamentally different conceptualization of the relationship between the world and the Bible. In many ways, Luther preserved the medieval division of temporal and spiritual, the two hierarchies of authority. For him, a person's relationship to God was something intimate, away from the temporal world; the "spiritual" remained shaped by his own experience as a monk. Calvin also recognized two swords, but those realms were coterminous in each human being's life: As he made clear at the end of the *Institutes*, everyone was subject to the Word of God, a God who was at once transcendent and everywhere to be seen, even as God saw each human life in its fullness. The world, for Calvin – who had never been a monk – did not exist apart from things spiritual. Everything one did in the world was, for Calvin, a manifestation of one's belief: how one dressed, how one spoke, how one conducted oneself in the everyday. Thus, if one was Christian, everything one did, from paying taxes to doing laundry, gave outward expression to that Christianity.

The world was the theater of God's glory, and worship was something one did every day, with every breath.

At the end of the sixteenth century, Reformed Christians looked closer to Anabaptists than to Lutherans: While Geneva and some of the Provinces of the Burgundian Netherlands had officially and formally embraced a Reformed vision of true Christianity, Reformed Christians had failed to win the support of any monarch – not surprising, when one considers the decentralized character of authority for them. A century later, Reformed Christians, drawing on their disciplined local organization and their conceptualization of the relationship between Scripture and the ordering of the world, had led the successful revolt of some of the Burgundian Provinces against the Holy Roman Emperor. Reformed Christianity is inseparable from the English Revolution in the seventeenth century, its congregationalism at once a touchstone for political theory and a mode of grassroots organization. The histories of the global commercial empires, Great Britain and the Netherlands, are unimaginable without Reformed Christians, and the new state that Reformed Christians forged on the northern shores of the Americas – as an extension not only of commercial and political empires, but of congregational Christianity – would become constitutionally inseparable from the Reformed ordering of the world.

A Spectrum of Christians: Catholics

How one tells the story shapes very much how one speaks about those European Christians who did not seek to order the world according to their understanding of Scripture. Most often in narratives of the Reformation, they have been cast as reactionary, as in "Counter-Reformation." And yet, that is to accept the terms of evangelicals, who expected all Europeans to embrace the vision of true Christianity they found in God's Word and who cast those who did not in the beginning as "simple," ignorant, or misguided, and then as recalcitrant, resistant, reactive, rejecting.

All evangelicals shared the belief in the power of the Word of God to convert human beings to right understanding of true Christianity. Even after it became clear in the 1520s that reading Scripture did not necessarily lead to a common vision of true Christianity, evangelicals believed that the intimate relationship between reader and text – increasingly, they came to argue, properly formed through careful education and discipline – was the only true foundation for that common vision. They shared a fundamental optimism that the Word of God would of its own power bring about change in every single Christian, correcting his or her orientation in the world and serving as the wellspring of correct understanding of God and his will.

By any measure, the majority of European Christians did not become evangelicals. Their reasons, as they gave in testimonies, were various. Some found the dizzying array of interpretations of Scripture compelling evidence that no one person had the truth. Others found the familiar rhythms of medieval Christianity spiritually nourishing in ways that the different practices of evangelical Christians were not. Still others accorded the Pope and the traditional hierarchy of the church definitive authority. Yet others found the bitter clashes a kind of war of words which held little connection to the lived Christianity of their day-to-day lives. In courts ecclesiastical and civil, European Christians spoke of their confusion – the bitterness of the debates, the savagery of the caricatures of opponents, the competing claims of expertise and certainty – and of their fear: of losing practices they found important in their own spiritual lives, of changes that disrupted the rhythms of their devotional lives, and, foremost, of losing their souls in eternal damnation, in a world so utterly divided on the nature of "true Christianity."

As early as the 1520s, European Christians began calling for a general, ecumenical council to resolve these terrifying divisions – though they did not agree as to who should call that council, where it should be held, or what, precisely, its agenda should be. In the past, general councils had been convened to address a broad range of controversies – from questions of the relationship of Christ to God the Father through questions about the nature of the priesthood and the jurisdiction of temporal rulers to questions of the relationship between the Eastern and Western Churches. In the past, representatives of the religious orders, bishops and cardinals, theologians, and representatives of temporal authorities had articulated positions that then became the position of the Church.

In 1545, Pope Paul III succeeded in convening the Council of Trent. By 1545, evangelicals had come to reject papal authority and – mindful of the fates of Jan Hus, burned at the stake, or John Wyclif (d. 1384), posthumously condemned, both at the Council of Constance in 1415 – did not accept invitations to participate. But in 1545, many, many European Christians, from the Emperor Charles V to handmaids, still hoped that a council might halt the fragmentation and restore unity, if not harmony. It was no accident that the representatives at Trent invoked the Council of Nicaea – which had addressed a deep division over the relationship of Christ to God the Father and articulated a statement of belief, the Nicene Creed, which Christians to this day profess.

That it did not turn out that way speaks foremost to the ever more divergent conceptions of the relationship between Scripture and the ordering of the world. From the perspective of the Vatican, whose residents were largely the clergy who had access to the Bible and were themselves authorized to celebrate the Mass, it was hard to imagine that a hunger for the Bible – to which the Revolutionaries of 1525, Anabaptists, Luther, Calvin, and Christians across France and the Empire had given voice – could sunder an institution, a phenomenon, which had just celebrated 1,500 years of existence.

The Council's first decrees after those organizing the Council itself took up the question of Scripture: Which text would be authoritative, which books would comprise the Christian Bible, and by what principles that text would be interpreted. In the Fourth Session, held on April 8, 1546, the Council

> decides and declares that the old well known Latin Vulgate edition which has been tested in the church by long use over so many centuries should be kept as the authentic text in public readings, debates, sermons and explanations; and no one is to dare or presume on any pretext to reject it.
> The council further decrees, in order to control those of unbalanced character, that no one, relying on his personal judgment in matters of faith and customs which are linked to the establishment of christian doctrine, shall dare to interpret the sacred scriptures either by twisting the text to his individual meaning in opposition to that which has been and is held by holy mother church, whose function is to pass judgment on the true meaning and interpretation of the sacred scriptures; or by giving it meanings contrary to the unanimous consent of the fathers.[10]

These decrees were the product of a process that many European Christians had trusted in the past. They were not a foregone conclusion, but carefully formulated in the midst of a number of sometimes conflicting concerns. Over a period of nearly two months, theologians, bishops, cardinals, and representatives of religious orders debated a number of questions concerning "the books of sacred scripture" – not the Word of God – different men bringing forward different dimensions of the problem: the positions of the Church Fathers, positions of medieval theologians, prior conciliar decrees, as well as pastoral experience in dioceses and parishes.

[10] *Decrees of the Ecumenical Councils*, vol. II, edited by Norman P. Tanner, S.J. (London: Sheed & Ward Ltd., 1990), p. 664.

With this particular formulation, the Council of Trent set the other end of the spectrum on the question of the relationship between the Bible and the ordering of the world. The Council claimed for itself the authority to determine which books constituted the Bible and which books would be excluded: the Catholic Bible and Protestant Bibles would henceforth be different. The world was not to be ordered according to any one understanding of the Bible, and the Bible's relationship to the world was to be mediated through a hierarchy of sacerdotal authority.

For those who hoped for unity, the Council was a failure. As these very first decrees on the Bible make clear, the Council rejected not simply the evangelical vision of Scripture – as the Word of God that each Christian should have access to and spend a lifetime studying – but even Erasmus's efforts to correct the Greek text and make more living the Latin translation. Evangelicals rejected all the Council's decrees on Scripture and, with them, the Council's claim to speak for Christendom in the west. For evangelicals, the Council had placed itself over the Word of God, and from that early session, there would be no common ground.

Instead, the Council of Trent ended up defining "Catholicism," at least until the Second Vatican Council in 1962–65. The participants wept at the close of the Council in 1563. For them, the Council had addressed the widespread longing for reform, as it called for the education of priests, the establishment of seminaries to educate priests, the increasing supervision of parish priests, and the regularization of bishops. It had defined the hierarchy of authority, the nature of the priesthood, the rituals of the Church, as well as core theological doctrines on original sin, free will, justification, predestination, purgatory, and the remission of sins. It called for a single missal, catechism for priests, breviary, and liturgical calendar to be used by all Catholics around the globe, though it left to the pope the actual drafting of these texts. But in 1563, most participants felt they had covered, if not all points of doctrine and practice, then at least core points definitive of what was called the Catholic Church.

They defined a "Church" consciously in contradistinction to particular positions of evangelicals. Called by one pope, the Council affirmed the authority of the papacy in 1563 when it placed in the hands of Pope Pius IV the formal confirmation of all its decrees. In its reform of bishops and parish priests, it confirmed both the episcopal hierarchy of authority and the singular status of priests, consciously and explicitly asserting the sacrament of ordination as a life-altering sacrament, once for all time, which separated those who received it from the rest of the world. The Council accorded the office of priest singular authority, based on that sacrament: to administer the sacraments of baptism, confirmation, last rites, confession, and communion; and to care for souls, that is, to oversee the spiritual lives of all those Christians living within a parish or diocese. The Council held that authority as inhering in the office itself, even as it also called for the persons of priests to be disciplined, celibate, embodying the person of Christ in every parish. With its emphasis on the transformative power of the sacrament of ordination and the representative function of clerical conduct, to make Christ present in each parish, the Council asserted an essential division between clergy and laity, setting the hierarchy of ecclesiastical authority apart from all laity, whether royal, noble, or common. Priests were to be educated, through the catechism and seminaries, which would reinforce their authority, but their authority inhered not in their person or their knowledge, but in their office.

It also articulated a different hermeneutic principle, a different approach to reading Scripture, directly challenging in that early decree divergent readings of Scripture as subjective, suggesting the capriciousness and arbitrariness of such readings – a sentiment that critics of the evangelicals had been voicing for some time – and locating the authoritative reading of Scripture in no one reader, but in "tradition." "Tradition" in the sixteenth century was the counterpoint not to the "new" – no evangelical was claiming a "new" reading of Scripture – but to the singular, the divergent. "Tradition" was multivocal, a "sense" that was arrived at over time through the consideration of many different readers who respected one another's readings and acknowledged the possibility that "truth" lay in the collectivity, not a single inspired reader. "Tradition," as the theologians at the Council of Trent explicated it, embraced both Church Fathers such as Augustine and medieval theologians such as Peter Lombard, as well as generations of laity whose acquiescence was itself a testimony to the veracity of the readings. From the perspectives of Rome and Paris, "tradition" was not a simple hierarchy of authority from apex to base, but a layering over time of authorities, in the plural, whose divergencies the theologians of the Sorbonne studied and the cardinals in the Vatican knew intimately from negotiating the papal court.

That sense of "tradition," which has subsequently been construed as a kind of reaction against the "radicalism" of individual evangelical theologians, was powerfully attractive to many European Christians. We who are heirs to the proliferation of readings of the Bible and its import for thinking about reading, books, and canons have found it hard to imagine what it felt like, around 1540, as theologians and street preachers promulgated mutually exclusive visions of "true Christianity," in which all pointed to the same text, Scripture, even as they offered contradictory readings. For those to whom the Gospels spoke directly, it was an exhilarating time: One heard Jesus speaking, one knew, with visceral certainty, how one was to live, in order to live in accord with God's will. For those who did not share that hermeneutical certainty, it was a deeply frightening time: Whom one believed determined whether one was saved or damned eternally – and all were calling for the radical change of the world as European Christians had known it, a world of familiar rhythms and known practices, and collectively acknowledged authorities. One was being asked to choose something new, based on a text that even the most learned could not agree as to its constituent parts, let alone its meaning or its import for daily life. "Tradition" offered a way of framing that demand, in which one's own knowledge of Scripture was not the test of another's claim to true Christianity.

At Trent, therefore, less than 300 representatives of "the Church" defined what they understood that Church to be, not through the assertion of any one person's insight, but by situating themselves within a 1,500-year tradition, of many different voices, whose insights they sought to draw on in order to discern "consensus," what abided over time. They defined:

- the canonical text of Scripture: its language, Latin, its specific translation, Jerome's Vulgate, and its constituent books
- the nature of a sacrament and the number of sacraments, seven
- the nature of clerical authority
- the Mass:
  - its parts, and in particular, the Canon of the Mass
  - its collective function
  - its meaning
  - who was authorized to celebrate it.

Over nearly twenty years, in the midst of a landscape ravaged by one war after another, they had worked methodically through the great questions of sixteenth-century Christianity, and they had arrived at "consensus": anchored in tradition, taking into account a number of different perspectives, and according no one position preeminence.

In hindsight, many have viewed the Council of Trent as simply affirming traditional Christianity. In some ways, that seems to be the case. It defined a Church with one head, the pope, and a clear hierarchy of authority, from the head through archbishops to bishops and, at the

lowest and also local level, parish priests. It affirmed and expanded on
the decrees of earlier councils, foremost the Fourth Lateran Council of
1215, with its decrees on clerical status and transubstantiation. It drew
on 1,500 years of theological discussion, even as some theologians were
privileged over others.

But the Council of Trent marks a watershed. The Council of Trent
self-consciously situated itself within a "tradition" reaching back to the
apostles, grounding the papal claim to singular authority in Jesus's words
to Peter, "on this rock I will build my church" [Matthew 16:18]. The
Council of Trent cast evangelicals as subjective, arbitrary, individualist
rather than communal, as breaking with rather than honoring tradition.
While the terms of the characterization have been softened, the Council
of Trent's core claim – that it spoke for an ancient and tried tradition –
has endured, despite evangelicals' claim that they were recovering a
tradition that had become deformed through innovation. In this way,
the Council of Trent won the battle of polemics, which Church would
be seen as "conservative," preserving what of Christianity was essential
and true over time. And it defined "tradition" for western Christianity:
Henceforth, "tradition" would encompass the Council of Trent. That,
perhaps, was the Council's most stunning achievement.

Set against earlier conciliar decrees, the Council of Trent's decrees
are more explicit, lengthier, and of greater numbers. No Council met
over as long a time as did Trent. No Council covered as many different
questions, from justification through the education of priests to which
books would comprise the authoritative Bible, in part because Christianity had become ever more densely layered and complex over time. It
had far, far more to say about transubstantiation and the meaning of
the sacrament of ordination than did the Fourth Lateran Council – carefully articulating positions that addressed and point-by-point rejected
evangelical understandings of worship, of the eucharist, and of the relationship between pastors and their communities. And as it defined each
term – priest, sacrament, sacred scripture – it did not simply set a bulwark
against the evangelicals. It gathered together heterogeneous discussions
and determined which position among the many would henceforth be
core, the point of departure, the foundation. Subsequent discussions of
such diverse questions as the role of images in worship or the particular content of a clerical education took the decrees of the Council of
Trent as their touchstone. The Council of Trent defined "Catholicism,"
and for all those who recognized its authority, it became the source for

FIGURE 4.1. Hans Holbein the Younger, Sir Thomas More, 1527. Copyright The Frick Collection.

determining what was "Catholic" and what was "traditional," that is, what had been definitive in the heterogeneity of medieval Christianity.

A World Shattered

By the end of the century, there were so many different "Churches" – Mennonite, Hutterite, Bohemian Brethren, Lutheran, French Reformed, Dutch Reformed, Swiss Reformed, English, Catholic – each with its own understanding of the relationship between the Word of God and the world. Each articulated its own doctrine, its own internal structure of authority, its own definitions of a sacrament, its own ethics – in conscious repudiation of all others. Each balanced a distinctive reading with a sense of something shared, forming a "Church" that would, as we shall see, provide its "members" with a community rooted to no place, a community constituted "wherever two or three are gathered in my name."

In 1521, Pope Leo X named Henry VIII, King of England, "Defender of the Faith." In 1535, Thomas More, who had risen to the highest public office in England, Chancellor, was beheaded for treason because he refused to take an oath recognizing the King of England as the supreme head of the Church in England. More's death was both familiar – one in a long series of violent confrontations between a Church that claimed universal authority and a monarch who sought to consolidate his authority within his domain – and epigrammatic of the century in which competing conceptions of the ordering of the world scissored the lives of Europeans. Even as the Word of God was brought to bear on the most intimate of human relations – marriage, family, friendship – the boundaries of the jurisdiction of monarchs and magistrates were being redrawn. Nothing remained the same.

5

The Ties That Bind

In 1522, Johannes Grießbeutel married. He did so in front of thirty-two witnesses, a number of whom, "in order to honor the groom, appeared as his brothers-in law."[1] In many ways, the wedding was typical. By 1500, the medieval Church had established the custom for couples to come to the thresholds of churches, to take their vows to one another before witnesses in this public formal way. And yet, in the wake of this wedding, the Augsburg City Council ordered some witnesses put in chains and fined others, among them the prominent and powerful citizens, Christoph Ehem, Anthony Rudolf, and Marx Pfister. This wedding was a transgression: Grießbeutel was an ordained priest. Those who witnessed the wedding were giving their public and legal support to an act the medieval church had forbidden in canon law, papal and conciliar decrees. Priests could not marry. Marriage was the sole sacrament restricted to the laity.

Finding no evidence in the Gospels that Jesus had called for a separate priesthood, marked by celibacy, evangelical priests married. Some, such as Grießbeutel, were known only locally, but word of the weddings of others travelled quickly across Europe: Huldrych Zwingli, who wed secretly in 1522, then publicly in 1524; Andreas Bodenstein von Karlstadt, in 1522; Martin Luther, in 1525; or Johannes Oecolampadius, in 1528.[2] Many, such as Luther and Thomas Müntzer, married women who had been nuns, who thus repudiated as well the cloistered life.

---

[1] Johannes Baur, *Bericht von Barfüßer-Orden* (Augsburg 1680), my translation.

[2] On January 19, 1522, Andreas Bodenstein von Karlstadt married Anna von Mochau. On April 2, 1524, Huldrych Zwingli married Anna Reinhard in a public ceremony; they had been married in secret two years earlier. In June 1523, Thomas Müntzer married Ottilie von Gerson. On June 13, 1525, Martin Luther married Katharina von Bora before witnesses. In 1528, Johannes Oecolampadius married Wibrandis Rosenblatt, who, at Oecolampadius's death in 1531, married Wolfgang Capito, and, at his death in 1541, Martin Bucer.

For all, evangelical priests were redrawing the western Christian map of human relations – transgressing an ancient and, by 1500, essential boundary between human beings. With these acts, evangelical priests publicly, before witnesses, rejected the medieval understanding of "religious" as celibate. They rejected precisely that state, sexual abstinence, that the medieval Church had taught was the living mark of the difference between the clerical estate and the laity, to whom marriage was reserved. A number of them had condemned in print the common practice among priests of living with women whom they could not, because of their ordination and their vow of celibacy, publicly marry. It was, they said, immoral for two people to live together, to have sexual relations, and not be bound in marriage.

In marrying, evangelical priests self-consciously and expressly denied the line separating "clergy" from "laity." There would be no separate caste of priests for any of the Churches those evangelical priests founded. Following the erasure of that line, everyone belonged to the same group, or, as Luther called it, "the priesthood of all believers." That phrase, among the most famous of the sixteenth century, did not simply signal the rejection of the medieval priesthood – a celibate caste defined by oaths, marked by dress, and set apart spatially and legally. Evangelicals altered the traditional relationship between ordinary Christians and "religion." Everyone could be a "priest." Every life could be "godly."

Human Nature

> If anyone says the holy Spirit is not given through holy ordination, and so bishops say *Receive the holy Spirit* in vain; or that no character is imprinted by it; or that someone who was once a priest can become a layman again: let him be anathema.
>
> Canon 4, Session 23, Council of Trent, 1563

> If anyone says the married state is to be preferred to that of virginity or celibacy, and that it is no better or more blessed to persevere in virginity or celibacy than to be joined in marriage: let him be anathema
>
> Canon 10, Session 24, Council of Trent, 1563[3]

From the first clerical marriage, European Christians no longer shared the same vision of human nature or the human community. Catholics continued to acknowledge an essential divide between "laity" and

---

[3] *Decrees of the Ecumenical Councils*, edited by Norman P. Tanner (London: Sheed & Ward, 1990), Vol. II, pp. 744, 755.

"clergy." Marriage and ordination were sacred acts defining and differentiating these two groups of human beings. The former lived "in the world." The latter, following the Council of Trent, was to model the perfect Christian life: humble, obedient, and celibate. Sexual activity separated the laity from "the religious"; it made them less religious and less perfect than the clergy. The Tridentine decrees applied to all Catholics, in both hemispheres. Whether one was in Quito or in Munich, the human community divided between those who did not marry and those who did, between those whom ordination had transformed into a more perfect representative of Christ and those who were less spiritual, less religious, less perfect.

> Now concerning the matters about which you wrote: "It is well for a man not to touch a woman." But because of cases of sexual immorality, each man should have his own wife and each woman her own husband. The husband should give to his wife her conjugal rights, and likewise the wife to her husband. For the wife does not have authority over her own body, but the husband does; likewise the husband does not have authority over his own body, but the wife does. Do not deprive one another except perhaps by agreement for a set time, to devote yourselves to prayer, and then come together again, so that Satan may not tempt you because of your lack of self-control.
>
> I Corinthians 7: 1–5

Paul's Letters had been the scriptural authority for the value medieval Christianity had placed on celibacy. His writings on marriage had also shaped the medieval Church's position on marriage, as something less spiritual than celibacy, but necessary for the control of sexuality and for procreation. In the time Franciscans and Dominicans were arguing whether the peoples of the western hemisphere were prelapsarian, evangelicals were reading Paul, finding there a vision of human nature divergent from the one that underlay the medieval doctrine of the seven deadly sins. The medieval Church's understanding of human nature had sought to balance the twin doctrines of free will – that every human being was free to choose good or evil – and original sin, that all humankind, through the fact of sexual generation, was born into a state of fallen nature. In sermons and images, medieval doctrine had emphasized human choice: Each human being could choose not to be angry, greedy, slothful, proud, envious, lustful, or gluttonous. Sins, in the plural, were a choice, and they were, moreover, susceptible to naming and to representation.

At the same time Bartolomé de Las Casas was arguing for human innocence, Martin Luther was preaching and writing on the bondage of

FIGURE 5.1. Hieronymous Bosch, The Seven Deadly Sins. Museo del Prado, Madrid, Spain. Photo credit: Erich Lessing / Art Resource, New York.

the will. Evangelicals all rejected the doctrine of free will, and with it, the notion that any human being could be "innocent" at all. They found in Paul a vision of human nature as itself, essentially, sinning. Sin was not a choice. Sin could not be represented as a thing. Sin was not a noun. It was a verb. Human beings sinned, active voice, with the drawing of their breath, throughout their waking hours, in their thoughts.

Following Paul, evangelicals held the great majority of human beings to be sexual creatures. They did not reject celibacy per se. They rejected the notion that celibacy was a choice any human being could make – though they allowed the possibility of a small number of individuals who, following an analogy of talent, were born able to live a celibate life, which, for many evangelicals, remained a superior state. Following Paul, they linked human sinning and sexual activity. Sex, like sin, was essential to human beings. It was also inseparable from the Fall of humankind.

Sin passed from generation to generation through sexual union. It was what human beings did.

Evangelicals divided on what that understanding of human nature meant for human relationships. Some evangelicals, foremost the Anabaptists, differentiated human relationships according to membership in the community of the faithful – a membership, for Anabaptists, marked by baptism. Those relationships formed after entry into the community of the faithful were different in their very essence. Some, such as Huldrych Zwingli and Martin Bucer, accorded human relationships the potentiality to help a person do and be good – communities of various kinds, from the most intimate to the body of the faithful, could affect human nature. Some, foremost, Martin Luther, held sinning to be so integral to human nature that nothing could separate the sinning from the nature. Human relationships, therefore, could serve to control, but not to change, human nature. Still others – foremost, John Calvin – held that human communities helped individual human beings work against their nature, fight that inner propensity to sin, in order to be godly. Human nature remained essentially sinning, but human beings could seek to be better than their nature.

For evangelicals, human relationships, from the most intimate to the most casual, were to serve the fight against sin. Marriage and family became primary sites for that battle. If human beings by their very nature actively sinned, and sexual activity was an expression of that sinning, then marriage, following God's command to Adam, became the institution within which sexual activity could serve a higher purpose, procreation, and be subsumed to the divine order. Marriage thus became the institution that offered the great majority of humankind the chance to live a godly life. Or, put another way, if every life could be godly and godliness did not reside in celibacy, then godliness might be found in exactly those relations excluded by vows of celibacy: marriage and family.

Marriage

The seventh is the sacrament of matrimony, which is a sign of the union of Christ and the church according to the words of the apostle: *This sacrament is a great one, but I speak in Christ and in the church* [Eph. 5:32]. The efficient cause of matrimony is usually mutual consent expressed in words about the present. A threefold good is attributed to matrimony. The first is the procreation and bringing up of children for the worship of God. The second is the mutual faithfulness of the spouses towards each other. The third is

the indissolubility of marriage, since it signifies the indivisible union of
Christ and the church. Although separation of bed is lawful on account of
fornication, it is not lawful to contract another marriage, since the bond
of a legitimately contracted marriage is perpetual.

> Council of Florence, Bull of Union with the Armenians,
> November 22, 1439[4]

Evangelicals and Catholics shared many points of agreement on marriage. They agreed that its divinely ordained purpose was procreation.
They agreed that marriage provided the fundament of the family, in
which children were to be raised to honor God. They agreed that the
marriage resided legally in the mutual consent of two adults. But they
disagreed vehemently on the question of marriage's sacramentality.

Catholics affirmed that marriage belonged with baptism, confirmation, penance, communion, last rites, and ordination as a sacred act, a
moment in which grace and human action met. Marriage was unique
among the sacraments. Unlike the other six, the "efficient cause" – what
makes it happen – was not any action or words of a priest, but the vows
exchanged between two lay Christians. By the end of the fifteenth century,
a priest could have a variety of roles in a marriage. He might announce
the banns – the public announcement of the intent to marry on the part
of two individuals – before celebrating the Mass. He might attend the
wedding. He might bless the union. But what made a marriage, according to common practice and canon law, was solely the vows exchanged
between two adults, mutual consent. All else was a matter of local practice. A marriage was "consummated," according to canon law, with sexual intercourse between the spouses. At that point, the marriage became
permanent.

When Grießbeutel married, he followed some, but not all of medieval
practice. He married before a church, though not his own parish church.
His witnesses seem to have been lay men, many of rank, but no priest
presided over or blessed the union. He did not publish any banns –
publicly announce in advance his intent to marry. Other evangelical
priests might choose, as Luther did, to marry at home. What the couples
said to one another was not recorded – it did not signify as much as place
and witnesses.

Medieval marriage had no specified text. Local custom might provide
consistency of acts and words, but, since the priest only served to witness,
possibly to bless, the medieval Church need provide no canonical text,

---

[4] *Decrees of the Ecumenical Councils*, vol. I, p. 550.

no script for the consistent performance of a ritual. Vows needed to be exchanged. Witnesses needed to be present. Legal contracts usually preceded the actual event. But the ceremony itself was not scripted before the sixteenth century.

Only after evangelical priests married did they turn to considering the form that an evangelical wedding service should take. Evangelicals agreed on what a marriage was – the exchange of vows between two adults – and what it was not, a sacrament. Christ blessed but neither commanded nor himself performed a marriage; Scripture offered no guidance how a Christian wedding should be performed. Evangelicals found in Genesis compelling evidence that God had instituted marriage in joining Adam and Eve. All, from one end of the spectrum to the other, held the central act of marriage to be the exchange of vows between a man and a woman. Mutual consent remained the essence of a marriage, although Anabaptists understood that consent as covenanting, something more than simple consent. Most, though not all, held as critical to the validity of the marriage the advance announcement of it: the banns. And all echoed the Council of Florence's evocation of Paul's analogy between Christ and the Church and husband and wife.

That said, evangelicals differed on whether the wedding fell under civil or ecclesiastical jurisdiction. Many evangelicals, such as Huldrych Zwingli, in rejecting the sacramental nature of marriage, called for weddings to be brought under civil jurisdiction. The civil authority was to have authority over the choice of spouse, the announcement of the engagement, the validity as well as any dissolution of the marriage. But Zwingli preached in a town whose magistracy embraced his vision of true Christianity relatively early. Elsewhere it was more complicated. Luther largely held the ceremony to fall under civil jurisdiction. In 1529, however, he asked pastors to be responsible for the formal declaration of the banns, done from the pulpit; the direction of the exchange of vows at the entrance to the church; and the blessing of the marriage at the altar of the church. It was important, Luther wrote, that the wedding honor God.

Calvin moved weddings into the church – as both structure and human community

Do you, N., confess here before God and his holy congregation that you have taken and take for your wife and spouse N. here present, whom you promise to protect, loving and maintaining her faithfully, as is the duty of a true and faithful husband to his wife, living piously with her, keeping faith and loyalty to her in all things, according to the holy Word of God and his holy Gospel?

Do you, N., confess here before God and his holy assembly that you have taken and take N. for your lawful husband, whom you promise to obey, serving and being subject to him, living piously, keeping faith and loyalty to him in all things, as a faithful and loyal wife should to her husband, according to the Word of God and the holy Gospel?

John Calvin, *Marriage Liturgy of 1545*[5]

In communities that looked to Geneva and Calvin for guidance, the wedding was no longer simply a rite joining families, which they and their connections witnessed. The wedding and with it, marriage, moved into the living community of Christians, physically and spatially as well as imaginatively. In Reformed communities, each wedding was itself "public": witnessed by the community of the faithful, within the space devoted to the collective and public worship of God, the vows now binding not only before God, but also before the entire congregation.

For much of their history, Anabaptists lived, at best, as a tolerated religious minority. They did not have courts of any kind. For them, marriage, which ideally occurred after an adult's baptism, belonged to the realm of redemption, to that life lived after one had made a conscious commitment to Christ. For them, marriage was a covenant formed between two consenting members of the community of the faithful. It became a part of the redeemed life, not a restraint on sinning human nature.

In each evangelical community, there was wide variation in the actual practice of marriage. Some Anabaptists, for instance, found in the Old Testament the scriptural justification for polygamy, a justification that Luther's powerful patron, Philip, Landgrave of Hesse, echoed in justification of his own bigamy. So, too, over the course of the century, different communities faced a new phenomenon, the "mixed marriage," in which two persons of different understandings of true Christianity married. Evangelicals and Catholics alike struggled with this. All had taken a common faith to be the foundation for this divinely ordained union.

Evangelicals and Catholics alike faced men and women who would no longer live together. Their thinking on the question of divorce shared a common opposition to it: Marriage remained for all a foundation of Christian society, divinely ordained and mutually binding. No one wanted marriages to dissolve easily; only Martin Bucer allowed for divorce

---

[5] Cited in John Witte, Jr., "Marriage Contracts, Liturgies, and Properties in Reformation Geneva," *To Have and to Hold: Marrying and Its Documentation in Western Christendom, 400–1600*, edited by Philip L. Reynolds & John Witte, Jr. (New York: Cambridge University Press, 2007), p. 461.

on grounds of incompatibility. Catholics and evangelicals differed on the framework within which they approached the question of divorce. Catholics had entered into a lifelong spiritual union. Its dissolution was not a simple legal act, as it was, for example, in Zurich. To break a Catholic marriage required demonstrating that it had not been valid in the first place: by reason of consanguinity, a close relation of blood or kin, or non-consummation. Adultery, as the Council of Trent reaffirmed, could not be grounds for divorce. Because evangelicals universally rejected the sacramentality of marriage, evangelical courts, whether civil or ecclesiastical, could not automatically draw on the extensive body of canon law to determine a case; in the sixteenth century, they had no well-developed body of cases to guide them. Different evangelicals preserved different parts of canon law. Luther, for instance, radically reduced the number of degrees of separation necessary, even as he recognized the medieval canonical principle of consanguinity, grounded in Leviticus, as a factor in the validity of a marriage. Following the Sixth Commandment for Lutherans, Seventh for Reformed Christians, evangelicals condemned adultery. Evangelical pastors sought to preserve the marriage if possible, to stop adultery rather than dissolve the marriage. As evangelical courts confronted the specifics of individual cases, they did grant divorce on grounds of adultery, though on a case-by-case basis. In Geneva, the court granted divorces when it found that a good Christian was being forced to live in an ungodly marriage with an immoral or wicked or un-Christian person.

By mid-century, Europeans Christians were divided over "marriage": what it was, what made it, what made it valid, if it was dissoluble, and on what grounds. Men and women appearing before ecclesiastical and civil authorities worried that their marriage was still valid: that they had married according to Catholic or evangelical practice, that they had married someone who did not recognize the ceremony as binding, that they had married without full understanding of true Christian doctrine. There were Catholic marriages and Reformed marriages and Anabaptist marriages and Lutheran marriages, and in the eyes of some married under each of these, the other marriages were not valid.

Catholics and evangelicals agreed on two things. They agreed that mutual consent was the foundation of marriage. And they agreed that the positive good of a marriage was the procreation of children. For many evangelicals, the family was the microcosm of the ordering of the world. For all, family and home were at the forefront in the battle for souls.

Family

Finally, if you really want to atone for all your sins, if you want to obtain the fullest remission of them on earth as well as in heaven, if you want to see many generations of your children, then . . . bring up your children properly. If you cannot do so, seek out other people who can and ask them to do it. Spare yourself neither money nor expense, neither trouble nor effort, for your children are the churches, the altar, the testament, the vigils and masses for the dead for which you make provision in your will.

Martin Luther, *A Sermon on the Estate of Marriage,* 1519[6]

Therefore, it is the duty of every head of a household at least once a week to examine the children and servants one after the other and ascertain what they know or have learned of [the catechism], and, if they do not know it, to keep them faithfully at it.

Martin Luther, Preface, *The Large Catechism,* 1529[7]

Erasing the line dividing laity and clergy brought family into Christian life as never before. The medieval Church had promulgated that marriage was for "the procreation and bringing up of children for the worship of God," as the Council of Florence decreed. But it had accorded the priesthood the responsibility to educate: Parents were to bring their children to church to be baptized, to hear sermons, to receive confirmation, to confess, to receive communion. Parents were responsible for modeling Christian virtue and bringing their children to church. They were not responsible for teaching their children Christian doctrine.

Johannes Brenz and Philip Melanchthon, schoolmasters and pastors, were among the first evangelicals explicitly to call for educating children in the tenets of Christianity: the Ten Commandments, which provided the moral code for Christians; the Apostles' Creed, which was, for all Christians, the core statement of belief; the Lord's Prayer, which became, for evangelicals, the one prayer all Christians should be able to recite from memory; and the sacraments – what they were, their number, and their meaning in the life of a Christian. Luther was the first to place that education in the home, to instruct fathers to oversee it. By mid-century,

---

[6] Martin Luther, "Sermon on the Estate of Marriage, 1519," *Luther's Works,* vol. 44: *The Christian in Society I,* edited by James Atkinson (Philadelphia: Fortress Press, 1966), p. 14.
[7] Martin Luther, Preface, "The Large Catechism," *The Book of Concord: The Confessions of the Evangelical Lutheran Church,* edited by Robert Kolb and Timothy J. Wengert (Minneapolis: Fortress Press, 2000), p. 383.

a number of popular evangelical catechisms were calling for fathers to educate their children.

The medieval Church had linked catechism and the sacrament of confirmation. Confirmation marked a person's entrance, normally at age seven, into the community of adult Christians. After confirmation, European Christians could take communion. Evangelicals all denied confirmation was a sacrament. Many, most explicitly Luther, also criticized the medieval Church for failing to educate. A number of evangelical Churches ended up retaining confirmation as a ceremony, albeit redefined to mark the completion of catechetical instruction. The Council of Trent affirmed that confirmation was a sacrament; it also called for a catechism, to be used first for the education of priests, who would then instruct their parishes. Over time, catechizing children became the common practice of most Churches.

In part, moving catechism into the home was the consequence of the political situation – as we shall see, the monarchs of Spain and France and the Emperor all remained Catholic; the monarch of England, as well as German princes and the northern provinces of the Habsburg Netherlands, became evangelical. In every place, therefore, some Christians found themselves a "minority," a concept to which we shall return. That meant, among many things, they did not control the schools or their curricula. In the places they controlled, Catholics and evangelicals built schools: schools for boys, (fewer) schools for girls, schools for training priests or ministers. All agreed on the importance of children – they were the next generation of Christians. By mid-century, evangelicals and Catholics alike were seeking to bring children into closely watched and carefully structured processes of education: catechism in church for every Church; catechisms at home for many evangelicals.

Nor was "education" restricted to texts. The medieval Church, in sermon and handbook, had called on parents to model Christian virtue in the home, to provide their children with living human embodiments of humility, obedience, temperance, patience, charity. In the sixteenth-century battle for souls, preachers, evangelical and Catholic, called on the men and women attending their sermons to model the virtues of that particular Church in the home, to make living for their children the virtues that would mark their Church in the world.

Wives, submit yourselves unto your own husbands, as unto the Lord. For the husband is the head of the wife, even as Christ is the head of the church:

and he is the savior of the body. Therefore as the church is subject unto
Christ, so let wives be to their own husbands in every thing.
Martin Luther, *The Order of Marriage for Common Pastors*, 1529[8]

As evangelical pastors preached of God the Father, they instructed their
parishioners in the proper ordering of marriage and household. The
household was to be "Christian" in its ordering as well as in what was
taught there. Wives were to be subject to husbands, children to parents,
servants to masters, and each of these relationships was to mirror Christian obedience to God and God's ordering of the world. Evangelicals
named their children for the evangelists, the patriarchs and matriarchs,
linking them by their very names to the Scripture that ordered their
lives.

Catholics shared with most evangelicals a vertical ordering of relations, but there were structurally two hierarchies. "Fathers" could be
priests or biological fathers. "Mother" might be an abbess or a biological
mother. Each family had its brothers and sisters, fathers and mothers.
Both kinds of mothers as well as biological fathers were subject to the
singular authority of priests. Catholics named their children for saints,
including the apostles, as well as for the Mother of God, Mary, and her
legal husband, Joseph, linking them to 1,500 years of martyrdom, testimony, good works, and embodied holiness.

Evangelicals preached God the Father and Christ the Son. The Catholic
Church affirmed a masculine sacerdotal hierarchy and the singular holiness of celibacy. In the midst of so many different assertions of authority's
essential masculinity, the Catholic Church fostered the cult of Mary, articulating her life in word and image. The interiors of churches presented
congregations with images of one or more of the stages of her life: from
the Annunciation, when the angel Gabriel tells the young and innocent
girl of her pregnancy and delivery of the child she was to call Jesus; to the
Crucifixion, and, most powerfully, the Pietà, when the still young mother
holds her dead son in her lap. Catechisms taught the Ave Maria, the
prayer based on Gabriel's words to Mary, which was both personal, in the
practice of the rosary, and liturgical, in the Mass. Palestrina, Orlando di
Lasso, and other composers set the Ave Maria to polyphony, and Jesuits
taught it to the peoples of the western hemisphere. Pure, but not divine,
Mary embodied the mercy and tenderness the devout sought from her

---

[8] Martin Luther, "The Order of Marriage for Common Pastors," *Luther's Works*, vol. 53:
Liturgy and Hymns, edited by Ulrich S. Leupold (Philadelphia: Fortress Press, 1965),
pp. 114.

FIGURE 5.2. Lodovico Carracci, The Apparition of the Virgin and Child to Saint Hyacinth. Louvre, Paris. Photo credit: Erich Lessing / Art Resource, New York.

son. Mary belonged to Catholics as she did not to evangelicals. Even as they attended to the families of their congregations, evangelicals denied the Mother of God her role as intercessor. For them, the Incarnation overshadowed the drama of that young girl or the young mother with her dead son. A number sought to substitute the name of the son for the mother in songs that were beloved, familiar, comforting among Catholics, seeking to translate the emotion for the mother to the son.

Christianity moved into the home as never before. Fathers were implicated in the process of teaching the doctrine that saved or condemned souls; mothers and wives were to model Christian obedience in a world shattering. But as communities split, the fragmentation thrust into homes in a number of different ways. Anabaptists, forced to worship clandestinely, held their conventicles in homes across Europe. Reformed Christians in Antwerp, Catholics in Amsterdam and London gathered for collective worship in the homes of members of their hidden communities. *Huguenots*, as Reformed Christians in France came to be called, increasingly met in homes, in the hundreds in Paris, as violence escalated. Their numbers ranged from a handful to hundreds in a single gathering. Luther sought to get Bibles and catechisms into homes, to link each home with his particular vision of true Christianity. Even as men and women married, their weddings belonged ever more to their Churches, as the wedding itself became a manifestation of religious affiliation, and the marriage was "Catholic" or "Lutheran" or "Reformed" or "Anglican."

The battle for souls was waged in the family. It became the first site for education in Christian doctrine, as it had been for education in Christian virtue. It was a microcosm of God's ordering of the world: the father serving as God's instrument within the domestic sphere of evangelical households; "fathers" marking hierarchies of authority for Catholics, from the biological father in each household, through the "father" of each parish, to the Holy Father who was God's representative on earth. But as the fragmentation of Christendom arced into the home, it tore apart the most intimate of ties that had bound one human being to another. For Reformed Christians, a "Catholic" wedding was an abomination; for some, the spouses were viewed as adulterous. For Catholics, evangelicals, in denying the sacramentality of marriage, desecrated that holy bond; evangelicals were not married in the eyes of their Catholic sisters, brothers, sons, daughters. The children of marriages of another Church were "bastards" in the eyes of some, born into an illegitimate liaison.

Over the course of the sixteenth century, one's understanding of "true Christianity" shaped one's family. It formed and informed the inner dynamics: between husbands and wives, parents and children. It shaped whom one had as household servants: Servants who belonged to a different Church could betray a family to hostile authorities, as Huguenots learned in France and Catholics learned in England. It could determine whom one married: As more and more places became divided between competing understandings of true Christianity, men and women married members of their Church, religious affiliation trumping ties of profession or neighborhood. It determined whether one had *godparents* – adults who offered another circle of protection and connection who stood with an infant at baptism – or not. It shaped one's experience as a child, adolescent, and young person, as well as one's wedding and one's marriage.

The fragmentation reached deeply, dividing family from family, within the same village, town, even the same biological group. The character of the authority of biological fathers differed from Church to Church. The Lutheran Church accorded fathers authority over the household and responsibility for the education of that household in the tenets of what would become Lutheran Christianity. The Catholic Church also accorded biological fathers authority over their wives, children, and all those who worked for the household, but placed those fathers under the authority of priests in all issues religious, spiritual, and moral. Anabaptist covenantal marriage placed women on the most equal footing of any Christian Church, a footing that had its counterpart in the fact that it was also the only Church in which women were permitted to preach. Calvin wrote more letters to women than any other sixteenth-century evangelical, addressing questions of marriages of mixed Churches, the raising of children, the limits as well as the extent of obedience. The Reformed Church placed fathers and families under the jurisdiction of the pastors and elders of the Church: Fathers and husbands were to be obeyed, but the home, with the wedding, had been brought into the church, to be supervised and regulated by it.

Over the course of the sixteenth century, European Christians grew up in households that grew more and more deeply different. Some had images of the Virgin Mary in an honored place. Some had no images. Some had large family Bibles. Others had small prayer books or saints' lives. In the sixteenth century, these came to signal not economic but religious differences between families. Some chose "religious" lives for their children. Some sought to live "religious" lives at home. The very word differed from household to household. Gone was any Christianity common across the European landscape. The home was where one first learned to be Christian. And the Christianity one learned at home one then carried across a fractured landscape in which sound and image were no longer commonly understood, in which the Christianity of home could be radically different from the Christianity of that particular place.

> My father was fond of reading good books and had some in Spanish so that his children might read them too. These books, together with the care which my mother took to make us say our prayers and to lead us to be devoted to Our Lady and to certain saints, began to awaken good desires in me when I was, I suppose, about six or seven years old. It was a help to me that I never saw my parents inclined to anything but virtue. They themselves had many virtues. My father was a man of great charity towards the poor, who was good to the sick and also to his servants – so much so that he could never be brought to keep slaves, because of his compassion for them. On one occasion, when he had a slave of a brother of his in the house, he was as good to her as to his own children. He used to say that it caused him intolerable distress that she was not free. He was strictly truthful: nobody ever heard him swear or speak evil. He was a man of the most rigid chastity.
>
> My mother, too, was a very virtuous woman, who endured a life of great infirmity: she was also particularly chaste. . . .
>
> I had one brother almost of my own age. . . . We used to read the lives of saints together; . . . I used to discuss with this brother of mine how we could become martyrs. We agreed to go off to the country of the Moors, begging our bread for the love of God, so that they might behead us there . . . but our greatest hindrance seemed to be that we had a father and a mother.
>
> *The Life of Teresa of Jesus*[9]

Christianity proved powerfully volatile in many families. The desire to teach a Christian life put in the hands of children such as Teresa of Ávila and her brother books that offered them models of lives of martyrdom, sacrifice, absolute devotion, and conviction. The desire to teach a Christian life filled evenings in pious Lutheran homes with the lives of the prophets and the parables of the Gospels. Christ had called for those who would follow him to leave family. Obedience was taught, but to whom? To what? As Teresa's parents learned, lives of martyrdom sat uneasily with the command to honor one's parents.

The desire to teach a Christian life filled the mornings and evenings of children with words, read, read aloud, or sung. Those words sketched

---

[9] *The Life of Teresa of Jesus: The Autobiography of St. Teresa of Ávila*, translated and edited by E. Allison Peers (New York: Image, 1991 [1960]), pp. 65–6.

many different lives: of martyrdom, of peripatetic preaching, of movement, and of unwavering belief. In Catholic homes, those who could afford to commission or purchase images placed before children representations of saints, none of whom had become a saint simply through filial obedience, some of whom, such as Francis of Assisi or the apostles, became holy by repudiating the careers their parents had chosen for them.

The absolute conviction rendered in the lives of saints and then the lives of evangelical martyrs set them apart from all others. The books of saints and martyrs bound together lives that were themselves severed in fundamental ways from family and kin, as those who embraced martyrdom looked not to mother or father, but to heaven. As Teresa understood as a child, the tie that bound the saints was to God. Her parents were a "hindrance" to martyrdom; she was "happier" in the convent than in her father's house. And she remained loyal to the Church of her parents.

> Said the mother, "My child, go straight to mass."
> "The mass," she replied, "is only abuse.
> Bring my books with my holy vows.
> I had rather burn, my ashes scattered,
> Than go to mass and break my oath."
>
> French song[10]

Belief, as sixteenth-century Christians learned, was a volatile thing. It sundered son from mother, daughter from father. Ties of affection within a family were supported in each Church's Christian education only insofar as they did not impede the practice of true Christianity. No tie, for any Church, was more binding than the tie between true Christians. Mothers, like the one recounted in the song, fathers, sons, and daughters informed authorities both ecclesiastical and civil of the stated beliefs and the private practices of children, parents – the ties from which we have our word, "familiar." Some, like the mother, even witnessed the execution of child or parent for heresy, when she or he would not recant for the sake of maternal love or filial duty.

Betrayals were a fear in every country, in thousands of households, as something said to a friend, within the home, on a street corner, suggested divergent belief. Rare were the families such as Michel de Montaigne's, in which evangelicals and Catholics continued to honor their ties to one another. Not eating meat on a Friday signaled Catholic membership;

---

[10] Donald Kelley, *The Beginning of Ideology: Consciousness and Society in the French Reformation* (Cambridge: Cambridge University Press, 1981), pp. 79–80.

FIGURE 5.3. Lucas Cranach the Younger, "The Difference Between True Religion and False," called "The Holy Communion of the Protestants and Ride to Hell of the Catholics." Kupferstichkabinett, Staatliche Museen, Berlin, Germany. Photo by Jorg P. Anders. Photo credit: Bildarchiv Preussischer Kulturbesitz / Art Resource, New York.

eating meat signaled evangelical. Praying the rosary signaled Catholic; refusing to pray anything other than the Lord's Prayer signaled evangelical. Prayers in Latin signaled Catholic; prayers in the dialect of the region signaled evangelical. Small acts and words became signals, as brothers and sisters, fathers and mothers embraced one ordering of the world or another. And each was a marker for a fundamental division, a fissure, between ways of entering the world.

Turks and Cannibals

Polemic translated the fragmentation of divergent understandings into stark oppositions. Polemic promulgated the practice of reading simple acts as signals. Polemic constructed simple bipolarities and with them, the clear delineation of two groups that were divided essentially from one another. One's brother might be related by blood, but if he prayed the rosary, he was not simply "Catholic." He was "papist," subservient to the Antichrist, and therefore the exact opposite of a true Christian.

In print and in sermon, pamphleteers and preachers, evangelical and Catholic alike, constructed opposing camps. Zwingli, for instance, wrote a widely read polemic, *On True and False Religion.* "True" religion comprised what Zwingli was seeking to institute in Zurich: specific doctrines, specific practices. "False" religion comprised what Catholics held and practiced. It was not simply that specific points of doctrine were "true" or "false," but that there were two "religions," the one true in all that it said and did, the other false in all that it said and did. One belonged to one group or the other.

Sixteenth-century religious polemics constructed two kinds of human being – true and false Christians; Christians and "papists"; Christians and "heretics" – who were diametrically opposed to one another in all practices and beliefs. The medium of print lent itself to representing bipolarities: black and white, left and right, top and bottom. The visual polemics drew upon each to separate humankind into two utterly discrete groups, as different as black and white, divided between right and left, saved or damned. They confronted their viewers with clear choices: right or wrong, true or false, saved or damned.

There was no grey zone in the polemics. If one accorded the Pope supreme authority, one was a "papist" – even if one called for the reform of the entire medieval Church. If one questioned the celibacy of priests, one was a "heretic" – even if one continued to attend Mass. Single practices could not be separated from "religion," whether true or false. Polemics did not allow for individual human beings to choose this belief, that practice – if one did a specific practice, that practice signaled membership in a group that shared the same beliefs and practices. One could not agree with one position and disagree with another and still be a member of the same group.

Polemic did not stop with the construction of simple oppositions. Pamphlets and sermons fused who a person was with what he or she did. Those who differed in practices or doctrine differed in essence. What one did was an expression of how one entered the world: Those small signals – praying in Latin, eating meat on Friday – were the external markers of someone "not us."

Polemicists deployed particularly powerful tropes to sharpen and deepen that division: being "not us" made a person horrifying and alien. In eastern Europe, "the Turk" was both a very real presence and a powerful image of a dangerous enemy. After taking Constantinople in 1453, the Ottoman armies had pushed into Habsburg lands in the east, culminating with Sultan Suleiman the Magnificent's siege of Vienna in 1529. In the 1520s, the greatest forces of Europe could not stop the advance of the Ottoman Empire. Tales and images circulated of "Turks" slicing

FIGURE 5.4. "A Seven Headed Martin Luther," 1698. British Library, London, Great Britain. Photo credit: HIP / Art Resource, New York.

FIGURE 5.5. Theodore de Bry, "Cannibalism amongst Brazilian Natives." From "Americae," part III, 1592. Color engraving. Photo by Knud Petersen. Kunstbibliothek, Staatliche Museen, Berlin, Germany. Photo credit: Bildarchiv Preussischer Kulturbesitz / Art Resource, New York.

Christian children in half, at once invoking the biblical tale of the slaughter of the innocents and representing the fear of losing one's children to enemies whose antipathy was religious in foundation. In 1529, the Catholic polemicist Johannes Cochlaeus linked Luther to the Turk: One of Luther's doctrinal positions mirrored Muhammad's repudiation of the divinity of Christ. In images that blurred the differences between the Sultan's turban and the Pope's tiara, evangelical polemicists linked the papacy and Islam. So, too, Lutheran polemicists linked Reformed Christians to Turks, through tales of Reformed Christians who fled the Empire and converted to Islam, drawn by the affinities, the Lutherans claimed, they found between the two "religions." And just as Ottoman swords sliced Christian children, other Christianities put innocent lives at risk.

In France, Huguenots accused Catholics of cannibalism. The accusation overrode distinctions medieval theologians had carefully articulated – between appearance and reality – as well as the range of experiences medieval Christians had of the sacrament of the eucharist. But it allows us to see at work a polemic that sought actively to sever human ties. Briefly, the caricature of "cannibalism" rested on the evangelical critique of the interconnected doctrines of "transubstantiation" and "real presence." Together the two doctrines held that when the priest spoke in the Mass the words from the Gospel account of Jesus's last meal with his disciples – "for this is my body," "for this is my blood" – the bread and the wine, there on the altar, were transformed in their substance, hence "transubtantiated," into the real body and the real blood of Christ, hence "real presence." With the word, cannibal, Huguenots attached the physicalities of every human body – its weight, its mass, its sinews and tissue, muscles and bones, blood and skin – to the act of collective worship of all Catholics.

The trope arced across the Atlantic, linking Catholics and Caribs or the Tupi in Brazil. The debate, whether one's nature was changed by eating human flesh, was transplanted to France. Those who believed the doctrine of transubstantiation and believed that Christ was present physically, "really," in the eucharist were thus, according to the polemic, ingesting human flesh, their own matter itself changed in substance by that consumption, their nature no longer common even with those who might share the same mother. Polemicists linked the strange new world with the ancient and familiar liturgy of the eucharist. Catholics, following that association, were "barbarian" precisely because they practiced a preeminent marker of barbarism.

A cannibal no longer rested in the western hemisphere – strange, but remote. A cannibal could be in one's own home, the person with whom one had grown up, the person to whom one had given birth. It was not simply that blood no longer bound one Christian to another. It was that a person essentially different could be born into the same family. Essential difference was not biological. It resided in what one believed and did. A Christian was not born into a legally constituted group. A Christian was something one became. A Christian was marked by certain practices. A Christian expressed "beliefs" in act and word.

Nor was polemics mere name calling. For the Huguenot Jean de Léry, there was no boundary between "cannibals" who consumed their God under the doctrine of real presence and cannibals who consumed their neighbors. All shared the thirst for human blood, the gluttony for human flesh:

Furthermore, if it comes to the brutal action of really (as one says) chewing and devouring human flesh, have we not found people in these regions over here, even among those who bear the name of Christian, both in Italy and elsewhere, who, not content with having cruelly put to death their enemies, have been unable to slake their bloodthirst except by eating their livers and their hearts? I defer to the histories. And, without going further, what of France? (I am French, and it grieves me to say it.) During the bloody tragedy that began in Paris on the twenty-fourth of August 1572 – for which I do not accuse those who are not responsible – among other acts horrible to recount, which were perpetrated at that time throughout the kingdom, the fat of human bodies (which, in ways more barbarous than those of the savages, were butchered at Lyon after being pulled out of the Saône) – was it not publicly sold to the highest bidder? The livers, the hearts, and other parts of these bodies – were they not eaten by the furious murderers, of whom Hell itself stands in horror? Likewise, after the wretched massacre of one Coeur de Roy, who professed the Reformed Faith in the City of Auxerre – did not those who committed this murder cut his heart to pieces, display it for sale to those who hated him, and finally, after grilling it over coals – glutting their rage like mastiffs – eat of it?

History of a Voyage to the Land of Brazil[11]

The polemical construction of the world divided humankind absolutely between true believers and cannibals or Turks. In the polemics, there was no difference between a Catholic and a Tupi – both were essentially different, not human in the same way a true Christian was. Both were "not." In the polemics, there were Christians – those who shared a specific understanding of the ordering of the world – and not Christians. The world divided, white and black, Christian and savage. If a Tupi converted, he became a child of God; if a Taino converted, she became a child of God. Tupis who did not convert, Catholics who continued to receive communion, existed together under a single rubric that named not simply their practices, but their nature: cannibal. In the polemics, the difference between Luther and an Ottoman soldier dissolved: Both brought violence, both sought to promulgate repugnant religious beliefs and practices, both threatened Christian children.

As polemicists constructed a world of bipolarities, they contributed to the shattering of the medieval Christian landscape in which different Christians behaved differently but shared a common geography of parishes, a common temporal structure – and a common definition of "Christian" as someone who was baptized, no more, no less. Baptism no

---

[11] Jean de Léry, *History of a Voyage to the Land of Brazil*, translated by Janet Whatley (Berkeley: University of California Press, 1990), p. 132.

longer defined Christian. A "Christian" was known by a range of words
and acts. And the world divided, according to the polemicists, between
Christians and savages, between human beings and non-Christians. Those
two kinds could exist anywhere: Cannibals could be in one's home, Christians could be in the new world. Christians were linked to one another
not by blood or proximity, but by common practices and beliefs. No
longer spatially or socially contiguous, Christianity was global.

"The Children of God"

in order to honor the groom, appeared as his brothers-in-law
                    Johannes Baur, Report on the Franciscan Order[12]

[the youngest daughter of Nicolas Le Mercier and his wife, . . . was dipped]
stark naked in the blood of her massacred mother and father, with horrible
threats that, if ever she became a Huguenot, the same would happen to her.
                    Jean Crespin, *History of the Martyrs*, 1564[13]

One's brothers might refuse to witness a wedding in which the betrothed
held the wrong vision of true Christianity. Those who shared that vision
became one's "family." Anabaptists called one another "brother" and
"sister," echoing the way Jesus spoke to the strangers to whom he
preached as well as the disciples who accompanied him. All who shared
in the same vision of Christianity were "the children of God," under the
protection of God the Father – no matter where on the surface of the
earth they might find themselves: Reformed Christians on the Brazilian
and northern coasts of America; Anabaptists in Münster and the Italian
countryside. And as they stood on the soil of the Viceroyalties of New
Spain or Peru, Franciscans called one another "brother" and "father," as
did the people whom they converted to join "the children of God." Each
Church built families that connected its members to one another, no
matter how hostile or unfamiliar the environment in which they found
themselves.

We do not know how often children were "rebaptized" in the blood of
their parents. But the children of adults who had been martyred were normally – that is, as a matter of course – taken from their biological families
and placed with those who shared the practices and beliefs of whichever

---

[12] Baur, *Bericht von Barfüßer-Orden*, my translation.
[13] Quoted in Barbara Diefendorf, *Beneath the Cross: Catholics and Huguenots in Sixteenth-
Century Paris* (New York: Oxford University Press, 1991), p. 102.

group was in the religious majority. Biological families were obliterated, with more or less violence, and families of faith were constituted.

While Catholics and evangelicals disagreed on human nature and the degree to which one might alter that nature, Catholics and evangelicals alike sought to bring populations into conformity with their respective understandings of true Christianity. Sermons and catechisms sought to teach conduct and belief. Catholics might place images of Mary in churches and homes, offering children and their parents at once an icon of Christian virtues that were preached and visualizations of a particularly holy life. Catholics and evangelicals brought images and words to bear, to reach the heart and mind of each Christian and move that person to practice and believe truly.

These were not enough, however. As the seizure of children demonstrated, for those involved, souls were at stake. Words and images brought some Christians into conformity, but they did not bring all. Thousands continued to practice what they had learned as children, for all sorts of reasons, including the simple fact that it was familiar and, as such, comforting. Others were persuaded that this or that practice or belief rang true, but not persuaded that all this or that preacher was calling "true" was indeed that. Many Christians listened to more than one preacher in these years, finding this one's understanding of worship compelling, that one's understanding of human nature made sense. We do not know what the overwhelming majority of European Christians believed. We know what many said and did in public, as various institutions interrogated hundreds of Europeans and then Americans about what they and those they knew did within their homes.

Catholics and evangelicals alike turned to laws and institutions to shape communities of faith, or what they called "the body of the faithful." One of the oldest and certainly one of the most feared was the Inquisition.

Pedro de Teva, resident of Almagro, sworn witness, etc., said, under the charge of the oath he just swore, that last year, 1492, while living in Cuidad Real, he was good friends with Francisco de Toledo and knew him well. Many times he ate with him in his house, consuming pork, strangled partridges, and other things, and Francisco's wife Marina did not eat any of it. One day, when he was eating a piece of wild pig with her husband, this witness said to her, "Lady, aren't you coming to eat?" and she said, "I cannot eat now." Her husband said to her, "I swear to God, woman, you are tempting fate." And she said to him, "Leave it alone, afflictions may come." From this point on, this witness watched her very carefully, and though he saw her many times,

she never ate pork or strangled partridges.... If her husband ate pork, she
did not want to drink out of the same glass as he did.

Inquisition trial of Marina González, Toledo, 1494[14]

In 1522, Charles, King of Spain and Holy Roman Emperor, introduced
the Spanish Inquisition into the Low Countries. For him, it was the
extension of a medieval instrument of orthodoxy that had been instituted
primarily to root out hidden apostates among the converted Jews and
Muslims and secondarily to discern heretics among Christians. Normally
comprising a board of theologians, often Dominicans, the inquisitors, as
their name implied, framed questions and enjoined answers expressing
orthodoxy.

While Charles's sense of evangelicals as "heretics" was common enough
among Catholics, and was fostered in Catholic polemics, the institution
of the Inquisition linked evangelicals to a fear that had arisen in the wake
of the forced conversions of the Reconquista, of "clandestine" religion.
Inquisitorial courts had long been concerned with hidden heresy or
apostasy – hidden in the sense that it was lived outright within the walls
of one's home. Before the sixteenth century, Spanish inquisitors had
pursued questions of belief into homes and interrogated family members,
drawing testimony against mothers, fathers, sisters, brothers. Heresy was
not restricted to the home, by any means, but inquisitorial courts, first
in Spain, then in the Netherlands, then in Rome, with the establishment
of the Inquisition there in 1542, were intensely concerned with what
was being done and said behind closed doors. In the eyes of Inquisitors,
whether one was singing psalms, as did Reformed Christians, or studying
the Torah, as did Jews, or refusing to eat pork, as did Jews and Muslims,
one was subject to prosecution, punishment, even execution. For each
group, the home – one's own or another's – was implicated in that charge
of "clandestine" religion.

That fear, of clandestine belief and its counterpart, "Nicodemism,"
as Calvin called it – the outward conformity to an enforced religion
while one kept "true faith" hidden – waxed in the sixteenth century, as
religious majorities moved to bring religious minorities into conformity,
often through force. It drove the twinned pursuits of surveillance and
discipline. Again, depending on one's understanding of human nature,
"apostasy" – the return to former religious practices and beliefs – and

---

[14] *The Spanish Inquisition, 1478–1614: An Anthology of Sources,* edited and translated by Lu
Ann Homza (Indianapolis: Hackett, 2006), p. 37.

"heresy," the breaking away from orthodoxy, could be exterminated or corrected.

The Inquisition was rooted in the medieval doctrine of freedom of the will. It sought to determine when a person had chosen – freely according to the premise of free will – to break with orthodoxy. Autos da fé, the mass execution of heretics by burning, frequently followed upon the confessions of those the Inquisition had brought to the declaration of heresy or apostasy. Inquisitorial courts could pardon or condemn, but they fell broadly within a penitential system: The confession of apostasy or heresy formally was to precede execution or pardon. The decision to pardon or to execute hung upon the conduct and the education of the accused: The ignorant, who could be easily confused, might be released after contrition and correction; if they appeared again before the court, they became intransigent in its eyes, and it called for their surgical removal from the body of the faithful – their *excommunication*, that is, exclusion from the sacrament of communion, and execution.

The Inquisition sought to shape faith through one kind of discipline: the formal interrogation of individuals on the full range of doctrine, from the prohibition of eating meat on Friday to the proper recitation of the Ave Maria. The Catholic Church also sought to strengthen other traditional forms of discipline, foremost that in the bishop's purview, and to extend both episcopal and parochial jurisdiction to adjudicate more kinds of religious heterogeneity. The Council of Trent called for the traditional episcopal visitation and the parish priest's responsibility for the care of souls to be intensified, that the church know more precisely the beliefs and practices of the Catholics within the bishop's and the priest's respective jurisdictions. It provided clear definitions of those who "are anathema" – heretical – and therefore to be denied communion and disciplined. The Council clarified dozens of specific points of doctrine that pertained to the daily lives of the laity. The grounds for divorce, for example, were specified for the episcopal courts that normally adjudicated petitions for divorce. Following Catholic doctrine of free will, adultery was a choice that a spouse could make and therefore choose to stop. It was not grounds for divorce because it was free choice. Catholics were to remain married, even when one spouse was promiscuous, or, following the seven deadly sins, lustful and therefore sinning. Contrition, confession, penance were the appropriate response to this crisis in a marriage.

Although evangelicals differed as to the degree any institution could affect human nature, they all agreed that legally constituted bodies could serve, at the very least, to control human behavior. In those places where they were in the political majority, such as free imperial cities, Swiss cantons, and principalities, evangelicals instituted different kinds of courts combining preachers and magistrates to adjudicate behavior and belief. In 1525 in Zurich, Zwingli, working with evangelical magistrates, formed the first marriage court, instituted to ensure the proper selection of spouses, the publication of the banns, the proper wedding ceremony, and afterward, the proper conduct of marriage. Basel followed suit in 1533, Geneva in 1545. The earliest Lutheran Consistories, founded by the princes of Saxony and Württemburg, were largely, if not exclusively, concerned with marriage. Each of these courts had its own procedures for determining membership of the court. Each court was a different balance of political authorities and pastors; some also included "Elders," senior, powerful members of the Church who served as leaders alongside the pastors. Each blended tradition and innovation. In many places, including Zurich, marriage had increasingly come under civil – as opposed to ecclesiastical – jurisdiction. Each of these courts substantially extended its jurisdiction, as each claimed jurisdiction over three stages – betrothal, wedding, marriage – and the conduct of the individuals within that marriage. In so doing, they effectively placed under the jurisdiction of "marriage" courts the conduct of most adults – especially given the evangelical affirmation of marriage as the way best to live a godly life for most Christians.

> Accordingly, as the saving doctrine of Christ is the soul of the church, so does discipline serve as its sinews, through which the members of the body hold together, each in its own place. . . . Therefore, discipline is like the bridle to restrain and tame those who rage against the doctrine of Christ; or like the spur to arouse those of little inclination; and also sometimes like a father's rod to chastise mildly and with the gentleness of Christ's Spirit those who have more seriously lapsed. . . . Now, this is the sole remedy that Christ has enjoined and the one that has always been used among the godly.
>
> John Calvin, *Institutes of the Christian Religion*, Book IV, Chapter XII[15]

By far the most influential of evangelical institutions of surveillance and discipline was the Consistory, whose archetypal form was instituted in Geneva in 1541, according to Calvin's directions. It was, according to Calvin, an ancient body for church discipline. In Geneva, Calvin set forth an institution whose jurisdiction extended over the entirety of human

---

[15] *Calvin: Institutes of the Christian Religion*, edited by John T. McNeill, translated by Ford Lewis Battles (Philadelphia: The Westminster Press, 1960), Vol. II, p. 1230.

conduct and thought. It was composed equally of pastors from the town and surrounding villages and elders, "men of good life and honest, without reproach and above all suspicion, above all fearing God and having good spiritual discretion."[16] One of the four syndics of the City Council presided over it each year. It met each Thursday throughout the year, in sessions of three to four hours. Like inquisitorial courts, the Consistory had the authority to summon witnesses and to ask any questions it deemed necessary. Unlike the inquisitorial court, it did not use torture to extract testimony. Its preeminent purpose, as Calvin envisioned it, was pastoral, not surgical – to correct and in that sense "discipline." Discipline, for Calvin, was what the community did to help weak Christians fight their sinning nature. The Consistory, therefore, also did not have the authority to execute: The strongest punishment within its authority was excommunication, excluding a Christian from participation in communion.

> Comparet's widow, mother of [Françoys and François], because she does not discipline her children, who are badly taught in all good morals. Answers that other young boys lead them astray and ruin them, and they are good children and obedient, and they were not at the scandal that was made thus, and she does not know what it is. And goes willingly to the sermons when she can, and above all on Sundays. The younger son does not come to Communion. The Consistory advises that she watch out from now on, that she teach her children and frequent the sermons and the catechism on Sundays; otherwise the Council will see to her. And that the children frequent the sermons.
> Registers of the Consistory of Geneva, 1542[17]

Each Church conceptualized discipline differently, according to its understanding of human nature. Discipline, for those who held a doctrine of free will, could serve to call the will's attention to its divergence from orthodoxy and, should that will not become obedient, to excise that person from the body of the faithful, first through excommunication, then through execution. Discipline, for those who held a doctrine of a will bound by sin, could serve, as Calvin said, as a bridle, a spur, or a rod – to correct behavior.

---

[16] "The Ecclesiatical Ordinances of 1541," *Registers of the Consistory of Geneva in the Time of Calvin*, Vol. I: 1542–1544, edited by Robert Kingdon, Thomas A. Lambert and Isabella M. Watt, translated by M. Wallace McDonald (Grand Rapids: Eerdmans, 2000), Appendix 1, p. 419.

[17] *Registers of the Consistory of Geneva in the Time of Calvin*, Vol. I: 1542–1544, p. 162.

While polemicists constructed bipolarities, each of those that became
Churches by the end of the century turned to discipline to build what
each called "the body of the faithful." No Church was geographically
coherent, spread seamlessly across a landscape. Discipline and polemic
forged boundaries that were not spatial, but personal – in the bodies
and minds of individuals. Individuals were to be bound to one another
through "belief" – learned statements of specific tenets, the texts of the
Apostles' Creed and the Lord's Prayer, as explicated by one's Church –
and through those practices that the Church taught were the proper
expression of that belief: eating meat on Fridays, or not; praying the
rosary, or not. In a world set in motion, as fathers drove out sons and
disinherited them, as wives and husbands left to emigrate to places where
their true family could be found, each Church sought to discipline "true
Christian belief and practice" in the places sons and wives left and in the
places where they arrived. Huguenots crossed the Atlantic, members of
the Society of Jesus, known as Jesuits, crossed every body of water, both
seeking to establish a place where true Christians might live their belief.
Each was bound to others through a new sense of "family" – not of blood,
but of belief – what the Jesuits called "a union of hearts and minds," what
others called "children of God." No longer rooted to any one landscape,
"Christianity" was something one carried within oneself, binding each
true Christian to others, brothers and sisters in a world of cannibals and
Turks.

6

Boundaries

Shifting Jurisdictions

When the king's highness was at Calais in the interview between His majesty
and the French king, and hearing mass in the church of Our Lady at
Calais ... God was so displeased with the king's highness that his grace saw
not that time at the mass the blessed sacrament in the form of bread, for it
was taken away from the priest (being at mass) by an angel, and ministered
to the said Elizabeth then being there present and invisible, and suddenly
conveyed and rapt thence again by the power of God into the said nunnery
where she is professed.

Testimony of Elizabeth Barton, the holy maid of Kent[1]

On April 20, 1534, Elizabeth Barton was executed for treason. She had
neither threatened the person of the king nor plotted to overthrow him
or Parliament. Like Thomas More, who would follow her a year later
to Tyburn hill, she had rejected Henry VIII's claim to be the head of
"the Church," opposed the severance of "the Church" in England from
the Church universal, and rejected Henry's divorce, which the Pope had
refused to grant.

As late as 1532, it was not treason in England to refuse to recognize the king as sovereign over the Church within the boundaries of
his kingdom. As late as 1532 in England, bishops, priests, monasteries –
clergy and all their lands and property – remained under the jurisdiction of the pope. As we have seen, over centuries, European Christians
had defined two discrete jurisdictions: the spiritual and the temporal.
The former extended from the Ottoman Empire in the east to the
westernmost reaches of the Spanish empire in the western hemisphere.

---

[1] Act of Attainder against Elizabeth Barton, *The Statutes of the Realm*, vol. III, p. 448, quoted
in Ethan Shagan, *Popular Politics and the English Reformation* (Cambridge: Cambridge
University Press, 2003), p. 73.

In 1520, there was one spiritual sword: a hierarchy of authority rising from parish priests, through bishops and archbishops, to the pope. That hierarchy was written on the landscape: parish churches and cathedrals marking land in the single spatial entity of "Christendom" over which the pope was sovereign. In contrast, as every monarch and magistrate knew, there were hundreds of temporal swords, whose jurisdictions often conflicted: duchies in some ways and not others under the sovereignty of kings; cities both autonomous and under the sovereignties of princes; counts, dukes, marquises, and magistrates who were in some ways and not others under the sovereignty of an emperor or a king.

In 1500, as critics and supporters alike recognized, the two swords did not divide between the immaterial and the material. The spiritual governed not simply matters of the spirit – questions of the practice and teachings of Christianity – but the persons of the clergy, who were immune from temporal jurisdiction, and all their property: vast tracks of land throughout Europe, houses and monasteries, paintings, sculpture, books, liturgical objects, candlesticks, jewels, and silks. Before the Encounter, the Church had become the single greatest landowner in Europe: More land belonged to it than any temporal lord could command; and tens of thousands of peasants worked that land for, as subjects of, the Church. It also received income from all Christians in the form of the *tithe* – in formal theory, a tenth of each Christian's income – and in the rents and dues the peasants who worked church lands paid their landlord, the Church. The spiritual sword, with its thousands of parish churches and monasteries, was more physically present, more visible, on the landscape of Europe than was the temporal.

Nor were temporal rulers "secular" in our modern sense. The very notion of a "temporal sword" had been defined within Christian political theory. And authority was not separable from the Christianity of the monarch – in 1500, all rulers from the coast of Granada to the edges of the Ottoman Empire were Christian. Thirteen years before the holy maid of Kent was executed for treason, Pope Leo X had named Henry VIII "Defender of the Faith," just as one of his predecessors had given Isabel and Ferdinand the title, "Most Catholic Monarchs." Both spiritual and temporal swords governed in "this world," *saeculum* in the Latin.

In comparison with the spiritual sword, temporal swords were poorer – when Henry VIII dissolved the monasteries, the wealth of the crown increased by as much as thirty percent. The dominion of no temporal ruler extended as far geographically – though Charles V, heir to the Spanish empire in the western hemisphere and Holy Roman Emperor, dreamed of a comparable universal empire. Nor had any temporal lord achieved the coherence of the Church's jurisdiction: Even within lands nominally under one temporal lord, his authority was discontinuous from one space to another, no more certain than he could make it through force of arms or ties of loyalty. Most subjects of temporal lords shared neither a single language nor body of law in 1500.

In 1500, no two temporal rulers had the same jurisdiction over their subjects. Over centuries, princes and magistrates had negotiated privileges and rights with their sovereigns. While the pope had successfully claimed the authority to adjudicate questions of doctrine and worship, and matters pertaining to the persons of clergy, temporal rules had no such clarity. Two jurisdictional divisions were relatively clear, and two alone: between the temporal sword and the spiritual, and, within the domain of temporal swords, between Jews and Christians. In England, France, and, after 1492, Castile and Aragon, in theory, all subjects were Christian in those lands. In those lands where Jews were permitted to live, they nonetheless lived as a discrete legal category of subjecthood, their freedoms and privileges more precisely specified and circumscribed than those of their Christian neighbors and more dependent on the will of the sovereign.

From the 1520s onwards, city councils, princes, parliaments, and kings obliterated the ancient distinction between two kinds of jurisdiction. The Kings of England, Scotland, and Denmark, the Elector of Saxony, counts, dukes, city councils, and cantonal governments severed "the Church" within that temporal sword's domain – kingdoms, principalities, duchies, cities, cantons – from papal authority. They declared all Christians, clerical and lay, under their exclusive jurisdiction. They claimed full authority over the lands and property that formerly had been "the Church's." The King of England did not simply dissolve monasteries; he laid claim to the lands, gold and silver chalices, patens, flabella, pixes, crucifixes, crosses, and the books of all the monasteries in the Kingdom of England. Henceforth, within evangelical domains, no lands were to be held apart, reserved to another authority – though bishops, archbishops, and the pope disputed these claims, in some places, successfully. In those particular places, the landscape would no longer be divided between two jurisdictions, but unified under a single authority.

Following the arguments of evangelicals, that Scripture provided no justification for a separate caste of clergy, temporal authorities brought clergy fully under their jurisdiction. No longer would ordination create a group of specific privileges and freedoms. Clergy and laity alike were under the same jurisdiction within the geographic boundaries of temporal authority. Freedoms and privileges still differentiated – between noble and common, between slave and free, between men and women, and between Jew and Christian – but the boundaries of temporal jurisdiction formed the territory within which all privileges and freedoms were defined. All were under the jurisdiction of a single authority and that authority was geographically specific.

"Reformation"

"Reformation" was a legal act. "Reform" was not new to the sixteenth century: The desire to return to an earlier, purer form is at the very center of Christianity, from Jesus's relation to Judaism through Francis of Assisi's mimesis of Christ to fifteenth-century efforts to reform the conduct of the clergy. In the sixteenth century, temporal rulers legislated "Reformation," the term they used to name the legal act. They were not disputing the spiritual sword's jurisdiction in this or that area. Through the enactment of laws they were claiming jurisdiction over Christianity in its entirety – doctrine and practice, persons and land, time and space. City councils, princes, parliaments, and kings enacted laws setting worship, establishing the means to determine true Christian doctrine, defining morality – all of which had been under the jurisdiction of the Church. Laws were the formal means through which they brought the clergy and their property under the jurisdiction of the temporal sword. If, in hindsight, we accept the power of law to establish universal authority and jurisdiction, that move was startling and new in the sixteenth century: The lives of Barton, More, and hundreds of others who were executed for refusing to acknowledge the legitimacy of the government's claim of jurisdiction testify to its novelty and its uncertainty.

Evangelicals had laid much of the groundwork. They accorded a written text, Scripture, singular authority, superior to any form of human authority – superior, therefore, to any authority the ecclesiastical hierarchy might claim. They rejected the division of humankind into two, clergy and laity, and with it, the claim that ordination made a person better able to discern God's will. If all human authority derived its very authority from the Word of God, then the test of the legitimacy of any claims to authority was Scripture. Human authority, evangelicals preached, was binding insofar as it accorded with the Word of God. Those rulers who moved to bring their regimes into accord with the Word of God, following evangelical preaching, were legitimating and solidifying their authority over the lives of their subjects.

Evangelicals were also preaching "God's Law," even as they rejected the medieval classification of sins. Luther opened his catechism with the Ten Commandments, those commands God had put into words that any person could hear and all who could, could read. God's law was accessible to all, written, and applied to all humankind equally. Luther, in particular, underlined the interdependence of what he called Law and Gospel: Law, the stipulations, written in the Old Testament, God had given to Moses that every human being ought to observe in conduct and thought; and Gospel, the New Testament, where Jesus's teachings offered hope of God's mercy and promise of God's love. For all evangelicals, God's law held force over all human institutions and human authority: All things human – offices and laws, institutions and practices – were to be judged against it. Insofar as any human office accorded with God's law, it partook of the authority of God's law.

Europeans divided on this too. Evangelicals accorded authority to the laws that individual kings, parliaments, princes, and magistrates passed, insofar as those laws invoked God's Word and God's Law. Those, such as Barton, More, the Holy Roman Emperor and King of Spain, the Kings of France and Bohemia, who rejected the premise of the absolute and supreme authority of Scripture also rejected the claim to authority over the Church. "Reformation" created a new patchwork of jurisdictions in Europe. It splintered the universal Church, which remained in some places – where it then continued to have authority over doctrine and worship – but not others, where local governments decided questions of true doctrine and worship.

"Reformation" engendered a landscape of mutually exclusive conceptualizations of authority itself. While Henry VIII prosecuted aggressively those who did not accept his claim to authority over the Church within England, he could not, in the end, force acquiescence on the part of all, any more than Henry II in France or Charles V within the Empire could force evangelicals to accept the authority of the pope. All rulers, whether they acknowledged the authority of the pope or not, faced subjects who did not share their understanding of authority: its source, its jurisdiction, its force.

Violence

The division over authority engendered unprecedented violence in sixteenth-century Europe. Thomas More and Elizabeth Barton were but two of the best known of hundreds who were decapitated, hanged, drawn and quartered, burned at the stake. The earliest may have been two

FIGURE 6.1. Jan Luyken, The Burning of Dutch Heretics by the Spanish Inquisition, Etching, ca. 1700. Photo credit: Bildarchiv Preussischer Kulturbesitz / Art Resource, New York.

members of Luther's order, the Augustinian friars Hendrik Voet and Jan van Etten, whom the Inquisition had burned at the stake in Brussels in 1523. Throughout the century, those who accorded the pope authority were executed in evangelical lands; evangelicals were executed in Catholic lands; Anabaptists were executed in both. There were waves of executions. In England, Henry VIII's Act of Supremacy in 1534, the ascension of his Protestant son, Edward VI in 1547, the ascension of his Catholic daughter, Mary, in 1553 unleashed convulsions of violence, as Catholics and then Protestants were condemned for treason. In France, Kings Francis I and Henry II both executed Protestants, though the Wars of Religion in that land killed far more, and far more violently.

The executions engendered martyrologies: narratives of the lives that ended in legal executions. Over the course of the century, the men, women, and even children who were led to the gallows, to the stake, to the block invoked the names of others who had preceded them in a death the government held legal and they did not.

FIGURE 6.2. Torture and Execution of Catholics in the Netherlands. Engraving, ca. 1586. 10 × 14 cm. Bayerische Staatsbibliothek, Munich, Germany. Photo credit: Bildarchiv Preussischer Kulturbesitz / Art Resource, New York.

Very much like the Revolutionaries of 1525, with whom they shared leadership at times, Anabaptists called for a world ordered root and branch according to the Word of God. They sang as they burned, welcoming the coming of the Kingdom of God. In 1534–35, a small group sought to realize "the New Jerusalem" in the episcopal town of Münster. It began with a choice that echoed 1492 in Castile: between expulsion and (re)baptism into the community of the faithful. It was a bloody regime, executing members of its own leadership before it fell to the combined forces of bishop and princes. The leaders' bodies were hung in cages from the spires of the cathedral, remaining long after the birds had picked clean their bones, to serve as a reminder: The effort to realize the Anabaptist New Jerusalem ended in pain and killing hunger. In 1535, some 300 armed Anabaptists seized an abbey in the northern Netherlands, where, again, they sought to institute a New Jerusalem. Again, the regime fell, the members either killed in battle or executed afterwards. Many, many Anabaptists repudiated the violence of these groups; many, such as Menno Simons, preached pacifism. All Anabaptists, however, became suspect. They were executed in numbers proportionately greater than any other religious group.

Anabaptists may well have been the single largest group of those who were executed, but they were not alone. Catholics – priests, foremost, but also monks and nuns, nobles and commons, lay men and women – were executed in the hundreds, as they continued to accord the pope authority over matters spiritual. Reformed evangelicals were seized and executed at first in France; between 1553 and 1558, under Queen Mary I in England; and with the Peace of Augsburg in 1555, which declared them illegal throughout the Empire, also in those lands that adhered to the Augsburg Confession. No one in these years was exempt: The Chancellor of England, French nobles, and urban patricians were executed at the command of their sovereigns.

Executions in significant numbers occurred in Scotland, England, France, and the Empire. In all these places, religious identity and state violence were dialectically defined. "Martyrs" did not simply reject their sovereigns' claim to the authority to adjudicate orthodoxy. They affirmed a sense of themselves in the face of that sovereign's express violence, a sense of *being* a "true Christian" – not simply doing or practicing Christianity, but being as an orientation to the world and to others "true Christian." Being a Christian could not be denied because it was not a thing apart from being alive. Again and again, martyrs chose the death of the body, the body serving as a dramatic site for the affirmation of one's essential Christianity. Persecution allowed a person, as evangelicals and Catholics alike preached, the opportunity to "witness," to "demonstrate" one's "faith," that inward conviction that martyrdom proved. It was the dramatic materialization of inner conversion and "faith." In that same moment of execution, their sovereigns demonstrated the existence of a new political entity that claimed jurisdiction over the lives of all of those who lived within its territorial boundaries, the authority to determine "true Christianity" as doctrine and as practice, and the ability to deploy sovereign violence not simply to silence or to ban, but to immolate dissent and extirpate non-conformity. Henry VIII as well as the sovereigns of Münster left the bodies as a display of their ability to extirpate; for the communities of whom the martyrs were members, those bodies were a testimonial to their faith.

Although Charles never claimed the same jurisdiction over persons as evangelical regimes did, the Inquisition shied from violence no less than did the Tudors or the magistrates of Geneva or Zurich in the effort to ensure religious conformity within the jurisdiction of the temporal lord. No longer were Jews the only "religion" whose members were, by that very fact, at risk. The selfsame violence – seizure of goods, expulsion, and execution – was turned against those whose Church was not the Church of the state, even as those Christians were likened to Jews, Muslims, and other "non-believers."

Rebellion and "Religion"

The Empire

The division over authority fostered what were, in the eyes of some, rebellions, and in the eyes of their opponents, legitimate efforts to redraw the boundaries of jurisdiction. While "rebellions" occurred in England and France as well, the Empire was singularly vulnerable to them: Its crown was elective, and it comprised dozens of dialects, hundreds of legal traditions, and innumerable local customs. If Henry VIII executed his subjects to enforce a new definition of the jurisdiction of the Crown of England, Charles, elected Holy Roman Emperor in 1519, ruled over lands, in the plural, united by neither language nor custom nor legal traditions. Before being elected Emperor, Charles had inherited some fifteen medieval titles of his paternal grandmother, most importantly Duke of Burgundy, Count of Artois, Count of Holland, and Duke of Brabant, each of which had its own legally defined authority and jurisdiction. In 1516, he inherited the Crowns of his maternal grandparents, Isabel of Castile and Ferdinand of Aragon, which had their own legally defined jurisdictions, such that the Cortes of Castile could require of him that he learn Castilian before it agreed to his succession to the Crown. As he traveled, Charles changed crowns and languages in order to speak to his subjects in each place – no figure better captured the fragmented quality of temporal jurisdiction, its deeply local character, and the heterogeneity of customs, laws, and ancient privileges.

The division over authority within the Empire first manifested itself in the Revolution of 1525 and its aftermath, in which first peasants and artisans killed monks and priests, then the mercenary armies of princes and Emperor slaughtered the Revolutionaries, and at the end, tens of thousands were dead. In 1529, at the imperial diet, or court, convened in the episcopal city of Speyer, the division over authority became clear at the highest levels of imperial governance. One of the Electors of the imperial crown, five other princes of the Empire, and representatives of fourteen free imperial cities filed a formal protest against the imperial decrees to ban Luther and his teachings and to restore traditional worship until such time as a Church council might be called. The protest was a legal act. The name, *Protestants*, which labeled the group who filed that protest, is an artifact both of the contest over jurisdiction at the heart of Reformation and of the centrality of law in the pursuit of Reformation.

From 1525 until the Peace of Westphalia in 1648, the Empire was volatile, no single claim to authority uncontested, no uniform conception of authority binding all subjects to a lord. The Habsburgs in these years achieved de facto, if not de jure, hereditary claim to the imperial crown: At Charles' abdication in 1556, he was succeeded by his brother, Ferdinand, who had been raised in the Spain of Ferdinand, his namesake, and Isabel. In these same years, the two brothers became ever more deeply committed to Catholicism. They saw themselves as protectors of the ancient Church, a position that put them in direct conflict with their most powerful subjects.

In 1531, the Elector of Saxony and the Landgrave of Hesse signed a defensive alliance against the Emperor at the Hessian town of Schmalkalden, which would give its name to the League and to the wars the League fought. To join the League, princes and free imperial cities were required to recognize and endorse the Augsburg Confession. Between 1531 and 1545, it grew in membership, as cities and princes legislated "Reformation" and, with that act, seized ecclesiastical property and consolidated their authority within the boundaries of their jurisdiction. During these same years, the formal "lord" of princes and cities, the Holy Roman Emperor, was caught up in wars with France and the Ottoman Empire. In 1545, however, Charles brought to bear the full force of his resources – mercenaries financed through his singular wealth – upon them. In 1547, he defeated them and sought, in 1548, to "restore religion" as he understood it – that which had pertained in his childhood – to his domains. Military defeat may have forced his subjects to kneel, the formal act of obedience, but when Charles's resources were once again redirected elsewhere, they waged war once again and forced a peace in 1555.

The Peace of Augsburg marks a watershed. It formally acknowledged two legal religions within the boundaries of the Emperor's jurisdiction – the Augsburg Confession and the Catholic – which was not itself new: Many places had legally recognized "the Jewish religion" and "the Christian religion." It recognized two religions that 1) could be the religion of the sovereign; and 2) would have, in each place where it was the religion of the sovereign, the same authority as the other in the places where it was sovereign. For the first time in Europe since the end of the Roman Empire, two "religions" were accorded equal legal stature in the same place, and "Christianity" was legally not one, but two discrete "religions."

Immediately after the Peace of Augsburg, Charles abdicated, dismantling the lands with which he had hoped to build a universal empire along the lines of the universal Church, reaching from the Ottoman Empire in the east into the western hemisphere. His domains divided between his brother, Ferdinand, and his son, Philip. His brother had already effectively become sovereign of the Habsburg lands in central Europe; in 1558, he was elected Holy Roman Emperor Ferdinand I. Though Ferdinand had helped negotiate the Peace of Augsburg in 1555, he pursued a policy of "recatholicization": providing political and financial support to priests and the new missionizing orders in their efforts to convert evangelicals back to Catholicism; providing financial support for the publication of Catholic catechisms and other devotional texts; as well as the founding of new colleges and new seminaries. Legally, the Peace of Augsburg required him to respect the jurisdictions of princes and free imperial cities with regard to religion, but he sought to reach subjects throughout the Empire, to foster in this way the rebellion of Catholic subjects against evangelical sovereigns.

The Netherlands

Charles's son, Philip, inherited, as Philip II, the crowns of Castile, Aragon, Catalonia, Naples and Sicily. Philip also inherited his father's very first titles, the duchies and counties in the Burgundian Netherlands, as well as provinces Charles had acquired during his reign. During his rule, Charles had introduced the Spanish Inquisition into the Netherlands, pursued an aggressive policy of suppression of evangelical preaching and printing, banned and ordered the burning of Luther's works, and fully supported the executions the Inquisition ordered.

Under Philip, the provinces rebelled. Many causes contributed to the Revolt, but among them were diverging understandings of Christianity. Beginning under Isabel and Ferdinand, the Spanish crowns had pursued a policy of religious uniformity, uniting the different kingdoms first in religion, then, much later, in law. In 1492, Isabel and Ferdinand had expelled all their Jewish subjects – those subjects, in the thousands, who subsequently found haven as "New Christians" in Antwerp and Amsterdam. Isabel and Ferdinand instituted the Inquisition in Spain, Charles, in the Netherlands, scrutinizing first "New Christians," then evangelicals. Spain, even more than Rome, had pursued *Counter-Reformation*: the active opposition of evangelical preaching and printing, banning all evangelical texts within its borders, burning those who preached "God's Word," as well as all bibles in vernacular languages. The Christianity pursued in Spain was imperial – with a capital in Rome and an administrative apparatus that radiated outwards from that center to the farthest corners – clerical, defined by those who had been ordained, and hostile to an industry deeply rooted in Netherlandish soil, printing. Spanish Christianity immolated books and persons it found "heretical."

The provinces of the Burgundian Netherlands had never been uniform in their Christianity. Cathedral spires did not dominate the landscape of the provinces as they did in other parts of Europe, where commerce and episcopal administration normally coincided. Dutch Bibles had been printed in the fifteenth century. Two of the most influential late medieval movements of lay piety – the Devotio Moderna, which so influenced Erasmus's own understanding of piety, and the Beguines – had their roots in the particularist soil of the provinces.

In 1559, Calvin published the final edition of the *Institutes of the Christian Religion* in Latin. By then, editions of the *Institutes* were circulating among Reformed communities in France, its first intended readership, as well as London, Scotland, and the Netherlands. Calvin had been informally training pastors in Geneva, who were spreading into France and the Netherlands. In 1559, the Geneva Academy, the formal institution for the training of pastors, was founded. The *Institutes*, with its vision of Pauline Christianity – isolated communities of the faithful in a hostile and persecuting empire – resonated powerfully in the Netherlands. In 1566, Calvinist preachers began preaching in fields throughout the Netherlands. In August of the same year, thousands broke into some 400 churches and smashed "the idols," claiming what had been Catholic churches for evangelical use. This year, known as "The Wonderyear," was followed by brutal suppression. Philip sent the Duke of Alba and troops to restore obedience. In 1572, the Duke laid siege to Leiden.

All Philip's efforts failed. Merchants and magistrates found in Calvin's writings not simply the terms for resistance. They found not simply a vision of "the Church" that contrasted starkly in its localism with the imperial claims of Rome and its protector, Spain. They found a way of conceptualizing the human community – as at once scattered over the

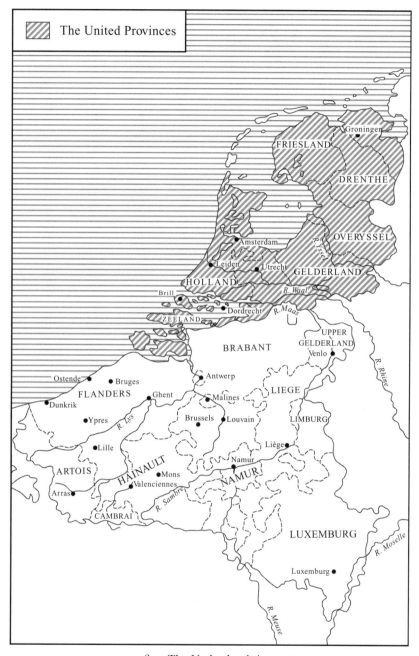

MAP 6.1. The Netherlands in 1559.

globe and bound to each other in their understanding of what it meant to be a Christian. They found in Calvin's writings a sense that the most mundane activities, when done in a consciousness of God, themselves became religious. They found in Calvin's vision of Christianity a way of being in the world that they could carry with them to the farthest corners of the earth, where the Dutch East India Company set up offices – Java, Indonesia – even as they could live that selfsame Christianity in the great metropole of Amsterdam, or in Delft, where Calvinist artisans reproduced the particular blue that merchants had brought back from China.

The Dutch Revolt lasted formally until the Peace of Westphalia in 1648, when a new political entity, the United Provinces, was formally and legally recognized. By then, the Spanish crown had abandoned the effort to bring the northern provinces to kneel. By then, a line had been drawn, in a treaty in 1609, which would, as it turned out, permanently sever the provinces to the north of that line, which became the United Provinces, from those to the south. By 1648, Reformed Christians from the Netherlands were carrying to New Amsterdam, on the coast of the North American continent, the blues of China and the particular understanding of being a Christian in the world that they had found in the writings of the Calvinist tradition.

France

Calvin also provided French nobles and merchants with a way of conceiving of community under a monarch who had been pursuing the unification of his domains through law and language. Calvin had dedicated the first edition of the *Institutes* in 1536 to Francis I, King of France. In his dedication, he had asked Francis to protect those Christians, who came to be called *Huguenots*, who looked to Geneva for leadership and who embraced the Reformed understanding of true Christianity.

Francis was a most unlikely patron. His family, the Valois dynasty, had successfully established its claim to the crown of France on the basis of blood lineage. For centuries, the Valois had sought to blur the line dividing temporal and spiritual rule, to expand royal prerogative and circumscribe papal authority. For centuries, the French monarchs had been distinguished by "the royal touch," the ability to heal scrofula through the touch of the king's hand. They had pursued far more successfully than other temporal lords control of the Church within their kingdom: the right to appoint bishops, and, during the period of the Avignon Papacy throughout the fourteenth century, the ability to shape who was elected pope. In France, "the Church" was not seen as Italian, but far more deeply

"Gallican," French. In response to evangelical placards calling the Mass an idolatry in 1534, Francis had participated in a procession of the holy sacrament. In keeping with Valois long-standing pursuit of autonomy from papal intervention, Francis and his son, Henry II, neither invited the Inquisition into France to determine orthodoxy nor sought to prosecute evangelicals through diocesan courts. In keeping with their sense of the French crown's particular configuration of "power," evangelicals were tried and executed by Parlement.

> It shall be pronounced that the court, on account of the scandalous, heretical, and sacramentarian blasphemies uttered by the prisoner against the honor of God, the Blessed Sacrament of the altar, and other sacraments of our Holy Mother Church, and its constitutions and commandments fully described in the proceedings, has condemned and condemns the prisoner, Marguerite Le Riche, to be taken in a cart from the prisons of the Conciergerie to the place Maubert and to be suspended from a gallows erected there, around which shall be built a fire in which her body shall be set aflame, burned, consumed, and reduced to ashes. And [the court] has declared and declares all her belongings forfeited to the king to be employed in alms and other charitable works, following the king's edict. The court nevertheless orders that before the execution of Marguerite Le Riche she shall be tortured and stretched on the rack to make her declare and name those who were her accomplices and supporters in the aforesaid crimes and also the location of the house in the faubourg of Saint-Victor where she went [for services] last Easter.
>
> Parlement of Paris, Conviction of Marguerite Le Riche for Heresy, August 19, 1559[2]

In 1559, Henry was killed in a jousting accident. His death left France, a country governed by Salic law and its insistence on the masculinity of sovereignty, with no adult male to rule: his sons were all children. For thirty years following that death, France was consumed by violence. The violence took all forms possible in early modern Europe: executions of "heretics" by the Parlement; military battles between "the Catholic League" and the Huguenots, who were led by princes of royal blood; street battles; and the random murders of individuals. Among the most famous incidents of violence was the Massacre of Saint Bartholomew's Day, 1572. Its violence began with an inept, albeit ultimately successful, attempt to assassinate the leader of the Huguenots. That in turn sparked violence first in the streets of Paris, as Catholics dragged their Huguenot neighbors from their homes and hacked them into pieces, then, as word

---

[2] Barbara B. Diefendorf, *The Saint Bartholomew's Day Massacre: A Brief History with Documents* (Boston: Bedford/St. Martin, 2009), p. 58.

Le Maſsacre fait a Vaſsy le premier iour de Mars. 1562.

A. La grange ou l'on preſchoit ou eſtoyent enuiron 1200 perſonnes.
B. Monſieur de Guiſe qui commandoit.
C. Le Miniſtre dedans la Chaire prinſt Dieu.
D. Le Miniſtre ſe cuydant ſauuer eſt bleſſé en pluſieurs lieux

& euſt eſté tué ſi l'eſpee ne fuſt rompue en deux.
E. Le Cardinal de Guyſe appuyé ſur la cimentiere de la paroiſſe.
F. Le voicy que les gens du preſche rompent pour eux ſauuer.
G. Pluſieurs qui ſe iettans ſur la muraille de la ville ſe ſauuent

aux champs.
H. Pluſieurs qui ſe cuydans ſauuer ſur le toict ſont harquebouſés.
I. Le tronc des pouures attaché.
K. Les trompetes qui ſonnerent qu deux diuerſes fois.

FIGURE 6.3. Jacques Tortorel, Massacre at Vassy, 1 March 1562. 1570. Ann Ronan Picture Library, London. Photo credit: HIP / Art Resource, New York.

spread, southwards to Lyon and Provence and westwards to the Loire valley. At the end of three days, thousands were dead, killed by their neighbors.

It was not so much the numbers – Europeans had died from disease or famine in comparable numbers – as it was the familiarity of the people doing the killing. The Wars of Religion in France were the collective extension of the shift in identity from kinship and blood to shared "belief" and religious practice. France, more than any other country, witnessed the deployment of polemics, the verbal and then physical severing of ancient ties to forge new communities "of faith" that identified with neither kingdom nor region nor town nor neighborhood nor kinship – solely with those "brothers and sisters" who shared their understanding of true Christianity.

Between 1530 and 1648, few places in Europe were free from religious violence. Every temporal ruler faced subjects who did not share the sovereign's understanding of "true Christianity" and who, therefore, questioned that sovereign's authority. The overlapping and contested jurisdictions of temporal swords proved to be faultlines, as subjects embraced conceptions of authority grounded in God's Word and God's law. More than any other domain, France made visible the specter of the body politic torn asunder. When the Bourbon Henry IV ascended the throne in 1589 with the promise, formally realized in the Edict of Nantes in 1598, of toleration of a formal religious minority (the Huguenots), and forgetting the transgressions of the majority (the Catholics), the mobs in Paris, Catholic and Huguenot alike, wept.

Religious Minorities and Nicodemites

If the Peace of Augsburg in 1555 recognized two Christianities, the Edict of Nantes formally acknowledged a Christian minority and defined its legal situation within a kingdom. While most sovereigns sought to impose at least the public conformity to a single religion within the boundaries of their jurisdiction, political realities made such enforced conformity impossible in many, many places. Before 1500, Jews had constituted a legal minority in those places they had been permitted to remain: legally distinguished from their Christian neighbors in the privileges and freedoms accorded them. With the Edict of Nantes, the French crown at once recognized a second Christianity, designated those places where, like Jews, they could live and practice their religion, and again, like Jews, restricted to specific places their rights to practice their religion and gather to worship.

In 1555, few places in Europe were religiously homogenous. Arguably the Iberian Peninsula was the only place, having expelled Jews and Muslims and suppressed evangelicals. There were pockets of evangelicals in the Italian peninsula, and Venice and Rome had instituted ghettos, legally defined spaces to which Jews were restricted at night and solely within which could Jews practice their religion. That said, European Christians did not abandon until 1648 their severally held dreams of religious uniformity. In Madrid and Nuremberg, Geneva and London, European Christians pursued religious conformity within the boundaries of their jurisdiction.

By mid-century, evangelical leaders across Europe faced fully that God's Word would not effect a revolution simply through preaching. In the same years, culminating at mid-century, in Valladolid and Rome, Catholics debated, often vehemently, both the efficacy of forced conversion in the western hemisphere and what methods might best result in durable conversion. In this as in so much else, European Christians divided. Some, such as the leaders of the Anabaptist Kingdom in Münster,

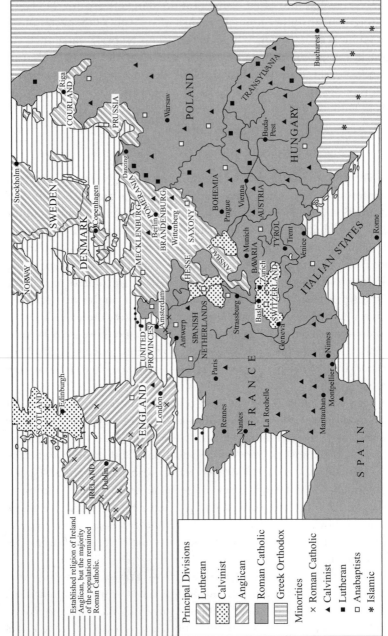

MAP 6.2. Religious minorities.

Established religion of Ireland was Anglican, but the majority of the population remained Roman Catholic.

Principal Divisions
- Lutheran
- Calvinist
- Anglican
- Roman Catholic
- Greek Orthodox

Minorities
- × Roman Catholic
- ▲ Calvinist
- ■ Lutheran
- □ Anabaptists
- ✳ Islamic

the Cardinal of Lorraine and the Catholic League in France, Philip II in the Iberian Peninsula and the Netherlands, brought force to bear – the sword, the gallows, the pyre – in pursuit of religious uniformity.

In their domains, some of their subjects practiced "true Christianity" as they understood it – and faced persecution, the loss of property, and perhaps their lives. Some, whose numbers we cannot discern, chose to live a divided life. Calvin named this phenomenon "Nicodemites": those who lived divided between public conformity and the private practice of a forbidden religion. It was by no means restricted to Reformed Christians. Every state was haunted by the fear of clandestine religious lives: at first, New Christians who lived privately as Jews in Granada, then evangelicals who attended Mass in Antwerp or Catholics who attended Lutheran services in Saxony. In London and Amsterdam, Catholics celebrated Mass in their homes. In Hesse, Reformed Christians sang Psalms in homes. Thousands of European Christians divided their lives, between the "religion" of their sovereign – legally recognized, defined in its doctrine and practice, which all could practice in every space within that sovereign's jurisdiction – and what they might hold to be "true," but which was, within the land in which they were subjects, illegal, forbidden any enactment in any space where others could see and report.

The fear of clandestine practices led sovereigns to institute mechanisms for peering into the lives of their subjects: the Inquisition in Spain and the Netherlands, the Consistory in Geneva. They sought through these institutions not simply to discover heterodox practices and beliefs, but to coerce conformity, to convey that no life lay beyond the jurisdiction of the sovereign, no activity was outside of the sovereign's sight. Praying the rosary within one's home was cause to appear before the Consistory in Geneva. Eating meat on Friday was cause to appear before the Inquisition in Spain or the Netherlands. They were the visible markers of "belief." Sovereigns might not be able to reach belief, but they could extirpate practices and destroy the persons who did them.

Confessions

Concerning public order and secular government it is taught that all political authority, orderly government, laws, and good order in the world are created and instituted by God and that Christians may without sin exercise political authority; be princes and judges; pass sentences and administer justice according to imperial and other existing laws; punish evildoers with the sword; wage just wars; serve as soldiers; buy and sell; take required oaths; possess property; be married; etc.

Condemned here are the Anabaptists who teach that none of the things indicated above is Christian.

Also condemned are those who teach that Christian perfection means physically leaving house and home, spouse and child, and refraining from the above-mentioned activities. In fact, the only true perfection is true fear of God and true faith in God. For the gospel teaches an internal, eternal reality and righteousness of the heart, not an external, temporal one.

> Article XVI: Concerning Public Order and Secular Government,
> *The Augsburg Confession*, 1531[3]

At the imperial diet in Augsburg in 1530, Philip Melanchthon, one of Luther's trusted inner circle, presented a statement of belief, a "Confession," to Charles V. The Augsburg Confession was not intended to be exhaustive, though it comprised twenty-one "Articles of Faith and Doctrine," including the nature of God, original sin, the nature of Christ and of "the Church," the function of the sacraments, and the bondage of the will, as well as seven articles on disputed topics, such as the Mass and monastic vows. It was intended to bring together Christians who disagreed – to find the precise formulation that allowed different understandings of "true Christianity" to find common ground. It failed in its initial purpose: to build a bridge between Luther and his allies on the one side and Charles V on the other.

It was not the first confession. The Anabaptist Michael Sattler had drafted a confession at Schleitheim in Switzerland in 1527, also intended to unite divergent Christians, to provide them with, in this case, seven points of doctrine to which they all could agree: adult baptism, the bann, "breaking bread" or their understanding of the eucharist, the role of pastors, separation from the world, and their refusal to take up the sword or take oaths. Sattler, like others who drafted confessions, learned that they could also serve as points for difference. Nor was the Augsburg Confession the only one offered at the diet in 1530. The cities of Strasbourg, Memmingen, Lindau, and Constance also submitted a confession, called The Tetrapolitan Confession. It offered a different vision of the Christian community, in which good works "proceed out of faith through love," and the chants of monks, the prayers of priests, and images were forbidden. The Tetrapolitan Confession, like the Schleitheim, did not succeed

---

[3] Article XVI: Concerning Public Order and Secular Government, "The Augsburg Confession – German Text," *The Book of Concord: The Confessions of the Evangelical Lutheran Church*, edited by Robert Kolb and Timothy J. Wengert (Minneapolis: Fortress Press, 2000), p. 48.

in unifying splintering evangelicals, though it did serve to unite, in a brief and important time, four separate cities that had legislated Reformation, and to provide each with a translocal core document.

The Augsburg Confession was quickly polished and printed as a pamphlet. If it failed to build a bridge between Luther and Charles, it succeeded in unifying those who came to be known as "Lutherans," who, between 1530 and 1540, came to oppose openly the emperor as well as the pope. It served as the core document of the League of Schmalkalden. It provided city councils and princes with a statement, approved by Luther, that they could then legislate as "true doctrine" and demand their subjects affirm.

Anabaptists, Martin Bucer, Heinrich Bullinger in Zurich, and other evangelicals in the south of the Empire drafted other confessions, such as The First Helvetic Confession of 1536 and the Second, of 1566, each of which sought to unify Christians across regions. None of these matched the Augsburg Confession in its durability: The Augsburg Confession was revised until 1580, when Lutherans, in the Council of Concord, restored the original Confession and declared it a core document of their Church. None received the same political support: The Anabaptist Kingdom of Münster lasted some sixteen months; most of the cities of the Tetrapolitan, First, and Second Helvetic Confessions would not be free of the threat of imperial suppression until the Peace of Westphalia in 1648. The Augsburg Confession had the initial support of the Elector of Saxony, the Margrave of Brandenburg, the Landgrave of Hesse – powerful princes – and the free imperial cities, Nuremberg and Reutlingen; it quickly gained the support of other cities, princes, and the King of Denmark. In each of these places, the Augsburg Confession became the foundation for determining questions of doctrine and practice. Following the Peace of Augsburg in 1555, each ruler who had adopted the Augsburg Confession had, de jure if not de facto, the authority to prosecute or expel those who were not willing to affirm it as a statement of true Christianity.

Most confessions did not receive the political support that princes and free imperial cities gave the Augsburg Confession. A small handful, however, served to unite dispersed and persecuted Christians, and, not unlike the Augsburg Confession and the League of Schmalkalden, to unite Christians in opposition to their sovereign. In France, the French Confession, drafted in 1559–60, and in the Burgundian Netherlands, the Belgic Confession, which appeared in 1561, provided dispersed communities of Reformed Christians with statements that served to unify them over distance and dispersion – something stable, translocal, and held to be "true" over distance as well as time.

> Whatever problems confronted the poor believers on every side, they were far from being daunted. On the contrary, it was at this time that God, through his special grace, inspired all the Christian churches set up in France to meet together to agree on a common doctrine and discipline in conformity with the word of God. Thus, on 26 May 1559, deputies from all the churches established by then in France met at Paris and there, by general agreement, the 'Confession of Faith' and 'Church discipline' were written down, as near as possible to those of the Apostles, in so far as the circumstances of the age allowed. This was truly done through the intervention of God's spirit to preserve unity, which has lasted since.
>
> Theodore Beza, *Ecclesiastical History of the Reformed Church in the Kingdom of France*[4]

In France, the French Confession gave Huguenots a core document, providing the small and scattered communities of Reformed Christians with a series of statements that, they knew, other Reformed Christians, equally isolated in expanses of hostile Catholicism, were also reciting. All those who affirmed the French Confession belonged to the same "Church" – though few could gather in any structure at all. All those who affirmed the French Confession constituted a single "body of believers," who, in their aggregate, as well as in the certainty of their faith, could live "under the cross," could form active, militarized opposition to "the Catholics," provide one another aid both military and financial, offer haven to those driven out, form a translocal, transregional, and ultimately, suprakingdom community of resistance.

> ... The true church can be recognized if it has the following marks: The church engages in the pure preaching of the gospel; it makes use of the pure administration of the sacraments as Christ instituted them; it practices church discipline for correcting faults. In short, it governs itself according to the pure word of God, rejecting all things contrary to it and holding Jesus Christ as the only head.
>
> Article 29: The Marks of the True Church, *The Belgic Confession*, 1561[5]

In the Burgundian Netherlands, the Belgic Confession provided Reformed Christians with one way to bridge the ancient provincial political

---

[4] *The French Wars of Religion: Selected Documents*, edited and translated by David Potter (New York: St. Martin's Press, 1997), p. 39.

[5] *Creeds and Confessions of Faith in the Christian Tradition*, edited by Jaroslav Pelikan and Valerie Hotchkiss, Vol. II: *Reformation Era* (New Haven and London: Yale University Press, 2003), p. 420.

divisions, to conceptualize a "Church" that was universal in its truth but regional in its practices and local in its organization. It began as a manuscript, soon printed, distributed clandestinely to communities of Reformed Christians who were living under the increasing suppression of Philip II. The text served to link Reformed Christians in Amsterdam, Delft, Antwerp, Groningen, discrete places in the sixteenth-century political landscape.

> The visible church of Christ is a congregation of faithful men, in the which the pure word of God is preached and the sacraments be duly ministered according to Christ's ordinance in all those things that of necessity are requisite to the same. As the Church of Jerusalem, Alexandria, and Antioch have erred, so also the Church of Rome hath erred, not only in their living and manner of ceremonies, but also in matter of faith.
>
> Article 19: Of the Church, *Thirty-Nine Articles*, 1571[6]

Promulgated by Queen Elizabeth's authority, drafted by the Archbishop of Canterbury, Matthew Parker, the *Thirty-Nine Articles* defined the Church of England. The Queen enforced each of the articles, which together defined orthodoxy within her domain. In the Book of Common Prayer, the book of liturgy for the Church of England, published that same year, she also commanded, "no man hereafter shall either print or preach, to draw the Article aside any way, but shall submit to it in the plain and Full meaning thereof: and shall not put his own sense or comment to be the meaning of the Article, but shall take it in the literal and grammatical sense." These articles were not to be allowed to provoke controversy. They were to establish, to define, to set doctrine within the boundaries of a realm that had seen the violent swings from Catholic to royal church to evangelical and Reformed, back to Catholic and now, to England's own distinctive Church. They outlined a Church that rejected the authority of Rome but preserved the hierarchy of archbishop, bishops, and priests; that rejected clerical celibacy but preserved the ancient form of preaching, the homily; and that forbade the calling of councils without the sovereign's authority. The Church of England shared with all evangelical Churches the authority it accorded God's Word, but the *Thirty-Nine Articles* defined an utterly distinctive Church, to which all English subjects were required to agree.

> The Estates of Scotland, with the inhabitants of Scotland who profess the holy evangel of Jesus Christ, to their fellow countrymen and to all other nations who confess the Lord Jesus with them, wish grace, mercy, and peace

---

[6] *Creeds and Confessions*, II, p. 533.

from God the Father of our Lord Jesus Christ, with the Spirit of righteous judgment, for salvation.

Long have we thirsted, dear brethren, to have made known to the world the doctrine which we profess and for which we have suffered abuse and danger; but such has been the rage of Satan against us, and against the eternal truth of Christ now newly reborn among us, that until this day we have had neither time nor opportunity to set forth our faith, as gladly as we would have done. For how we have been afflicted until now the greater part of Europe, we suppose, knows well.

Article 16: The Kirk

As we believe in one God, Father, Son, and Holy Ghost, so we firmly believe that from the beginning there has been, now is, and to the end of the world shall be, one kirk, that is to say, one company and multitude of men chosen by God, who rightly worship and embrace him by true faith in Christ Jesus, who is the only Head of the kirk, even as it is the body and spouse of Christ Jesus.

The Scots Confession, 1560[7]

When Mary of England died, John Knox was able to return to Scotland from Geneva, where he had lived as a refugee. In 1560, the Scottish Parliament commissioned Knox and five others to write a confession for the Kingdom of Scotland. Though it could not be ratified until after the Queen Mary Stuart abdicated in 1567, it, too, was the statement of faith for the entire kingdom. The French, Belgic, and Scots Confessions shared many core points of doctrine. They differed in their relationship to the temporal sword. In Scotland, Parliament ratified the Confession, made it a legal document governing the lives of all Scottish subjects. Unlike the French Reformed Church, which would ultimately be driven out of France with the Revocation of the Edict of Nantes in 1685, or the Dutch Reformed Church, which only received formal legal recognition with the Peace of Westphalia in 1648, from 1567, the Scots Reformed Church was not simply the majority Church, but the Church of government in the kingdom.

Confession, a statement of belief, became the public document of either political jurisdictions – under the Peace of Augsburg and then the Peace of Westphalia – or of those "Churches," the French and Belgic, that were "under the cross," facing the persecution of temporal sovereign and those sovereigns' effort to suppress. In both cases, confessions served to define precise boundaries. Each gathered in a single document statements on the nature of God, of Christ, of humankind, of sin; definitions

---

[7] *Creeds and Confessions*, II, pp. 389, 397.

of "sacrament" and its function within the community of the faithful; stipulations on the conduct of members both in their daily lives and in relationship to temporal authority – in so doing, they brought together dozens of points of dispute, precise points on which individual Christians could and did dissent. Those who affirmed the confessions were united in many ways: On each of these topics, they had declared their agreement, that these statements were "true." Those who disagreed, therefore, no longer simply disagreed on a point of doctrine, but on a point on a circle defining a Church – they were outside.

Each of these confessions served to delineate the boundaries of membership and thereby to define "non-members": "heretics" – those who rejected the orthodoxy, the correct teaching each confession professed – or "non-believers," persons polemically linked with Jews and Muslims. Each confession was reinforced through catechisms, taught to children and adults, replicating the precise formulations that the confessions had achieved. Even as the French and Belgic Confessions provided Christians living "under the cross" with a means to think of themselves as belonging to a transregional Church, they also articulated boundaries of membership for that Church – membership within, "non-believers" without. The consequences of dissent differed in some ways: Sovereigns could seize property and execute, whereas Churches could only expel. But in both cases, Christians took to the roads and the seas to find communities to which they could belong.

Exile

In 1500, Christians traveled throughout Europe with greater freedom than either Jews or Muslims. By 1555, every Christian Church was illegal in some parts of Europe, each life at risk in some places and not in others. This world set Christians in motion as never before. Catholics fled England under Edward VI; Protestants, England under Mary I. Protestants fled Philip II's troops in the Netherlands and Catholic mobs in France. Catholics fled Geneva, Basel, Zurich, Strasbourg. In the Empire, Lutherans fled Catholic princes and magistrates, Catholics fled Lutheran princes and magistrates, Reformed Christians fled both, finding, over the course of the century, islands of welcome under the protection of a handful of princes. They fled the places of their birth – whether Deventer or Strasbourg, London or Paris, Groningen or Granada – to find communities of those who shared their definition of true worship and true doctrine. They fled the ancient ties of loyalty, citizenship, patronage. They fled the complex and delicate webs of knowledge and human relations of that place: its laws, customs, familiar faces.

In the sixteenth century, "home" was no longer where a person had been born or married or had children. Home became Saint Peter's church in Geneva, where Calvin preached to swelling numbers of refugees. "Home" became Amsterdam, where small hidden communities of Anabaptists, Reformed Christians, Mennonites, Lutherans each welcomed "their own" into their houses. "Home" might be the coast of new continents, among plants and peoples their parents had never imagined. It was a century of "pilgrims." Some sought to build the New Jerusalem where "true Christianity" as they understood it was sovereign. Some understood themselves adrift on a path only God could see. For each, the world was a mix of brothers and sisters in Christ and treacherous lands.

PART III

RELIGION RECONCEIVED

7

Christians

Towards evening on the first Sunday in Lent, 1524, in the choir of the Strasbourg cathedral, the monks were singing Compline [the liturgy of the night].
Earlier that day, Martin Bucer had preached there. From the nave, where he had
remained since the sermon, a carpenter, Strübel Hans, began squawking like a
quail. He asked the monks, "what are you mumbling? Do you think it pleases
God? It is appropriate to God?" Some of the monks approached him, asking,
"dear friend, what concern is it of yours, what we sing or read in our church? If
you do not wish to hear it, then go outside and leave us be." More words were
exchanged. Then Strübel Hans took a one of the stools the laity brought with
them for sitting during sermons, and hit a monk on the head with it, putting
his hand to his sword as he did. All the monks left the choir and surrounded
him, seizing his sword from him and striking him with it, wounding him twice
in the head. They threw him out of the choir. Strübel Hans went home, on the
way telling first other carpenters, and then, anyone who would listen, what had
happened. Some 300 men gathered with him. They returned to the cathedral,
where they cried out, should a city allow a citizen to be struck thus?

The Imlin Family Chronicle[1]

In the 1520s, in words and acts, Europeans from Erasmus to Strübel Hans
called attention to the paradox of late medieval Christianity. Christianity
was everywhere to be seen and heard. It had blanketed the landscape
of Europe with steeples; marked townscapes with cathedrals, monasteries, and parish churches; placed crosses on roads in every land; and
divided time through processions and performances into the liturgical
year, through bells into monastic hours. Christianity was inescapable
physically and temporally, and yet, thousands of Europeans, like Strübel
Hans, found themselves at once surrounded and outside – they were
"Christians," but that landscape, those spaces, that time were not "theirs."

---

[1] "XXVI. Strassburg im sechzehnten Jahrhunder (1500–1594): Auszug aus der Imlin-
'schen Familienchronik," edited by Rudolf Reuss, *Alsatia* 10 (1873–74): 395, my translation.

In 1500, as the Strasbourg monks said to Strübel Hans, Christian time
and Christian spaces belonged to "the religious." The term was reserved
for a minority of European Christians: those who had taken vows, bound
themselves, following the ancient Latin meaning of "religio," to lives of
celibacy, poverty, and obedience. That minority both claimed and had
been accorded the authority to set the "hours" of each day, to designate
certain places as sacred and not others, to define and instantiate "Christianity" spatially, temporally, and personally. They defined what a Christian was: a person who had been baptized. They distinguished among
humankind different kinds of Christians: laity and clergy; tertiaries and
nuns; cloistered and uncloistered. They differentiated qualitatively ways
of being Christian, from the lowest – laity who work with their hands – to
the highest, the pope. They kept, in 1500, the majority of Christians in
the nave of the Church, observers of worship, not participants; witnesses,
not agents. Most European Christians, even kings, to Henry VIII's great
frustration, depended on that minority to do the most sacred acts, to
bring their children into Christianity, and to bless their marriages. In
1500, one could legally be a Christian, be "pious" – seek to live a life in
accord with what Christ and the Church taught – and yet, as a carpenter
or a mother, not be "religious," and therefore, be less "Christian" than
priests, monks, or nuns.

Following their readings of Scripture, evangelicals rejected the
medieval definition of "religious." The same principles that led them
to reject ordination and with it, a separate caste of priests, led them to
reject the vows that made a person "religious": There was no foundation
in Scripture; vows, like good works, rested upon the false premise of
human free will and a human capacity to change human nature. Evangelicals rejected the medieval configuration of two worlds and the value
it placed on a life enclosed behind walls. They rejected all the medieval
marks of an "otherworldly" life: celibacy, enclosure, poverty. For them,
the world divided not between laity and "religious," but between true
Christians and false, the saved and the damned.

Being a Christian

Question. Of which religion are you? Answer. I am of the Christian religion.

Question. From what cause? Answer. Because I believe in Jesus Christ, and
I am baptized in the name of Jesus Christ.

Johannes Brenz, Catechism[2]

[2] Johannes Brenz, *Catechismus pro Iuventuti hallensi* (Nuremberg: Johann Petri, 1541),
p. A3v, my translation.

The war for souls forged a different understanding of what it meant to *be* a Christian. European Christians agreed that baptism was one part of it. They differed on the relationship between baptism and the Christian life. Anabaptists held baptism as the sacrament marking the adult's voluntary entrance into the community of the faithful. Other evangelicals and Catholics held it to mark an infant's initiation into the community of Christians. Catholics in Europe baptized infants in the expectation that they would grow up "within" the Church. Catholics in the western hemisphere struggled with the relationship between baptism and being a Christian.

As baptized Christian accused baptized Christian of false worship and false doctrine, evangelicals and Catholics alike – some implicitly, some explicitly – rejected the notion that baptism alone made one a Christian. In the polemics of the 1520s and 1530s, evangelicals and Catholics came to define "Christian" as one holding certain beliefs about the nature of God, of Christ, and of humankind. In the polemics, baptism no longer separated Christian and "non-Christian": If one did not hold certain beliefs, did not define worship in certain terms, then one was not "Christian" – one was, in some polemics, not even human. In that battle, what one said, what one held to be true – what one "believed" – defined one as a "Christian." Being a Christian meant certain words and not others, certain kinds of behavior and not others, certain practices and not others, certain ways of dressing and not others.

The problem that confronted all European Christians in the 1520s was how to teach "belief." Evangelicals sought to teach belief through preaching, Bible study, and catechisms. In the early years of Reformation, evangelicals held that the study of Scripture could effect change in belief. They founded schools for the study of the biblical languages – Hebrew, Greek, and Latin. In the Great Minster in Zurich, Huldrych Zwingli began a school for boys in which they first learned ancient languages, then turned that knowledge to the close study, over years, of the texts of the Old and New Testaments. Luther's trusted friend, Philip Melanchthon, was a school teacher, as was Johannes Brenz; by 1521, both were seeking to teach boys to read the text of Scripture, as those boys were learning Latin. Luther himself called for fathers to instruct their families through reading Scripture aloud.

As it became clear that there could be as many readings of Scripture as there were readers, evangelicals sought to teach the hermeneutic that their particular Church held to be true.

Concerning the second order, which we have called Doctors

The office proper to doctors is the instruction of the faithful in true doctrine, in order that the purity of the Gospel be not corrupted either by ignorance or by evil opinions. As things are disposed today, we always include under this title aids and instructions for maintaining the doctrine of God and defending the Church from injury by the fault of pastors and ministers. So to use a more intelligible word, we will call this the order of the schools.

Draft Ecclesiastical Ordinances, 1541[3]

When he returned to Geneva in 1541, John Calvin insisted on a fourfold organization of the Church in Geneva: In addition to pastors, deacons, and elders – who preached the Word, cared for the poor, and disciplined members, respectively – there were to be teachers, who were to train the congregation in the proper understanding of the Word of God. In 1556, Geneva instituted the first evangelical Academy, divided into two schools, one for boys, the other for ministers. The school for boys was divided into seven grades; in them, boys studied Latin, Greek, and later, Hebrew. It required all boys to attend public worship, to learn Calvin's catechism, and to sing Psalms. All students began their day with a prayer at dawn and ended each day by reciting aloud the Lord's Prayer, the Genevan Confession of Faith, and the Ten Commandments. By the end of their education, each boy was deeply conversant with the tenets of Reformed Christianity: its reading of Scripture, its core statements of faith, its understanding of the Ten Commandments.

At the same time that Melanchthon and Brenz were teaching boys to read Scripture correctly, they were writing catechisms – handbooks of instruction in Christian doctrine and ethics. Catholics and evangelicals alike wrote catechisms: for boys, for families, for adults. Catholics called for catechisms to be used within the context of formal instruction, in the presence of a teacher or parish priest. Luther published two catechisms in 1529: *The Small Catechism*, for pastors to use with their congregations; and *The German Catechism*, for

every head of the household at least once a week to examine the children and servants one after the other and ascertain what they know or have learned of it, and if they do not know it, to keep them faithfully at it.[4]

---

[3] "Draft Ecclesiastical Ordinances (1541)," *Calvin: Theological Treatises*, translated by J.K.S. Reid (Philadelphia: The Westminster Press, 1954), p. 62.

[4] Martin Luther, Preface, "The Large [German] Catechism," *The Book of Concord: The Confessions of the Evangelical Lutheran Church*, edited by Robert Kolb and Timothy J. Wengert (Minneapolis: Fortress Press, 2000), p. 383.

He was the first to send catechisms into the home. John Calvin called for his catechism to be taught on Sundays, preferably within churches, if a community had such a building. Many, many catechisms were small enough to travel in a pocket or a hand – to carry into the home the lessons learned in church and school, to carry onto the road "true Christianity." Catholics and evangelicals alike sought to reach children, to have those children carry home their lessons, and, in bringing Christianity into each home, to form "Christians" who moved from place to place, able to recite aloud, as Luther had it, "what every Christian should know."[5]

Through the medium of print, Catholics and evangelicals sought not simply to teach correct doctrine – the correct understanding of God's nature, Christ's nature, human nature, and the relationships among them – but to inculcate "belief." "Belief" was not new to the sixteenth century: The Latin word, "credo," was to be found at the very center of the medieval Mass. But that formal statement had become, as evangelicals and Catholics alike recognized in the sixteenth century, at once familiar, rote, and at the same time remote – that which too often the priest alone recited.

Equally important, the credo did not encompass all the points of doctrine and practice that were disputed in the sixteenth century. Even if all Christians agreed on the Apostles' Creed, they disagreed on its meaning. Most catechisms written in the sixteenth century sought to teach Christians what each sentence in the Apostles' Creed meant – what one was actually saying, as one recited the familiar words of the Creed. Most also sought to teach the Lord's Prayer, both the text itself and the precise meaning of each of the sentences. Many sought to teach the definition of a sacrament according to its tradition; the correct number of sacraments (two or seven); and what those sacraments did, effected, in the life of each Christian. Most sought to teach the Ten Commandments, but they numbered the commandments differently – the Catholic Church, Luther, and Calvin broke apart the text of Exodus at different points – and, with their different numbering, emphasized different commandments.

As Christians in the eastern and western hemispheres learned their catechisms, they became able to state, with predictable regularity, across geographic and linguistic distances, precisely the same answers to dozens of questions. What is a Christian? What is the purpose of each human life? What is a sacrament? Over distance, individuals spoke the very same

5 Martin Luther, Preface, "The Large [German] Catechism," p. 383.

sentences, depending on the catechism they had learned. Lutherans answered these questions differently than did Reformed Christians or Catholics, but over time, all Lutherans drew on the same words, no matter if they were speaking in Danish, German, or Swedish. Reformed Christians numbered the Ten Commandments differently than either Lutherans or Catholics, no matter if they were in Leiden, Plymouth, or London. Catholics grounded their definition of "Christian" in baptism in Lima and Munich as well as Rome. By the end of the sixteenth century, "being" a Christian depended on what "I," first person singular, or "we," first person plural, "believe," a sequence of sentences, formulated by pastors and priests, that each Christian was required to be able to repeat at will. Over time, the sentences became more uniform, consistent, and were spoken on both sides of the Atlantic, deepening each community's sense of itself as physically anywhere on the globe, united in that subjective I or we.

1. Whoever wishes to be a soldier of God under the standard of the cross and serve the Lord alone and His vicar on earth in our Society, which we desire to be designated by the name of Jesus, should, after a solemn vow of perpetual chastity, bear in mind that he is part of a community founded principally for the advancement of souls in Christian life and doctrine and for the propagation of the faith by the ministry of the word, by spiritual exercises, by works of charity, and expressly by the instruction in Christianity of children and the uneducated.
First Sketch of the Institute of the Society of Jesus (1539)[6]

If the correct reading of Scripture drove evangelical schools, the Society of Jesus, whom Pope Paul III formally instituted in 1540, took as the first step of their missionizing the education of children. In so doing, they posited a complex process by which belief was not simply taught through words, but was the ground and the frame for all knowledge.

In this city of Goa, God our Lord moved certain individuals to serve him by founding a college, which is more needed in these regions than anything else. Work on it is progressing day by day. There is reason for giving many thanks to the Lord that he bids his servants erect such material edifices for the edification of numerous spiritual temples, that is, he orders his servants to teach and convert many infidels.
Letter of Francis Xavier to Ignatius of Loyola, September 20, 1542[7]

---

6 "The First Sketch of the Institute of the Society of Jesus (1539)," *The Autobiography of St. Ignatius Loyola, with Related Documents*, edited by John C. Olin (New York: Harper Torchbook, 1974), pp. 106–7.
7 *The Letters and Instructions of Francis Xavier*, translated by M. Joseph Costelloe, S.J. (St. Louis: The Institute of Jesuit Sources, 1992), document 16, p. 52.

The Society of Jesus, the Jesuits, worked along two deeply interconnected lines: missionizing around the globe – by mid-century, they were in south Asia, south America, as well as the Empire – and educating children, the next generation of Christians. They founded schools and colleges in Italy, France, the Empire, Central and South America, South and East Asia. In those schools, Jesuits, in those habits that signaled the lives they had chosen, taught boys Latin through the performance of plays, such that those boys spoke Latin as a living language – as Erasmus had hoped. They taught older boys Greek, as well as ever more sophisticated Latin grammar and style. They taught mathematics – Galileo may have first encountered mathematics as a Jesuit novice. They taught physics and metaphysics. They taught music: instrumental and polyphonic. Around the globe, the first Jesuit act of conversion was often teaching people to sing. In their colleges, they taught theology to young men they had, ideally, formed since childhood, that theology not a discrete study so much as the extension of what those students had learned as boys. A Jesuit education did not parse "knowledge," but consciously and over years sought to bring bodies, as well as minds and souls, into the Church, to teach "faith" as "a way of proceeding."

Living as a Christian

While all Churches sought to inculcate specific definitions of what a Christian believed, evangelicals and Catholics divided on the question: What is the Christian life? All Churches taught the Ten Commandments. All condemned murder, theft, and slander. All punished blasphemy and adultery. All taught children to honor and obey their parents, especially their fathers – so long as their parents and fathers adhered to that Church's particular understanding of Christianity. Consistories attended to and sought to enforce, but could not command, weekly attendance at Sunday services. In no place in Christian Europe were shops or workshops open on Sundays. And yet, adherence to the Ten Commandments did not make a life Christian. They were fundamental to, but did not constitute, a Christian life. As Churches fragmented from one another, they divided on what made a life Christian – what were the outward marks, the signs of a Christian life – and on the relationship of those signs to faith.

The Council of Trent affirmed and strengthened the medieval differentiation of two kinds of Christian: the "laity" and those who take vows. There would continue to be two kinds of Christian life, one "of this world," that of the laity, and one sanctified, that of the clergy. For

FIGURE 7.1. Rembrandt Harmensz van Rijn, The Syndics of the Amsterdam
Drapers' Guild. 1662. Oil on canvas, 185 × 274 cm. Photo by Hermann Buresch.
Rijksmuseum, Amsterdam, The Netherlands. Photo credit: Bildarchiv Preussis-
cher Kulturbesitz / Art Resource, New York.

Catholics, the cloistered life remained an ideal (even as Jesuits were
instantiating a new model, of global mobility and martyrdom). Teresa
of Ávila would be canonized – formally recognized as a holy person –
in the next century for her efforts to reform her order, the Discalced
Carmelites, women who lived enclosed behind walls. For Catholics, vows
would continue to mark a "religious life," a life more perfectly Christian –
vows freely chosen, freely taken, in the conscious pursuit of an ever intensifying faith.

Evangelicals rejected the premise of vows – human free will – and
reversed the sequence: One did not take vows or enter a cloister to
become a person of faith; one received faith from God, a gift of God's
mercy, and in humble gratitude, one sought to live a life that pleased God.
There were not two kinds of Christian lives. All Christians lived, more
or less, in accord with God's will. The "reprobate," or damned, whom
Calvin and Luther held to be known only to God, did not place their
lives under God's will. God's Word stipulated the specifics of a Christian
life. For evangelicals, "Christians" lived in the world God had made, a
world that embraced the field, the workshop, labor, and commerce. For

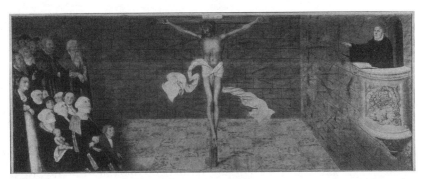

FIGURE 7.2. Lucas Cranach the Elder, Martin Luther preaches before the Crucifix. On the left is the family, 1540. Stadtkirche, Wittenberg, Germany. Photo credit: Bildarchiv Preussischer Kulturbesitz / Art Resource, New York.

evangelicals, living as a Christian was an orientation in the world, to see oneself under God's eyes, God's law, and God's will.

European Christians differed on exactly what God's will encompassed – the precise details – but they agreed that the Christian life was marked, in evangelicals' word, by outward action and spoken words. True Christians did (evangelicals) or did not (Catholics) eat meat on Fridays. In the Iberian and Italian peninsulas, what foods one ate and when marked one as a Christian, a heretic, a Jew, or a Muslim. True Christians did (Catholics) or did not (evangelicals) pray the rosary. All Christians were, increasingly, required to be able to recite at command the words of the Lord's Prayer. Living as a Christian became, in the sixteenth century, increasingly detailed and demanding. The records of the Consistory in Geneva are filled with accounts of confused men and women who thought themselves living as Christians, but found, before the Consistory, that they were in error: an old woman who prayed the rosary, a mother who swore at her sons when they behaved wickedly, a man who struck his wife for swearing.

European Christians divided on the parameters of a Christian life. In places that legislated Reformation according to Reformed Christian criteria, residents of those places were normally forbidden to gamble, to play cards, to procure or visit prostitutes. Governments guided by Reformed Christian ethics restricted clothing as well as conduct: Pearls, especially the exceptionally large and lustrous ones from the east, were forbidden; lace, the product of intensive and intricate, highly skilled manual labor, was forbidden; as were all colors but black and white. Sobriety was to be visible in the black dresses, cloaks, leggings, vests, and sleeves of the upright, as well as in their conduct. If habits and cassocks had marked "the religious" in medieval Europe, dress was the visible sign of all true Christians in Reformed communities.

Lutherans and Catholics did not seek to regulate dress to the same degree, but both Churches promulgated "modesty," which was to have its expression in dress. Reformed Christians appeared more austere, but austerity was a spectrum in the sixteenth century, and all Churches endorsed it. Black predominates in portraits of Lutheran ministers and their families, signaling sobriety and austerity.

But black was also the color the most bellicose Catholic monarch, Philip II of Spain, chose for his portraits, when not wearing armor for his battle against Protestants, and he pursued austerity in habits of dress, eating, and conduct. Black became the color of lay men and women in the sixteenth and seventeenth centuries, as merchants and monarchs signaled their piety in the color of their clothing.

Exile

> He so conducted himself as to be beloved among the men of our profession, if any one was. Esteemed as such among men who were endowed with some degree of authority, and so as to be neither a shame nor a disgrace to them. At length, when he could no longer bow the neck to that voluntary bondage which even yet we bear, he departed to take up his residence with you, having no prospect of return. But, as the matter stands, it fell out, contrary to his expectation, like the shifting scene of a play, and he could find no settled abode, whither he might betake himself.
>
> John Calvin, letter to Martin Bucer, September 4, 1532[8]

Many things forced Europeans onto the roads and seas in the sixteenth century: expulsions of Jews, Muslims, and Christians of illegal Churches; persecutions. At the heart of exile was that one could no longer live in the place of one's birth, childhood, marriage, and work. For some, such as Calvin's colleague, the departure was technically voluntary: He could no longer bear the "bondage." For others, departure was mandated, forced. But for all, such questions as the food they ate, the clothes they wore, as well as the beliefs to which they gave expression had made hostile what had been home.

For thousands of Europeans, exile forged their sense of themselves as Christians. Martin Luther, John Calvin, evangelicals who spoke to

[8] Calvin to Martin Bucer, 4 September 1532, in *Letters of John Calvin. . . .*, edited by Jules Bonnet, translated by David Constable, 2 vols. (Edinburgh, 1855), 1: 9–10.

transregional communities, preached and wrote a complex message. They urged Christians to be obedient to their sovereigns, insofar as they could. But if those sovereigns sought to force belief, then they had become like Pharaoh, a ruler seeking the enslavement of God's people:

> However, your departure must be like that out of Egypt, bringing all of your effects along with you. For all this, I believe you will need stedfast and very determined courage. But you are able to do all in Him who strengthens you. When He has brought you hither, you shall see how He will guide you farther. For my part, I would gladly help thereunto cheerfully and steadily, as bound as I am to do. I am confident, that after leading you by the hand in greater things, He will not fail you on this occasion. But he is sometimes pleased to exercise and try our faith, so that while quitting hold of that which is within our grasp, we know not what we shall receive in place of it. We have an example of this in our father Abraham. After having commanded him to forsake his country, his kindred, and everything else, He shewed him no present reward, but put that off to another time. "Get thee out," said He, "into the land which I shall shew thee." Should it please Him at this time to do the like with us, that we must quit the land of our birth, and betake ourselves into an unknown country, without knowing how it may fare with us there, let us surrender ourselves to Him, that He may direct our way, and let us honour Him, by trusting that He will steer us to a safe harbour.
>
> John Calvin, letter to a French noble, October 18, 1548[9]

In the sixteenth century, the landscape of Europe became treacherous for all Europeans. It had been treacherous for Jews for centuries. But in the sixteenth century, the "Christianity" of one place was different from that of another, and the same legal acts of expulsion and analogous acts of violence made each place hostile to some Christians: Catholics in England and Lutheran states; Reformed Christians in the Empire; evangelicals in the Habsburg Netherlands and Spain; Anabaptists almost everywhere.

For thousands of Europeans in the sixteenth century, being a Christian came to mean being placeless – not only driven from one's home but detached from any one place. Thousands left the parish churches where their families had been baptized for generations. Thousands no longer had a parish church at all: They gathered in the houses of members of their Church in the places where they had found refuge. Thousands landed in places surrounded by people who spoke a language they could not understand. And that landscape was not stable. Shifting jurisdictions could transform a place from familiar to hostile in a matter of months.

---

[9] Calvin, *Letters*, 2:167.

The death of Edward VI put English evangelicals at risk; the death of Mary put English Catholics at risk; the conversion of princes and the shifting balance of power in town councils moved territories from one Church to another. One government might tolerate Anabaptists; the next might seek to exterminate them. Betrayals severed human connections in a place. One place might become dangerous, another prove fatal.

For so many, being a Christian meant being in movement, as Calvin wrote, on a path only God could see. In the sixteenth century, it meant being prepared to leave the familiar for unknown destinations – unknown both in the sense of never before seen and in the sense that one did not yet know, where one would find safe haven, where one would land. Calvin invoked exodus: enslavement to an oppressive tyrant, flight into a desert, the promised land not yet seen. These images permeated sermons, as Christians scattered in search of a place where they might be Christian as they understood it, worship God as they held God should be worshiped. The promised land was unseen, its precise location unknown, but thousands put themselves in movement, over years, even decades, to find that place where they could be "Christian."

For no one was Europe uniformly "Christian" in that sense that Isabel and Ferdinand had pursued. It was not only that their sense of "Christian" had become more complex, involving for each person certain words and certain behaviors. But the landscape itself had changed and with it, how each Christian experienced that landscape. For each Christian, as for each Church, the landscape of Europe divided between hostile and Christian places. Neither of those labels were fixed, as governments shifted from one Church to another, and Christians of one kind became illegal as Christians of another became, once again, legal. So, too, the Christianity of any place could be precisely or loosely defined, depending on the government. Nor was the map of hostile and friendly places the same for each Christian: Places hostile to Anabaptists might permit Catholics to exist, so long as they were peaceful; places hostile to Reformed Christians might permit Lutherans to live there. The map of Europe was both splintered and constantly shifting.

For all European Christians, being a Christian no longer meant that one lived in a parish, that one took communion once a year. Being a Christian could not depend on any single place or on any objects that could not be carried. It had to be portable: All Churches faced persecution and exile in one place, if not another. Catholics continued to look to Rome for their leadership and as the capital of all Christendom, though they themselves might be adrift in hostile seas. Evangelicals had no such capital – the Word of God was the site of authority, not Rome. But for all Churches, one carried one's belief across a volatile landscape. One's Christianity inhered in a person.

Nicodemites

Some Christians fled. Others stayed. Some converted to the Christianity in force. Others, as court records attest, divided their lives between a Christianity visible to neighbors and authorities that conformed to the norms those authorities imposed, and a clandestine Christianity, beliefs and practices that had been condemned. Calvin called such persons "Nicodemites." Those who lived two lives – one seen, one hidden – were the fear of evangelicals and Catholics alike.

Over the course of the sixteenth century, so many were forced to "convert": Jews and Muslims to the Christianity of their sovereigns; Catholics to the Lutheran or Reformed Christianity of their sovereigns; Lutherans and Reformed to the Catholic Christianity of their sovereigns; and peoples of the western hemisphere to the Christianity of their conquerors. In each place, court records testify to persons who lived one life visible to authorities, another hidden from the eyes of consistories, inquisition, neighbors, pastors.

The fear of Nicodemites was not new in the sixteenth century. The forced conversions of 1492 and earlier had created "New Christians," men and women whose families had been Jewish, or Muslim, for generations, whom their sovereign required "become Christian," normally through forced baptism. Some seem to have become "genuinely" Christian, that is, they lived entirely as Christians – fasting on Fridays and during Lent and eating pork being two signs of the authenticity of their Christianity. Many, however, preserved such practices of their former life as they could, and like sixteenth-century Christians, lived divided between hidden but authentic practices and speech, and public practices and speech that were designed precisely to cloak what they held to be true.

Nicodemites were the counterpoint to those efforts on the part of both ecclesiastical and civil authorities to inculcate "belief," to bring speech and acts into conformity with norms that priests or ministers were articulating. Not all willingly embraced those norms. Not all were willing to abandon home to be the kind of Christian they held to be true. In order to survive and to remain "Christian" in their understanding, they divided their lives. A handful articulated a sense of a life that carefully severed the practices and beliefs they held to be true from all the spaces where others might hear or see and report – a sense of two worlds, the one hidden and true, the other visible and false.

In the eyes of authorities, they were practicing clandestinely – out of sight of supervision, regulation, admonition. Driven by widening suspicion of Nicodemites – the sense that human beings could act one way and believe another – courts ecclesiastical and civil crossed thresholds into houses. Driven by the sense that one gesture, one thing eaten, one word revealed a person's "true" beliefs, courts examined, scrutinized, gathered information. In Madrid and Geneva, Granada and Edinburgh, "true Christians" behaved in certain ways, ate certain foods, did and said certain things – both inside and outside their households. As Calvin wrote and preached, Nicodemites were not "true Christians," precisely because their lives were divided between hidden authentic faith and visible false practice.

Deception is an age-old problem, but in the sixteenth century, people feared it as never before. People testified before courts that their neighbors, even their spouses were practicing it. Neighbors listened and reported. In Dutch cities, as glass became more available in the sixteenth and seventeen centuries, windows became larger, allowing at once more light and greater visibility of the lives within. "Transparency" became both a personal and an architectural value in the sixteenth and seventeenth centuries. In the seventeenth century, Puritans closed theaters in London, in part because they were sites where deception was regularly practiced. The desire to root out deception shaped conduct, architecture, theater, literature.

Persecution engendered complex understandings of the Christian life among those who sought to survive the persecution. And those who sought to survive, in turn, were the catalyst for the intensification of interrogation, surveillance, and regulation. No government and no Church possessed the means to enforce perfectly or consistently ideals of conduct or speech. In every place, no one could be sure what another believed. In every place, some held true the Christianity the authorities were promulgating – both those who had been born in that place and those who had emigrated there to live the Christianity that place practiced. In every place, some conformed in speech and habit to the practices of the majority – to outward appearance, they were "Christian" in the sense of the place. But among them were those for whom the outward signs were no more than that – outward signs – whether attending Mass or participating in the Supper. What was true for them was hidden: For them, to survive was to hide the truth and to perform a Christianity they held false, but inescapable and lethal.

Poor Christians

Evangelicals rejected the monastic vow of celibacy. They also rejected the monastic vow of poverty. They repudiated what they called voluntary poverty as both a burden on the community of Christians and a kind of arrogance, a willful choice to pursue a life God had not ordered. At the same time, evangelical preachers worked with city councils to formulate new programs of civic care for those Christians who, through no fault of their own, were destitute.

Evangelicals drew on an ancient concept, "the deserving poor," and refined it. Like their medieval predecessors, they held widows and orphans to be "deserving": the death of a spouse or parents was not in the control of any person. The "deserving poor," however, were also to conform generally to evangelical notions of a "true Christian": to be modest in dress and demeanor, not to gamble, play cards, dance, or engage in any "immoral" behaviors or practices, and, increasingly, to attend sermons, to be visibly a member of the community of the faithful. Catholic authorities, both spiritual and temporal, also refined their notions of "deserving poor," in response to the evangelical critique of waste, restricted resources for care, and the growing fear of "false" beggars and Christians. While Catholic poor relief remained more inclusive and expansive, over the course of the sixteenth century, it attended increasingly to the demeanor of its recipients.

Catholic poor relief had one great advantage over evangelical programs. Catholics could call on the doctrine of "good works." Good works were, following medieval doctrine and usage, various acts replicating what Jesus had done – feeding and sheltering the poor, caring for the sick, burying the dead. They were acts of "charity," that is, acts expressive of the Christian virtue of brotherly love, love of one's neighbor. Over time, medieval preachers had firmly connected good works and one's own salvation – one should do them for the sake of one's soul. Medieval images presented European Christians with the consequences of failing to do good works: The miserly were frequently depicted suffering the pains of hell. Catholics gave alms, the particular name for goods and wealth intended for the care of the poor. They gave alms in their churches. They gave alms at the doors of churches and in public spaces. If their programs of relief were, in the eyes of evangelicals, haphazard, random – that gift of alms to a beggar in a street – those programs could also count on consistent support.

Here, too, evangelicals applied the principle that no human action of any kind could affect God's judgment of a human soul, no human action of any kind could place any constraint on God's absolute power. They did not, therefore, repudiate "good works" as much as what they saw as the self-interest of acts of charity as well as monastic vows of poverty. All were done, they argued, not to honor God, but to gain one's own salvation. Thus as evangelicals moved to "reform" the care of the poor, they also reframed "good works": No longer acts meriting salvation, but acts expressive of the grace and faith God had given.

Different evangelicals arrived at different formulations. Zwingli preached that Christian brotherly love was the way that human beings could honor God in day-to-day life. Caring for the poor became in Zurich one piece in a complex of worship performed in everyday life. The poor in Zurich, therefore, were to mirror true Christianity in their demeanor and their conduct: Recipients of Christian brotherly love were to behave like the donors, to differ only in their material circumstances, not the conduct of their lives. In Strasbourg, Martin Bucer preached an analogous understanding of acts of Christian brotherly love as expressive of faith and grace. Luther preached brotherly love as a consequence of faith, as its expression. Caring for the poor in Lutheran communities became one way that the community manifested its faith. Calvin established a specific office, the deacons, whose defining responsibility was the care of the poor. In Reformed communities, the Church as a body was responsible for all its members, and the deacons were responsible for determining both need and worthiness. Well into the seventeenth century, individual Reformed communities struggled to find ways to raise funds to support their poor – they tried lotteries and other fund-raising mechanisms, plays to encourage the daily practice of Christian brotherly love.

Catholics and evangelicals divided on the question, which poor Christians deserved help? Catholics and evangelicals came to share, over the course of the sixteenth century, a hostility to itinerant poor: In Catholic and evangelical towns alike, the poor were increasingly screened for residency. But they divided on what "Christian brotherly love" meant: its scope and implications for its recipients. For the people of Zurich, Christian brotherly love encompassed all those who were like them, "brothers," in their Christianity. Reformed Christians in Scotland and the Netherlands shared something of that sense of the necessary precondition of brotherhood, and accorded their deacons the authority to determine the precise direction of the community's love. Catholics retained a more heterogeneous understanding of Christian brotherly love: For some, such as Las Casas, it was what was to be extended to the peoples of the western hemisphere, to those who were not yet Christian, as well as to one's neighbors in Seville or Macerata.

Holy Lives

I began to deck myself out and to try to attract others by my appearance, taking great trouble with my hands and hair, using perfumes and all the vanities I could get – and there were a good many of them, for I was very fastidious.

...I had a sister much older than myself from whom, though she was very good and chaste, I learned nothing, whereas from a relative whom we often had in the house I learned every kind of evil.... I became very fond of meeting this woman. I talked and gossiped with her frequently; she joined me in all my favorite pastimes and talked to me about all her conversations and vanities.

...So excessive was my father's love for me, and so complete was the deception which I practised on him, that he could never believe all the ill of me that I deserved and thus I never fell into disgrace with him.... I had made the greatest efforts to keep it all secret, and I had not considered that it could not be kept secret from Him Who sees all things.

The Autobiography of Teresa of Ávila[10]

The Council of Trent affirmed the ancient doctrine of human free will and human beings' capacity to choose a life (hence the vows) more perfect. For Catholics of the sixteenth century, "religious" continued to belong to *orders* – to taking vows, entering a group defined by particular dress, its "habit," and living a life regulated by a rule. Some Catholics, such as Teresa, entered medieval orders and worked to reform the lives within them: to restore the stark rhythms of that particular life, its patterns of prayer, fasting, and charity.

Other Catholics founded new orders. One order in particular articulated a way of living as "religious" anywhere on the face of the globe: the Society of Jesus, founded by Ignatius of Loyola.

Up to the age of twenty-six he was a man given to the vanities of the world; and what he enjoyed most was warlike sport, with a great and foolish desire to win fame.

The Autobiography of Ignatius of Loyola[11]

---

[10] *The Life of Teresa of Jesus: The Autobiography of Teresa of Ávila*, edited and translated by E. Allison Peers (New York: Image, 1991), pp. 69–72.

[11] "The Autobiography," *Ignatius of Loyola: The Spiritual Exercises and Selected Works*, edited by George E. Ganss, S.J. (New York: Paulist Press, 1991), pp. 68.

Ignatius's life offered a particularly compelling model for a Catholic "religious" life. That life began, significantly, at the age of thirty – not at birth. Wounded in battle, he read. He was drawn, as he lay, leg shattered, to mendicants – to those who sought to live a mimesis of Christ's peripatetic and preaching life. His life was marked by places – points on an itinerary he did not set, but followed. In Manresa, he set the rhythms of the life he formally instituted some fifteen years later: He prayed, seven times a day, he begged for his own food, he gave alms to the poor in each place. In Manresa, he first had visions:

> Often and for a long time, while at prayer, he saw with interior eyes the humanity of Christ. The form that appeared to him was like a white body, neither very large nor very small, but he did not see any distinction of members. He saw it at Manresa many times. If he should say twenty or forty, he would not dare judge it a lie. He has seen this another time in Jerusalem and yet another while traveling near Padua. He has also seen Our Lady in a similar form, without distinguishing parts. These things he saw strengthened him then and always gave him such strength in his faith that he has often thought to himself: If there were no Scriptures to teach us these matters of faith, he would be resolved to die for them, solely because of what he has seen.
>
> *The Autobiography of Ignatius of Loyola*[12]

These visions – which the Church took to be an essential sign of the holiness of his life – preceded formal training in theology. They came into a life of prayer, begging, charity, placelessness, and an orientation to a God who could be addressed anywhere at any time of the day. When formally instituted, Loyola's order had no house, owned no land, no dwellings, but moved from place to place as they believed God wished.

> Four Weeks are taken for the following Exercises, corresponding to the four parts into which they are divided. That is, the First Week is devoted to the consideration and contemplation of sins; the Second, to the life of Christ our Lord up to and including Palm Sunday; the Third, to the Passion of Christ our Lord; and the Fourth, to the Resurrection and Ascension. To this week are appended the Three Methods of Praying. However, this does not mean that each week must necessarily consist of seven or eight days. For during the First Week some persons happen to be slower in finding what they are seeking, that is, contrition, sorrow, and tears for their sins. Similarly, some persons work more diligently than others, and are more pushed back and forth and probed by different spirits. In some cases, therefore, the week needs to be shortened, and in others lengthened. This holds as well for all

[12] "The Autobiography," p. 80.

the following weeks, while the retreatant is seeking for what corresponds to their subject matter. But the Exercises ought to be completed in thirty days, more or less.

Ignatius of Loyola, *Spiritual Exercises*[13]

Shaped by medieval devotional works, *The Spiritual Exercises* differed from them in two ways. It was written in a world comprising continents medieval Europeans had not even imagined. And it was written in a world in which even the most familiar texts had proven vulnerable to multiple, mutually exclusive readings. *The Spiritual Exercises* instructs its reader both how it is to be read – over weeks, working in each of its sections until that section is internalized – and with whom, a teacher, himself already instructed in the exercises, such that he knows the text without reading. The *Exercises* explicitly formed bonds between men, teacher and exercitant, generation after generation, in an intimate spiritual journey that preceded the physical movement of the member of the order. It founded "the union of hearts and minds," a sense of community far more flexible for a shifting landscape and an expanding Church.

> 1. Whoever wishes to be a soldier of God under the standard of the cross and serve the Lord alone and His vicar on earth in our Society, which we desire to be designated by the name of Jesus, should, after a solemn vow of perpetual chastity, bear in mind that he is part of a community founded principally for the advancement of souls in Christian life and doctrine and for the propagation of the faith by the ministry of the word, by spiritual exercises, by works of charity, and expressly by the instruction in Christianity of children and the uneducated.
>
> First Sketch of the Institute of the Society of Jesus (1539)[14]

The Society of Jesus differed from medieval orders in three ways. Its organization was modeled on the military hierarchy of the Roman Empire: a general, provincials who governed "provinces," and the members of the order, who were to be "soldiers of God." It owed absolute obedience to the pope – to no other person in the hierarchy of the Church, not bishop, not archbishop, not cardinal – its fourth and distinctive vow. And it was founded for the express purpose of spreading Catholicism: both restoring Catholic doctrine and practice in those parts of Europe where

---

[13] "The Spiritual Exercises," *Ignatius of Loyola: The Spiritual Exercises and Selected Works*, p. 122.

[14] "The First Sketch of the Institute of the Society of Jesus (1539)," *The Autobiography of St. Ignatius Loyola, with Related Documents*, edited by John C. Olin (New York: Harper Torchbook, 1974), pp. 106–7.

evangelicals ruled, and carrying that doctrine and practice to the far corners of the earth.

> I am writing to Father Nicolò to take care of the brothers who are in São Thomé and on Cape Comorin or in Quilon; and I am writing to the brothers on Cape Comorin that they should obey Father Nicolò, and that they should write to Father Nicolò in Quilon or Cochin, wherever he may be, about all their needs, both their own and those of the Christians; and I am writing to Father Nicolò that he should write to the College of the Holy Faith in Goa about all their needs, both their own and those of the Christians. And you, Antonio Gomes, take special care to provide for the brothers with great diligence, charity, and love. Father Nicolò will always be under the obedience of Father Micer Paulo, in keeping with the order which I left when I departed from there. Those who are within the house and those who are outside it should thus obey those who were appointed by me when I left there. Both the native and the Portuguese students will obey Antonio Gomes, and Antonio Gomes will be obedient to Micer Paulo, as I have indicated in writing. Those who are in Bassein and Hormuz will be obedient to Micer Paulo, as I have already said; and take care to write to me in great detail about everything.
>
> Letter of Francis Xavier to Fathers Paulo, Antonio Gomes, and Baltasar Gago, from Malacca, Malaysia, June 20–22, 1549[15]

Before Loyola died, Xavier, one of the first companions, had traveled to the South Asian peninsula, Malaysia, Japan, and China, in each place seeking to convert and educate. Jesuits carried with them a sense that "Christians" were bound together not by place, not by buildings – though they built schools and churches around the earth – but by that union of hearts, something at the very center of each person's being, something affirmed and strengthened with each letter that Jesuits circulated and shared. They also carried, as Xavier's letter makes explicit, a hierarchy of authority that organized those dispersed communities and linked them, through a chain of obedience, to the pope in Rome. "Christians" in Bassein, Cochin, Malacca, were physically scattered, but, as persons, bound to one another and situated within a hierarchy of authority that claimed the world as its domain. As Jesuits said, "We are not monks. The world is our home."

> In January of this year, 1549, I wrote to you at great length about the fruit which is being produced in souls in these regions of India, both in the fortresses of the king and in the lands of the infidels, by means of which our most holy faith is increasing; and all the brothers of the Society have also

[15] *The Letters and Instructions of Francis Xavier*, document 84, p. 276

written about the fruit which God our Lord is producing in souls through them.

Letter of Francis Xavier to the Society of Jesus in Europe,
June 22, 1549[16]

Jesuits brought "infidels" and "natives" into "our most holy faith." Evangelicals in England and the Netherlands feared the Jesuits, who were the single most successful order in returning European Christians to the Catholic Church. In the Empire, Peter Canisius was credited with returning hundreds to Catholic practices and belief. The particular Jesuit attention to a process that began with self-examination and contrition and culminated in the contemplation of God's glory proved powerful in Europe, the Americas, and Asia, a way of being a Christian that was independent of place or even immediate society. Jesuits did not distinguish souls: Anyone whom they converted was a Christian; any male could join the Society of Jesus. For the Jesuits, any human being – in Goa, in Malaysia, in Bavaria, in Antwerp – could be brought into "our most holy faith." There was no natural boundary to Christianity, no limits that could not be overcome – not Chinese distance, not cannibalism, not evangelical fervor, not Muslim infidelity – with the help of "God our Lord."

Teresa of Ávila and Ignatius Loyola were the first sixteenth-century Catholics to be canonized – formally recognized as holy persons, saints, in the Catholic Church – in 1622. Although they belonged to different orders, their lives shared attributes the Catholic Church accorded particular meaning in the sixteenth century. Each entered adulthood without a sense of vocation to the life they ultimately lived. Each, as an adolescent, was adrift in a world of possibilities. Each *found* a holy life. Teresa, a woman, remained cloistered – this would be one of the holiest of lives for Catholic women. Ignatius, a man, was itinerant and founded the first order dedicated to converting the world. Traveling the globe, seeking to convert the peoples they found – in Asia, in the Americas, in the Pacific, in the Indian Ocean – would be one of the holiest of lives for Catholic men. Teresa and Ignatius each wrote, with the help of another, a narrative of a life in which a frivolous adolescent came, over years, to be a servant to God. Neither was particularly learned. The life was found – through prayer, introspection, self-examination, and the conscious entrance into the discipline of an ordered life. The life was at once portable – one could pray anywhere at any time – and inseparable from the Catholic Church, which provided the frame and the authorization for

---

[16] *The Letters and Instructions of Francis Xavier*, document 85, p. 277.

that life. Both saints were "religious" in the medieval sense of the word, even as their lives were fully rooted in the deep shifts of the sixteenth century.

The other holy life, for Catholics as well as evangelicals, was one that ended in martyrdom. In a world in which outward acts were construed as signs of faith, both Catholics and evangelicals commemorated martyrs, those who consciously, publicly, expressly were willing to offer their bodies for the sake of their souls. Marble images of them would grace Saint Peter's Basilica, the center of the Catholic world. John Foxe would gather hundreds of individual stories of evangelical martyrdom in a compendium of the surest testimony of true and authentic Christian belief.

Priests and Ministers

> If they are not rightly brought up, those of adolescent years tend to make for the world's pleasures and, unless trained to religious practice from an early age before habits of vice take firm hold on so many, they never keep to an orderly church life in an exemplary way without very great and almost extraordinary help from almighty God. Hence the holy council decrees that every cathedral, metropolitan and greater church is obliged to provide for, to educate in religion and to train in ecclesiastical studies a set number of boys, according to its resources and the size of the diocese: the boys are to be drawn from the city and diocese, or its province if the former do not provide sufficient, and educated in a college chosen for the purpose by the bishop near to these churches or in another convenient place. Those admitted to the college should be at least twelve years old, of legitimate birth, who know how to read and write competently, and whose character and disposition offers hope that they will serve in church ministries throughout life.
>
> Canon 18, Decree on Reform, Session 23, Council of Trent, July 15, 1563[17]

Even as the Council of Trent affirmed the sacrament of ordination and the sanctity of vows, bishops attending it acknowledged that there were priests who fit evangelical complaints: illiterate, indifferent to the forms and texts of worship, some venal. In its call to reform the priesthood, the Council of Trent specified greater care in selecting priests, more consistent and frequent episcopal supervision. The foundation of the reform, however, was to be education. This was new.

---

[17] *Decrees of the Ecumenical Councils*, edited by Norman P. Tanner, S.J., Vol. II (London: Sheed and Ward, 1990), p. 750.

The sixteenth century became a world of texts. Printing put far more texts in circulation. Evangelicals called for specific kinds of literacy that were inseparable from reading and listening to texts. Evangelical preachers called for the faithful to read or, failing that ability, to listen to Scripture read aloud. Evangelical catechisms drew children into reading practices. While literacy remained a facility of a minority, the faithful everywhere were being asked to be familiar with texts: the Lord's Prayer, the Apostles' Creed, the Ten Commandments, and, for evangelicals, the Bible.

Thus, in the sixteenth century, the sense of what qualities Church leaders should possess changed. The decrees of the Council of Trent capture that shift. One calls for priests to model the person of Christ in their conduct, to serve, as they were supposed to have served in the medieval Church, as a visible and audible embodiment of Christian virtues, foremost humility, celibacy, and obedience to the Church. But another calls for priests to be educated, not simply as adults in Christian theology, but beginning as children, to be formed by years of formal study, of languages, and of specified texts. The priesthood was, in part, to draw its authority from formally acquired knowledge.

In the swirl of texts, leaders of the Catholic, Lutheran, and Reformed Churches needed not simply to be able to read – though literacy quickly became an essential attribute of leadership. They needed to be able to judge words: their orthodoxy or heresy, their capacity to clarify or obscure truth. By mid-century, each of the Churches that would be accorded legal status had called for and begun to establish both schools for boys and seminaries or colleges for the training of the pastorate, whether priests or ministers.

Priests and ministers remained divided from one another by the sacrament of ordination. Evangelicals' "ministers" ministered to congregations, but were not different in nature from anyone else in the Church. But ministers and priests were to have in common by the seventeenth century that they acquired their leadership through the channel of education. That education varied from person to person, but each Church set forth an ideal of knowledge that each man who mounted a pulpit, who administered the sacraments, who cared for his flock, was to possess. Even Teresa of Ávila and Ignatius of Loyola, though not learned, were nonetheless both readers and writers. The models of the Christian life that proliferated in the sixteenth century, from those of Catholic saints to Martin Luther's or John Calvin's, were literate. Teresa and Ignatius might read devotional works, while devout evangelicals read the Bible, but they all read, and those texts informed their lives. Their leaders, therefore, were to be conversant with those texts, able to negotiate them and to lead their congregations in the proper reading and understanding of those texts.

Alone among Churches, Anabaptists held that the Holy Spirit could come to anyone and illumine his or her understanding of Scripture. Alone among Churches, Anabaptists remained wary of formal education. They separated "revelation," God's self-disclosure in both nature and Scripture, from university education, and in keeping with their conviction that revelation – insight into God's nature, intent, will – could come to anyone: women as well as men, the illiterate as well as the learned.

The Catholic, Lutheran, and Reformed Churches all called for their leadership to be grounded in formal education. Education became the channel through which a man passed to become priest or minister. Any man might become a minister or priest: All three Churches actively reached out to poor boys, to bring them into that process of formation. Over time, the sons of ministers often themselves became ministers, the particular configuration of humble economic situation and spiritual authority intimately familiar.

The educations that Catholic priests and Lutheran and Reformed ministers received differed in their content and their structure. Catholic priests were required to have a mastery of Latin, which was the language of doctrine, the liturgy, and the sacraments. Their education began with the study of Latin and moved into the catechism, the books of the liturgy, as well as works of doctrine. Evangelicals were particularly concerned that ministers acquire mastery of three biblical languages, Hebrew and Greek for the study of original texts and the Greek Church Fathers, and Latin for the study of the Vulgate and the Latin Church Fathers. Scriptural knowledge was the foundation of ecclesiastical authority in evangelical Churches. Thus, the education of evangelical ministers also began with Latin, the universal language of scholarship, but then moved to the study of Greek, then Hebrew, all three of which were understood as mandatory, not optional. The focus of Catholic study was a language and a body of texts that brought a man more fully into an ancient tradition, complexly understood to encompass a number of voices. The focus of evangelical study was three ancient languages, which were to give the student access to the Word of God, the focus of lifelong study. Other texts were important – Church Fathers, Luther, Calvin – but their purpose, at least in the sixteenth century, was to inform the direct study of Scripture.

So, too, both Luther and Calvin sought to shape reading Scripture in faraway places – through thousands of letters, through treatises, and, for Calvin, through the *Institutes*, a frame through which ministers were to approach God's Word. Education, too, was to serve to shape, to inculcate certain understandings of words as well as explanations why other understandings were wrong; to situate words within certain textual communities and not others. For all three Churches, education was to "form" their leadership – education, in Erasmus's understanding of it, as a process. Priests and ministers did not simply acquire knowledge. They were informed by it. It was to shape how they read, how they read to others, and how they helped others to read.

In emphasizing education, the Catholic, Lutheran, and Reformed Churches transformed the pastorate. With learning, parish priests no longer belonged in the same way to their parishes: Even though they might still be sons of the parish, their education set them apart. They possessed knowledge that belonged to the office of priest: of Latin, of certain texts, optimally, of doctrine and theology. And in bringing poor boys into the ecclesiastical hierarchy of leadership, each Church also began a slow erosion of social status as a foundation for spiritual power. With learning, ministers at once acquired their authority in their congregations and became persons apart. Like priests, they possessed knowledge – of the languages of God's Word, of the text of Scripture – inaccessible to their congregations, a knowledge that evangelicals prized as the most important.

By the end of the century, readers and writers of texts had become Church leaders and models. Not simply literacy, but certain kinds of literacy carried with them spiritual authority. In theory, any man might enter the priesthood or the ministry: That knowledge was not restricted to any particular social stratum. It was restricted to men. Women's spiritual authority, as Teresa of Ávila's life made so clear, might draw on reading and writing, but it was denied access to the institutions that would, for the next four centuries, form the leadership of the Churches of the Reformation. Spiritual authority would increasingly come to be grounded in the mastery of languages and texts.

"The World Is Our Home"

In the sixteenth century, being a Christian was no longer rooted to place. Exile drove some Europeans onto roads, some, across the Atlantic to settle in the western hemisphere. Jesuits – singly, in pairs, and in small communities – traveled to "the corners of the earth," a notion transformed with the changing understanding of that earth's expanse and human settlements. That world had not ever been Christian. The things and buildings that had been inseparable from a medieval Christian life would, over time, be imported in some places, but they were not there. Not in the Americas, not in Asia, not in Africa, on no coast of the Pacific Ocean at all.

Thus when first Catholics, then Reformed Christians traveled to uncharted lands, the Christianity they carried resided not in things – though evangelicals carried bibles, Jesuits carried images; Dominicans, Franciscans, and Jesuits carried missals or breviaries as they could – nor in structures. They built churches, as they could, but none were there before they arrived. The Christianity of Europeans resided in their words, their actions, and their persons. Standing before the Emperor in China, standing in a court of a Japanese warlord, standing alone in the forests of South America, South Asia, North America, Jesuits embodied the Christianity they sought to promulgate. It required no cloister, no consecrated ground. As Jesuits said, "we are not monks. The world is our home."

The world is our home. The simple statement marked a tectonic shift. The world, when that sentence was written, had been revealed to be much larger and largely unknown – a strange place, and all the unknown areas never touched by Christianity. Even the more familiar world of Europe had shattered into places of estrangement and danger on the one hand and, on the other, safe havens, the location of which itself shifted with the currents. One could be at "home" in that world not through things or buildings, but because of what one carried within oneself – for Jesuits, a "union of hearts and minds," for other Christians, that sense of "brothers" and "sisters" that had been forged in the polemics on European soil. Reformed Christians shared a sense that each Christian was visible to God and made visible his or her faith, no matter where on the face of the globe he or she might land, whether the forests of North or South America or the streets of Amsterdam or Lyon. For Jesuits, obedience bound each member to one another and ultimately to Rome. By the end of the century, "Christian" was not geographic, but personal – portable, a way of entering the world, no matter where one found oneself, forests or cities, western or eastern, northern or southern hemispheres.

8

Things and Places

Iconoclasm

The plundering of the Churches... began in West Flanders on the 14th of August, 1566, the day which preceded the great Festival of the Papists, the Ascension of the Virgin Mary.

Some few of the vilest of the Mob, to whom several Thieves and Whores had joined themselves, were those that began the Dance, being hallooed on by nobody knows whom. Their arms were, Staves, Hatchets, Hammers, Ladders, Ropes, and other tools more proper to demolish than to fight with; some few were provided with Guns and Swords. At first... they attacked the Crosses and Images that had been erected in the great Roads in the Country; next, those in Villages, and lastly, those in the Towns and Cities: All the Chapels, Churches, and Convents which they found shut, they forced open, breaking tearing, and destroying all the Images, Pictures, Shrines, and other consecrated things they met with: nay, some did not scruple to lay their hands upon Libraries, Books, Writings, Monuments, and even the dead bodies in Churches and Churchyards. Swift as lightning the evil diffused itself, insomuch that in the space of three days above four hundred Churches were plundered.

Geeraert Brandt, *The History of the Reformation in the Low Countries*[1]

From the earliest years of evangelical printing and preaching, individuals had entered churches and smashed things. In Wittenberg in 1521, Augustinian friars smashed an altarpiece. In Zurich in 1523, the assistant in the Great Minster pulled down an enormous wooden retable – one of the carved and painted images above altars; by 1524, the City Council had moved to complete a process they could not stop, of removing lamps, crucifixes, images, frescoes, sculpted figures. In Basel in 1529,

---

[1] Geeraert Brandt, *The History of the Reformation and Other Ecclesiastical Transactions in and about the Low Countries, From the Beginning of the Eighth Century, Down to the Famous Synod of Dort, inclusive*, vol. I (London: Timothy Childe, 1720), p. 191.

some 200 men broke into the Cathedral and smashed hundreds of things inside its walls. The violence of August 1566 was new in its sheer scale and scope, but the violence itself – the smashing of the things of late medieval Christianity – belonged to "Reformation."

The violence directed collective attention to the many roles things had played in late medieval piety. In Antwerp and Basel, mobs cleared spaces exceptionally dense with exquisite things – golden candelabra, jewel-like paintings, ivory figures, silver and gold crosses, stained-glass windows. Elsewhere, individuals singled out particular kinds of objects. In some places, members of families or corporations smashed or removed objects their ancestors had commissioned, gifts whose skill and value in precious metals and stones was a public testament to the piety of the donors. In Strasbourg, some moved relics – those physical remains – of a beloved saint into a charnel house: These things were, their act said, no more than the bones of a dead person, like all the other bones. Others smashed the altars, the physical site for the Mass. In Zurich, three artisans smashed oil lamps, "eternal lights," that burned incessantly above the pulpit in the Great Minster. Across the countryside, individuals and their friends pulled down wayside shrines and the crucifixes that so frequently marked intersections of roads and trade routes. In Antwerp, the first target was an image of Mary, which the attackers taunted before bringing down.

Those who smashed things did not themselves agree which things, if any, belonged in the places of worship. Martin Luther rejected the violence and preached that each congregation could decide for itself what to keep: Things, for him, were unimportant. Andreas Bodenstein von Karlstadt found throughout the Old Testament prohibitions against idolatry and the making of images of God, and published a widely circulated pamphlet, "On the Removal of the Images." John Calvin renumbered the Ten Commandments: For him, the second was a prohibition against making any images of God, whether God the Father or God the Son. Individual iconoclasts, when they were brought before courts, articulated many different principles they had found in Scripture. In Zurich, iconoclasts invoked Christian brotherly love, which should take the wealth invested in beautiful things and feed the poor. In Strasbourg, Martin Bucer had preached that Christ alone saved, and repudiated the cult of saints and all its material expressions – the preservation of bones, reliquaries, altars dedicated to saints. Others invoked the doctrine of the resurrection of Christ, which, for some, removed him from the physical realm entirely, negating any connection between his person and a thing. Still others testified that all things simply drew the weak away from the one and only true savior.

FIGURE 8.1. The Breaking of Images by Calvinists in the Netherlands, 1566. Engraving. Photo credit: Foto Marburg / Art Resource, New York.

At the heart of the violence was a splintering of Christians' understandings of the relationship between the physical and spiritual worlds. In each place where some smashed, others cried out in anguish at the loss – not of beauty, but of things that had, for them, been inseparable from "honoring God." For them, it was "sacrilege": the transgression of something essential. And if those who held it a sacrilege were in power, then those who had done the smashing faced fines, imprisonment, even execution – "sacrilege" was a transgression of the law of God. And for those who willingly faced death in order to smash the things in churches and on roadsides, the "sacrilege" lay in the presence of those things and the danger they posed to true worship.

Idols

No Christian would endure the aggravating idol in the chapel in the cathedral. It is a grave affront, not only to our community but even more to those in the surrounding lands. Every day, without interruption, people can be seen bowing before it, praying to it. Some obstreperous persons seek particularly while the Word of God is being preached to bring attention to the same [idol] and disrupt those who wish to hear [the Word of God]. So, too, the silver idol behind the altar in the choir in the cathedral and the idol in the entrance to the cathedral, for which a retable was recently made, disturb. Also the idolatrous specter of the Mount of Olives, where more often than not a lamp is lit during the day – such a travesty against God and pious Christians. And also the idols in Saint Anna's [church], more for sport than for honor, which also have no basis in Scripture. In sum, we see and hold that all idols are a disturbance, in all churches, not to righteous Christians, but to the weak and those who have not yet taken on the Word, which is so urgent – for all idols are against the Word of God and therefore arise from the devil and can bring no good fruit.

Complaint of Six Citizens of Strasbourg, March 1525[2]

The word "idol," like the word "barbarian," has an ancient history. As Karlstadt documented, it was to be found in the Old Testament, a word in use from the time of Moses. By the mid-1520s, the label resonated across the Atlantic: As Hernan Cortés wrote in his letters from the Aztec Empire, Cortés himself, his soldiers, and accompanying priests, labeled objects "idols" as they were smashing them. In the western hemisphere as well as the eastern, the name "idol" authorized violence.

Within Europe, the word was used to label objects that some continued to hold central to Christian worship. In another way, then, it marked a chasm between two very different ways of thinking about the relationship among human beings, the objects they create, and God. Medieval Christians had commissioned objects and themselves made objects of as great beauty and worth as they could. They did so to honor God – both the making and the preciousness of the materials demonstrated devotion. Each object in a church was a testimony of piety.

Then God spoke all these words: I am the LORD your God, who brought you out of the land of Egypt, out of the house of slavery; you shall have no other gods before me. You shall not make for yourself an idol, whether in the form of anything that is in heaven above, or that is on the earth beneath, or that is in the water under the earth. You shall not bow down to them or worship them; for I the LORD your God am a jealous God, punishing children for the iniquity of parents, to the third and the fourth generations of those who reject me, but showing steadfast love to the thousandth generation of those who love me and keep my commandments.

Exodus 20: 1–6[3]

[2] Archives du Chapitre de St. Thomas de Strasbourg, 87, no. 29, my translation.
[3] *The New Oxford Annotated Bible*, Third Edition, edited by Michael D. Coogan (Oxford: Oxford University Press, 2001). I have elided paragraph breaks.

Having themselves come of age in churches which were treasure houses of all these acts of piety, evangelicals read Exodus differently. Unlike medieval Christians or contemporary Catholics, evangelicals such as John Calvin found a full stop between "you shall have no other gods before me," and "You shall not make for yourself an idol." For them, these were two discrete commandments, not having and not making. For Luther, who found things indifferent, the stop came after this paragraph, between not having, not making, and not worshiping, on the one hand, and not taking God's name in vain, on the other – things did not command Luther's attention as they did Karlstadt's or John Calvin's.

Calvin was wary of any thing that a human being had made. For him, as well as for those who shared his understanding of human nature, the essential sinfulness of human beings precluded their being able to make any thing that reflected God's power. All things that were human-made were by that fact flawed. They had no place in the honoring of God. Huldrych Zwingli was wary of human-made things because, themselves the product of human imagination, such objects were comfortably familiar – they reflected human understanding, not divine mystery. For both Calvin and Zwingli, "idols" had to do not with the things themselves, but with the fact that human hands had made them, human imagination had formed them, human frailty framed what they could and could not represent.

Evangelicals severed the making of things from piety. Things could, Calvin wrote in the *Institutes*, be beautiful – the ability to make was itself a gift from God – but they could not represent anything of God because of the chasm of sin between humankind and God. Only God, nothing a human being could make or do, could reach across that chasm. That same argument, as we shall see, was extended to human actions, specifically the actions of the priest in the Mass. Not all evangelicals shared that sense of the inseparable connection between human hands and human sinfulness. For Luther, "faith alone" made unimportant everything in the churches. For him, the presence of things did not matter one way or the other, but their commissioning and making could have no effect in the central drama of human salvation and divine love. For all evangelicals, making things played no role in salvation, not craft, not gift.

Images

In 1520, Uly Anders, a peasant from the county of Toggenburg in Switzerland, beat, broke apart, and threw out a window a small carved image of Christ on the cross, with Mary and John on either side. As he threw it out the window, he cried, "the idols bring nothing and they will help nothing."

Anders paid for his act with his life: The Zurich City Council executed him for the crime of blasphemy. For the city councilors, as for authorities across Europe who prosecuted the crime of blasphemy, it was no simple act of vandalism. The things so destroyed were not simply beloved, familiar. They were "images." The word had two fundaments largely lost to modern sensibilities. The first was mechanical: Medieval theories of optics conceptualized the relationship of object and eye in terms that were abandoned in the seventeenth century. Before Johannes Kepler posited light refraction as the mechanism of sight, classical and medieval theorists struggled with the question: How does the eye see? Greek and Arabic theorists of optics posited a range of possible solutions to the question, which might be broadly organized into two kinds: one in which the eye reaches across distance; and the other – which proved more popular – in which the object moves through space, through a series of "species," to reach the eye and enter the mind. "Images," in other words, did not remain on the wall or the altar, but reached out, to enter the eye and mind. Modern thinking about sight, which places light between eye and object, recognizes a distance between thing and mind that medieval theorists did not.

> I worship one God, one Godhead, but I adore three persons: God the Father, God the Son made flesh, and God the Holy Spirit, one God. I do not adore the creation rather than the Creator, but I adore the one who became a creature, who was formed as I was, who clothed Himself in creation without weakening or departing from His divinity, that He might raise our nature in glory and make us partakers of His divine nature. . . . Fleshly nature was not lost when it became part of the Godhead, but just as the Word made flesh remained the Word, so also flesh became the Word, yet remained flesh, being united to the person of the Word. Therefore I boldly draw an image of the invisible God, not as invisible, but as having become visible for our sakes by partaking of flesh and blood. I do not draw an image of the immortal Godhead, but I paint the image of God who became visible in the flesh . . .
>
> John of Damascus (d. 749), *First Apology Against Those Who Attack the Divine Images* [4]

---

[4] John of Damascus, *On the Divine Images: Three Apologies Against Those Who Attack the Divine Images*, translated by David Anderson (Crestwood: St. Vladimir's Seminary Press, 1980), pp. 15–6.

The second fundament for late medieval thinking about "images" was the Incarnation. From the earliest conventicles, Christians had grappled with what it meant, in the words of the Gospel of John, "And the Word became flesh and lived among us" (1:14). In the fourth century, the Council of Nicaea sought to define succinctly the relationship between God and Christ:

> [T]he Son of God, the Only-begotten begotten from the Father, that is from the substance of the Father, God from God, light from light, true God from true God, begotten not made, consubstantial with the Father, through whom all things came to be, both those in heaven and those in earth; for us humans and for our salvation he came down and became incarnate, became human, suffered and rose up on the third day, went into the heavens, is coming to judge the living and the dead.[5]

But Christ's person eluded concise definitions, catalyzing thought on the nature of divinity and the nature of humanity. What was "flesh"? Was it the material body, as in flesh and bones? Was it more complexly the human person? What was the relationship of "flesh" to humanity? Was "flesh" more broadly the physical world? What is the relationship of "flesh" to all Creation? By the eighth century, Christians were confronting the ways in which God's decision to "become flesh," literally, Incarnation, implicated the physical world and connected it to divinity – as they explored in all media God's decision to become visible and tangible.

In the eighth century, the Church divided, East and West, on the question of the relationship of human-made representations of the person of Christ to the Son of God. Those opposed to the making of images of Christ invoked, among others, the same passages in the Old Testament that Karlstadt cited seven centuries later. But the Church in the West would ultimately follow principles John of Damascus articulated, principles that would shape thinking about images into the sixteenth century. John linked the "flesh" of God Incarnate, Christ, to the visible world: In taking on that "flesh," God chose to become visible – a principle that Calvin echoed seven centuries later. Thus, John argued, God offered human beings, who longed to see God, a form they might then draw, paint, sculpt, in their desire to come closer to God. John explicitly rejected any identification of image and Christ – the image could not be Christ – but he connected "flesh" not simply to the visible world, but also

---

5 "The First Ecumenical Council: The First Council of Nicaea, 325: The Creed of Nicaea," *Creeds and Confessions of Faith in the Christian Tradition*, edited by Jaroslav Pelikan and Valerie Hotchkiss (New Haven: Yale University Press, 2003), vol. I, p. 159.

to the material world. The Incarnation, following that thinking, invited human beings to take up stone, wood, tempera, to fashion images of the visible God. And the desire to see, to touch God engendered thousands upon thousands of images.

Medieval Christianity grappled with the interplay of Incarnation and materiality in a number of ways. Not only did artisans fashion images of Jesus, his mother, and the apostles. They fashioned images of saints. By 1500, each town had its own patron saint, as well as those saints – the apostles, the early Christian martyrs, Church Fathers such as Jerome and Augustine, the founders of religious orders such as Benedict or Francis – who were shared among all Christendom. When living, they had manifested "holiness": patterns of behavior, such as humility, that were mimetic of Christ; attributes, such as sweetness of scent, that set their bodies apart. In the later Middle Ages, moments in the lives of saints were rendered in panels and sculpted figures, as individual saints became embedded in the liturgical year. "Images" provided their viewers with instances of holiness: conduct, gesture, bearing, manner. Images of saints, Thomas Aquinas argued in the thirteenth century, belonged on a continuum: At one end was Christ, God Incarnate; at the other, images of saints; and between them were Mary, then the apostles, then the saints, then images of Christ, of Mary, the apostles.

If Erasmus criticized the simple-minded for confusing images of saints with God, he had nonetheless come of age in a world that engaged multiply with the Incarnation: God's choice, in John of Damascus's words, to become visible. Incarnation, as other apologists for images argued, invited representation, the effort not to make God present, but to make present that form God had chosen to become visible. Images entered the eyes and minds, and images of Christ belonged, according to medieval theory, on a continuum of Incarnation. They were not mere decoration. Their beauty served piety, itself an effort to render, in all the skill human beings could summon, God's perfect being. To attack them was, for many sixteenth-century Christians, to attack a place that took up the mystery of Incarnation. God was not present in the image, but the image spoke directly and complexly to God's choice, to become "flesh," to become material.

For many contemporaries, then, the violence against things was, if anything, greater in force and horror than the violence against persons. It drove Erasmus from Basel, the city where he had been able to publish the Greek New Testament. For them, the violence was not against things – objects human beings had made – but against a site of intense devotional

FIGURE 8.2. Correggio, Noli me tangere. Museo del Prado, Madrid, Spain. Photo credit: Erich Lessing / Art Resource, New York.

meaning, a direct and multilayered engagement with Incarnation and all its implications for the physical world. Nor did images function the same for each Christian, long before the sixteenth century. For many, including Luther himself, images offered one means to contemplate the life of Christ – to consider it in detail, to "imagine" it in the late medieval understanding of visual cognition. For others, images were where they focused prayers to persons – Jesus, Mary, Joseph, local saints – who were no longer walking the earth but who were, in part through that image, "present" in devotional lives of Christians.

As Uly Anders shows, iconoclasts attacked things outside of churches. In 1523, Claus Hottinger, a shoemaker from a village near Zurich, brought down a great crucifix at the intersection of two roads, something that Dutch iconoclasts would do in greater numbers some forty years later. For many, "idols" resided not in their proximity to collective worship, but in the thing itself, its function as an image. The targets of Anders's and Hottinger's attacks were of radically different scale: the one small enough to be thrown out of the window of an inn, probably no more than a foot in height; the other so large that Hottinger had to have help, as well as ropes, to bring it down. But they were the same "image" in an important way. Both depicted Christ on the cross. Both were images of Christ's death, images that had become particularly implicated in medieval teaching on the sacrifice of the Mass. Both were exceptionally complex: in their devotional function, in their connotations, and in their engagement with the interplay of the physical world and divinity.

Anders's and Hottinger's acts of violence remind us of the pervasiveness of Christian imagery across the landscape of Europe – in inns, at the intersections of roads. They help us recover the visual density of late medieval Christianity. They also remind us that those images, though they might have been in place for decades, even centuries, still caught the eyes of passers-by and, following medieval optical theories, entered their minds. The images of Christ on the cross, Mary holding the infant Jesus, Peter holding the keys, Saint Francis preaching – all the images in churches, on roads, in homes and inns – engaged their spectators, who, as the violence testified, were not unmoved by "images."

Iconoclasm did not differentiate, as we tend to do, between "things" and "images." For iconoclasts in Zurich and Antwerp, oil lamps were "idols." For iconoclasts in the southern Empire and the Habsburg Netherlands, altars were "idols." Each thing in its own distinctive way visualized something of the medieval understanding of Incarnation, something that iconoclasts were willing to risk their lives to destroy. None provoked more consistent or geographically widespread violence than altars.

Altars and Tables

Of the "images" that iconoclasts attacked, none was more ancient than altars. The earliest altars have been dated to the third century. They had

FIGURE 8.3. Anonymous, The Mass of Saint Gregory. Louvre, Paris. Photo Credit: Art Resource, New York.

been made of wood, stone, or marble. Some were box-shaped, others were more table-like, with columns supporting a slab. A large number drew on Roman sarcophagi, with their long, rectangular shape and their panels depicting narratives. Some had images of Abraham and Isaac, as the father prepared to sacrifice the son to God. Many contained relics, those material remains of saints – their bones, the clothing they wore. All were called "altars."

Complexly embedded in late medieval engagements with the Incarnation, altars had been the site for thousands of Masses, that surface on which rested the chalice, the paten, the wine, and the host. Most altars, by the sixteenth century, were decked with cloths that marked the liturgical seasons, integrating the site into the temporal cycle of Christ's year. So, too, like crucifixes, altars – with their slab tops and their embedded relics – participated in the meaning of the Mass as a sacrifice.

Reformed Christians removed all altars from the churches they claimed for their worship. There would be no sepulcher, no tomb. In its stead, whether they built their own church or used an ancient site, Reformed Christians installed simple wooden tables. They differed on where those tables belonged within the space of worship – beneath the pulpit, to the side – but they agreed that a table was the appropriate site for "the Supper." The table was the object named in Luke's narrative of the Last Supper: "When the hour came, he took his place at the table, and the apostles with him" [22:14]. The table was scriptural. In choosing as the site for their eucharist the table, Reformed Christians also shifted the temporal focus of the eucharist, from the Crucifixion – all images of which were also gone from Reformed spaces – to the meal Jesus shared with his apostles. From Golgotha and its skulls to the interior of a home. The table was to be simple, both in keeping with the simplicity of the Gospel narrative and to reflect human humility – the human inability to make anything that approximated in importance the Last Supper.

Lutheran congregations, as Luther himself had encouraged them, retained altars for the most part, though some adopted simple tables, for the "Supper." Some Lutheran churches removed side altars and altars that impeded their members' view of the pulpit. Reformed and Lutheran alike reduced the number of sites for the eucharist to one. Whether altar or table, in evangelical churches, there was only one place where the congregation together celebrated the eucharist – one focus, one center, for all the Christians within that space.

FIGURE 8.4. The Protestant Church in Lyon, called "the Paradise." Seventeenth century. Bibliothèque Publique et Universitaire, Geneva, Switzerland. Photo credit: Erich Lessing / Art Resource, New York.

Catholics kept their altars. They kept multiple altars in their churches, many endowed with their own altarpieces. In the places they reclaimed from iconoclasm or evangelical use, they restored the altars, consecrating the new, reconsecrating those reclaimed from false worship. For them, altars were again the site where the great mystery of transubstantiation – that dramatic and multifaceted engagement with Incarnation – took place.

Altars and tables signaled deeply different understandings of the relationship between things and God. For Catholics, altars continued to participate in the Mass's singularly complex engagement with the mystery of Incarnation, the nature of Christ's sacrifice, and the relationship of both to humankind. In adopting tables, Reformed Christians rejected the temporal complexity of the altar, its linking of Incarnation, death, and sacrifice to an eternal present through that altar's very materiality, its abiding presence within the space of each church. Tables did not engage with either death or sacrifice at all. Tables linked one moment, discrete in a fixed past, to a living congregation, who recited the narrative of that moment as they looked upon the table. Tables linked two points in time – a past moment and the here-and-now – presenting those who approached them with a very different sense of Incarnation. Tables belonged, as altars did not, in a "house of God."

The Spaces of Worship

In 1547, when Protestant cities and principalities capitulated to Charles V's forces, the Bishop of Augsburg, Otto Truchsess von Waldburg, entered the city to reclaim the cathedral. His first act was to reconsecrate the church and then its altars. In his eyes, Lutheran use had desecrated the church: Their worship was false; that they had done so in this particular space had polluted it – it was no longer a sacred place. With the ancient ceremony, the bishop did not simply reclaim the cathedral for Catholic use. He marked it as a space apart from mundane life, a place of sanctity, which housed sacred things and was the location for sacred acts. Each Catholic church, in every site around the globe, was consecrated, each altar, consecrated, each a site of sanctity, sacred objects, and sacred acts – no matter if the site were the forests of Brazil, the Philippines, or South Asia.

In 1500, the structures we call churches were far more than architectural forms. They were places that European Christians had marked as set apart from "the world" – markets, courts, workshops, homes. The more beloved the church, the richer its sculptural programs, the greater the number of things, themselves beautifully crafted of precious materials. Within the great churches, those who entered found spaces transformed by stained glass that produced mystical light – patterns of blue, red, green across the floor. Each direction the eye looked, it encountered color, texture, story: images in wood, stone, tempera. Within those spaces, priests baptized infants, celebrated the Mass, chanted vespers; the particular colors in banners and altar cloths and vestments marked the seasons of the liturgical year. If "churches" have largely become places within which people gather to worship, the sixteenth century introduced that sense of the space.

In the first years, evangelicals took over medieval churches; they did not build new ones. Following Luther's repudiation of the violence of the Wittenberg iconoclasm, most Lutherans preserved the medieval interiors. Some removed choir screens that separated the high altar in the choir from the nave. Some moved the altar forward into the nave. For the most part, Lutherans tended to leave most of the medieval things in their churches, from altarpieces to tabernacles, from chalices to crucifixes. They celebrated the eucharist at only one site, what had been the main or high altar in medieval use. Other altars survived, no longer in use – no longer a site for a sacred act – simply a part of the structure of the space, unless those using the space found that they blocked the faithful's sightlines to the pulpit or the site of the Supper. Over time, Lutherans installed pews, fixed seating that faced the pulpit, structuring the space and giving physical form to "the congregation."

In keeping with their location on the spectrum of the ordering of the world according to Scripture, Lutheran churches shared some things with Catholic churches. Perhaps foremost, they shared the presence of organs: an instrument for creating sound within the space for worship. Lutheran churches retained much of the visual imagery of the medieval church, though the images existed in an altered relationship to worship. Luther accorded images didactic functions – they could make visible moments in the Gospel narratives of Jesus's life or instances when saints, persons of exceptional piety, enacted Christian virtues. Images were permitted to remain, so long as they did not "distract" – draw people's eyes from the central acts of worship: preaching, hymn singing, communion. They were to educate. Nothing more. Altar cloths, bells, even chalices and patens were, for Luther, things indifferent: They could remain, they could be set aside. And in that, Luther broke most fully with late medieval Christianity: No things were essential to worship at all. For him, a "church" was wherever the faithful gathered.

The iconoclasm of the Wonderyear, 1566, was inseparable from Reformed Christians claiming spaces for worship. More than any other Church, Reformed Christians sought to rid their spaces of "idols" – because all things in churches were human-made, and therefore flawed; because human beings were drawn to look at what they themselves had made; because those things were the diametric opposite of an uncircumscribable and invisible God; because they represented wrong understandings of Incarnation, sacrifice, and Resurrection. Their spaces were to be free of the clutter of medieval things, of those many engagements with Incarnation through human-made objects.

Reformed Christian spaces for worship looked to apostolic Christianity, to a time before medieval image-making. When they could build churches, French Reformed Christians built "temples," the name signaling that they had broken with Romanesque and Gothic practice of a cruciform church of elongated nave. The French temples – eradicated with the Revocation of the Edict of Nantes at the end of the seventeenth century – were circular or hexagonal or even duodecanal, without choirs, without apses, without a transept. French Huguenot churches in the western hemisphere, as well as Scots Reformed churches, were predominantly rectangular: a simple structure within which congregations gathered to hear the Word, in some, to sing psalms, in all, to receive communion, which in the Scots churches was closely restricted to those "worthy" to receive. Reformed churches were to be the place where both the visible church – all those who attended – and the invisible church, the righteous, gathered. In Dutch Reformed churches, as in the Temple of Lyon, the pulpit was the focus of the space; in Reformed churches in general, the congregation was oriented towards that site where the Word of God was preached. The faithful might be given pews, but pews were to be neither comfortable nor things that displayed human artistry.

Reformed churches, in the eyes of Catholics and many Lutherans, were "empty," structures marked by absences. "Absent" were carvings of any kind, crucifixes, candlesticks, chalices, patens, murals, frescoes, the Virgin Mary in her signature blue, the red of blood of martyrs, and crucifixions. Often Reformed Christians whitewashed the walls of medieval churches they claimed for service. For them, the absence of human-made things made room for God's Word, grace, mercy, and "light." Reformed Christian churches often carried the motto, "post tenebras lux" – "after the darkness, light." Their interiors, without the intervention of stained glass, were most often illumined by natural light – the light, as Calvin said, God had made – the sun, whether in the eastern hemisphere or the western, the northern or the southern.

In the sixteenth century, Anabaptists rarely had access to churches. When they did, as in the Kingdom of Münster, they purged the place of all things. Most often, however, they gathered in homes, clandestinely. And unlike those Catholics who were the religious minority in places such as Amsterdam or London, Anabaptists did not build altars or consecrate a site for worship. They gathered. They listened to preaching. They sang. They broke bread. All these could take place anywhere.

One church frames Reformation debates on the spaces of worship: Its renovations sparked some of the earliest confrontations, its completion

FIGURE 8.5. Pieter Jansz Saenredam, St. Katherine's Church, Utrecht. Upton House, Banbury, Oxfordshire, Great Britain. Photo by Christopher Hurst. Photo credit: National Trust Photo Library / Art Resource, New York.

in the seventeenth century visualized an expanding, monumental, and vibrant Church. In the pursuit of funding for a new basilica that would both replace the crumbling Constantinian church and serve as the architectural and artistic apex of all Christendom – more urgently since Hagia Sophia had been converted to a mosque in 1453 – Pope Leo X authorized the sale of indulgences. Evangelicals viewed indulgences as a piece

FIGURE 8.6. Giovanni Paolo Pannini, Interior of Saint Peter's Basilica. Ca. 1750. Museo del Settecento Veneziano, Ca' Rezzonico, Venice, Italy. Photo by Alfredo Dagli Orti. Photo credit: Bildarchiv Preussischer Kulturbesitz / Art Resource, New York.

of paper selling a fiction – Luther would write the Ninety-Five Theses for debate in 1517 in direct reaction against them – but for Catholics, they belonged to late medieval penitential culture: That piece of paper promised release from a specified time in purgatory, that place where souls went before entering heaven. It testifies both to the scale of the project and to the powerful popularity of indulgences that Leo chose them to fund the largest building project in all of Europe, the physical capital of Christendom: Saint Peter's Basilica.

Saint Peter's was one of the four churches the Emperor Constantine constructed in the imperial capital after his conversion to Christianity in the fourth century. By 1500, Saint Peter's alone had become the seat of the Pope, the primary church in western Christendom: As the Pope had become the head of the western Church, so only one structure had become its physical center. Renaissance popes pursued a vision of a singular church, to mark its primacy as structure and location. They drew

FIGURE 8.7. Giovanni Paolo Pannini, The Outing of the Duc de Choiseul on St. Peter's Square in Rome. 1754. Gemaeldegalerie, Staatliche Museen, Berlin, Germany. Photo by Joerg P. Anders. Photo credit: Bildarchiv Preussischer Kulturbesitz / Art Resource, New York.

on artists of the genius of Michelangelo to design floor plans, elevations, façades – to design a building that reflected the most sophisticated visual values of the Renaissance: proportion, perspective, design.

When completed in the seventeenth century, Saint Peter's was the largest church in western Christendom. The structure symbolized the position Rome had claimed in relationship to Catholics: a scale at once apart and encompassing all. Its interior could house more persons than any other church in Christendom, dwarfing individuals in the grandeur of its scale. It rendered in marble and gold the scale of God's Church on earth. Within its walls, the faithful could – and can – contemplate objects of as much beauty as their makers could fashion: Michelangelo's Pietà, saints larger than life rendered in pure white marble, Bernini's tombs of popes – all engaging with Incarnation, the tombs engaging as well with Resurrection. Here was the exuberant affirmation of images' centrality, both in the center of western Christendom and in the life of Catholics throughout the world.

Gian Lorenzo Bernini completed the piazza and colonnades in front of Saint Peter's in 1667. On the colonnades he placed dozens of martyrs, many recent, representing a Church whose most devout members went out into a dangerous world. Thirty years earlier, he completed the baldachin, a bronze and gold canopy over the high altar in Saint Peter's. His singular brilliance was brought to bear, to give the site of the highest Masses in the world a staging that dwarfed its celebrants and framed the event. The martyrs who witnessed all those approaching the center of the Catholic world reminded them of its history of sacrifice, as they approached the site of the most honored sacrifice.

The Interiors of Churches: Pews, Pulpits, Confessionals, and Fonts

Reformation also engendered changes in the interiors of churches. In the sixteenth and seventeenth centuries, pews were introduced into most spaces. They differed in look: Catholic and Lutheran pews could display all the artistry local wood sculptors possessed. But their function was similar. They provided seating for sermons that could, in any church, last more than an hour, in some churches, as much as four hours. They structured order into the congregation, organized people into rows and sections, so that they could no longer cluster, gossip, knit, or do business with the same anonymity. Pews belonged to the intensification of discipline in the collective life of congregations, a move not simply to seat those attending, but to place them in regular and visible order in relationship to the pulpit.

When evangelicals mounted pulpits in the sixteenth century, those pulpits were medieval. That said, evangelicals' attention to the Word of God moved pulpits more centrally into both spatial and spiritual orientation. As they built pews, evangelicals oriented them towards pulpits, structuring into the space itself the orientation they were seeking to inculcate through preaching, catechism, and discipline. Some pulpits were moved, and when evangelicals built churches, they placed the pulpits in the midst of the congregation.

If pulpits acquired greater significance in evangelical churches, in Catholic churches, a new form manifested changes in Catholic piety. Both Teresa of Ávila and Ignatius Loyola held confession central to their lives of piety. The Catholicism that emerged at the end of the sixteenth century emphasized the intimacy of confession as well as its spiritual

FIGURE 8.8. Antwerp confessionals, author's photo.

importance in the life of each Christian. As a praxis, confession inculcated both self-examination and the regular experience of God's love
and mercy. Prior to the Reformation, the sacrament of penance required
confession, but, for the most part, that confession did not have its own
formal site. In the wake of the sixteenth century, the form of the private
confessional emerged. This form structured a relationship between penitent lay person and priest, sometimes cloaking the priest, turning the
penitent to face the hidden priest, often in a space constructed for kneel-
ing. The physical, material shape of these confessionals inculcated spatial
and gestural relations between laity and clergy, even as they celebrated
in their exquisite craftsmanship the spiritual importance of confession
in each individual's life. Confessionals provided a place for each person
to speak to a priest, to review his or her life, examine it, and place that
life in the care of the hidden priest. They marked a place as Catholic,
where the sacrament of penance was offered regularly, in places at once
visible and artistically celebrated.

Catholics, Lutherans, and Reformed Christians agreed on the principle of infant baptism, even if Catholics and evangelicals divided on the
function and the meaning of the sacrament of baptism. Fonts did not

divide Catholics and evangelicals as altars did. Baptisms continued at
fonts in Catholic, Lutheran, and Reformed Christian churches – babies
brought into communities that would seek to form them far more deeply
than their medieval predecessors.

Bells

On Saint George's Day, April 23, 1526, the great bronze bell of the
Cathedral of Our Lady in Strasbourg was mysteriously removed from its
bell tower – one of the highest in Europe. The following week, it was
shattered before the doors of the cathedral. Bells, like chanting monks,
were the target of evangelical violence.

In a world of few clocks, no watches of any kind, bells marked time.
They did not mark regular hours such as govern the world today, of sixty
minutes of sixty seconds each. Bells marked time as the church divided it
and defined it: liturgical "hours," eight in number, which varied according to the length of daylight; holy days, set apart in the calendar year to
celebrate saints and events in Jesus' and Mary's lives. Bells marked Matins,
in the middle of the night; Lauds, at dawn; Prime in the early morning;
Terce in mid-morning; Sext, at mid-day; None, at mid-afternoon; Vespers,
at dusk; and Compline, at night. They marked the great feast days with
lengthy pealing. They were the means by which the medieval Church
claimed all time in its soundscape for the liturgy it had articulated and
enacted.

In smashing bells, evangelicals destroyed the means by which the
medieval liturgy was marked – as far as the sound carried – and the
means by which the laity, in the shadow of the tower as well as out in
the countryside, were called to churches. They did not simply silence the
bells. They silenced the medieval Christian structuring of time.

Monasteries and Convents

In 1536, King Henry VIII of England dissolved all the "lesser" religious
houses – those abbeys, canonries, convents, friaries, monasteries, pri-
ories which were "small," requiring their inhabitants to move into the
"greater" houses, and laying claim to all their "all the sites and circuits
of every such religious houses, and all and singular the manors, granges,
meases, lands, tenements, rents, reversions, services, tithes, pensions,
portions, churches, chapels, advowsons, patronages, annuities, rights,

entries, conditions, and other hereditaments appertaining or belonging to every such monastery, priory, or other religious house, not having, as is aforesaid, above the said clear yearly value of two hundred pounds."[6] Three years later, he did the same for the "greater" monasteries.

The coffers of the English crown were enriched as never before, and the landscape of England was redrawn. Gone were all the places where "the religious" gathered, lived within the rhythms of liturgical hours, and used the many different things – chalices and patens, missals and breviaries, altar cloths and altarpieces – to honor God. Henry's "Dissolution," as the legal act was called, was more dramatic than elsewhere, but in place after place that became evangelical, the cloistered life – its rhythms, its practices, its spatial articulation, its differentiation from "the world" – was legally erased.

In some places, nuns, friars, or monks simply handed over their property to civil authorities, transferring lands and goods that the Church of Rome continued to claim as its own to those authorities whose jurisdiction over their lives and things the members of that place now recognized. "Cloister," an ancient concept, had no place, either literally or figuratively, in Christian life, as evangelicals saw it. The walls that set some Christians apart from others were human constructs. Like bells, they were human artifice, not divine design.

In Catholic states, the cloistered life abided, normally protected, in places actively fostered by the temporal sword. Following Luther's recognition that some may choose lives of celibacy, Lutheran states permitted Lutheran (but not Catholic) cloisters, but those lives fell under the broad repudiation of good works as effective for salvation – the human beings who lived within the walls were no different in their nature, the place no different in valence, from the rest of the world.

Reformed Christians rejected cloister absolutely. For them, "this world" *was* God's world. For them, Creation did not divide between "this world" and an "other world." Organized and ordered according to God's will, Creation should not be repudiated or shut out. The pious life was not enclosed. God could see human beings wherever they were. The pious lived always in the world that God created. Cloister was at once artificial – a human construct – and an affront, a rejection of the world that God had made for a world defined by human beings. And cloister made no

---

[6] http://home.freeuk.net/don-aitken/ast/h8a.html, accessed on 10 April 2010.

difference, because no matter where one was on the surface of the earth, God could see one.

By the end of the century across Europe, one knew, as one entered a space, whether it was Catholic, Lutheran, or Reformed. Catholic churches retained their multiple altars, their altar cloths, their altar retables, their sculpture, all their images. Lutheran churches retained images, but they had only one altar in use. Reformed churches presented a new aesthetic, which the faithful saw as beautiful, and which their enemies saw as "empty." So, too, churches were the physical emplacement of the congregation within the whole Church. Catholics retained their sense that their church was oriented towards Rome, its center. Lutherans had bishops, but not dioceses, and no Rome: Wittenberg was a guide, not the center. Following Luther's own guidance, the space of worship was local – its accoutrements determined by the local congregation and its leaders. Over time, Lutheran churches came to have on their walls portraits of pious families in the congregation. Reformed Christians gathered in structures of simplicity and humility. No matter where they were – in the forests of North America, in the highlands of Scotland, in the southwest of France, in Swiss cities – their spaces of worship were houses of God: places scattered, dispersed, where the faithful gathered.

The churches reflected in the physical terms of stone and wood each Church's sense of itself, its sense both of the relationships among congregations and also of itself across space. Catholic churches continued to be oriented towards the east, Jerusalem, and increasingly after the Council of Trent, each place was brought into a universal Christendom, its particular congregation under the government of parish priest, bishop, archbishop, and Rome. Lutheran churches might have a special pew for king or prince, and pews inscribed an ordered world into the space, but the orientation within each Lutheran church was the Word of God and its physical site, the pulpit. Reformed congregations, too, were oriented internally toward the pulpit. They needed no eastern orientation – wherever they were, whether Leiden or Plymouth, they were directly beneath God's eye.

In the western hemisphere, Reformed Christians built structures where the faithful were to gather to hear the Word, to sing psalms, to take communion. In the western hemisphere, Catholics built churches with doors open, in which the mystery of the Mass might be observed by anyone. In arrangement of interior space – the placement of altar or table, the presence or absence of confessionals, the placement of pulpit, in density of images – each place articulated a different understanding of the relationship between the world of matter and God, between the faithful and God. For each Church, the relationship among things, place, and God set that Church apart.

9

Incarnation

Idolatry

Inasmuch as the Mass of the pope was a reprobate and diabolical ordinance subverting the mystery of the holy supper, we declare that it is execreable to us, and idolatry condemned by God; for so much is it itself regarded as a sacrifice for the redemption of souls that the bread is in it taken and adored as God. Besides there are other execrable blasphemies and superstitions implied here, and the abuse of the Word of God which is taken in vain without profit or education.

The Genevan Confession, 1536[1]

Evangelicals labeled so much of medieval Christian practice "idolatry": images, the cult of saints, pilgrimages, crucifixes, the Mass – with its chalices and patens, the priest's elaborate and scripted movements, his hands now drawing a cross in the air, now lifting the host, the chalice above his head. The term and the concept – the worship of false gods – were ancient. The prohibition of making or honoring images, "false gods" to evangelicals such as Karlstadt, was to be found among the Commandments in Exodus, whether encompassed within the First or, as Reformed Christians held, constituting a Commandment unto itself, the Second. But in the sixteenth century, the word acquired new resonances, of strange lands and alien practices, as European accounts of the western hemisphere labeled the practices of each people they encountered – the Tainos and Caribs of the Caribbean, the Aztec and Inka empires, the Tupi in Brazil – with the same word.

"Idolatry" named for evangelicals, as it did for Catholics and evangelicals in the western hemisphere, not just false worship, but fundamentally

---

[1] "The Genevan Confession (1536)," *Confessions and Catechisms of the Reformation* edited by Mark A. Noll (Grand Rapids: Baker Books, 1991), p. 130.

wrong conceptualizations of the relationship between God and human-kind, between God and the material world. For all, idolatry named a way of thinking about God that misplaced God, located him in things and actions where he was not to be found. Idolatry was looking away from God. And for evangelicals, it was the celebration of the human, raising human-made things, human imagination, human actions to the level of God. It was, for them, a kind of self-worship.

Evangelicals called medieval Christians – and Catholics who affirmed the orthodoxy of specific medieval practices – "arrogant." For them, medieval Christians, and the Catholics who endorsed medieval practices, failed to grasp the magnificence, the omnipotence, and the enormity of God; failed to acknowledge their own essential sinning natures, their essential baseness; failed to recognize in their practices the chasm between humankind and God; and failed to honor the God who alone could traverse that chasm. For evangelicals, the Mass was human-made, its gestures, objects, and connotations, the product of human imagination. As such, that ancient and familiar rite was no different from what Aztecs, Inkas, and Tupinamba were doing.

> Well, however that may be, said Villegagnon and Cointa, the words "This is my Body; this is my Blood" cannot be taken other than to mean that the Body and Blood of Jesus Christ are contained therein.... they wanted not only to eat the flesh of Jesus Christ grossly rather than spiritually, but what was worse, like the savages named Ouetaca... they wanted to chew and swallow it raw.
>
> Jean de Léry, *History of a Voyage to the Land of Brazil* [2]

For Reformed Christians such as Léry, the misconception of the relationship among God, the world of matter, and humankind at the center of the medieval and Catholic Mass aroused exactly the same visceral horror as the cannibalism of the western hemisphere – the very notion that one could "chew and swallow" "raw" the body of God.

At the epicenter of divisions among European Christians were different understandings of the Incarnation: when "the Word became Flesh," when God took on human form and became visible, audible, tangible.

> [The Protestants] indignant that this bell-ringing stopped their preacher from being heard, went in great numbers to the church of Saint-Médard, which they pillaged, mortally wounding several parishioners and smashing the images of the church. It happened that a poor baker of the parish, father

---

[2] Jean de Léry, *History of a Voyage to the Land of Brazil*, translated by Janet Whatley (Berkeley: University of California Press, 1990), p. 41. According to Léry, Villegagnon rejects the doctrine of transubstantiation, but nonetheless insists on Christ's corporeal presence.

of twelve children, seeing the massacre in the church, took the ciborium with the served sacrament [the host], saying to them, 'My masters, do not touch this, for the honour of he who reposes within.' But a wicked man ran him through with a halberd, killing him next to the high altar and said to him: 'Is this your pastry God who now delivers you from the torments of death?' And they crushed under foot the precious body of Our Lord and smashed the ciborium into a thousand pieces.

Christmas, 1561, Memoires of Condé[3]

For medieval Christians and for Catholics, the Incarnation changed the relationship between God and the world. Following it, God was not some ineffable being, remote, observing humankind from a great distance. God was a Father; he had a son, who, in turn, had a mother. God had chosen to enter the world of humankind, to take on materiality, dimension, to become not simply visible, but imitable. For them, the Incarnation invited representation – altarpieces and crucifixes, panels and statues, plays and performances – and mimesis: mendicancy, peripatetic preaching, humility. It was no esoteric doctrine, some subject of arid theological debate in universities. Over 1,500 years, it had engendered thousands upon thousands of images, objects, and structures; it had invited a multiplicity of enactments, from the lives of the religious to the Passion plays in towns. It had inspired layers upon layers of meaning for human action and the making of things. For medieval Christians and Catholics, the Incarnation had made porous the boundary between the world of matter and God.

The Mass had become complexly intertwined with multiple engagements with the Incarnation. At its center was the moment when the priest gave breath to the words, "Hoc est enim corpus meum," "This is my body," and then, "Hic est enim calix sanguinis mei," "This is the cup of my blood," and the bread – the host – and the wine, held in a chalice, were transformed into "the precious body and blood of Our Lord" the living and bleeding body of Christ. That sense, that in an instant God could be where mundane matter had been, may not have been universally held among all medieval Christians, but it brought to objects valences, potentialities, and confounded any simple division of the world into matter and spirit.

The medieval Church had nurtured a complex understanding of the Incarnation, through its patronage as well as through innumerable decrees. Specifically, with regard to the Mass, the Fourth Lateran Council

---

[3] Bruslatt, Mémoires de Condé ou Recueil pour servir à l'histoire de France, vol. I, pp. 68–69, in *The French Wars of Religion: Selected Documents*, edited and translated by David Potter (New York: St. Martin's Press, 1997), p. 42.

of 1215 had linked the person of the priest through his office to Christ's person. Over time, that identification accrued meanings to the Mass: As the priest spoke the words, his movements were to evoke Christ's sacrifice on the cross, to connect "the sacrifice of the Mass" to Christ's "sacrifice" on the cross – a connection which the crosses and crucifixes, above his head, upon the altar, carved into the altar, and stitched on the back of his uppermost vestment reinforced. The priest's clothing and move-ments connected his person to Christ's in a space that usually also held a number of representations of Christ: as infant, as preacher, as son, in the temple. Images of that living body were there, in the same space, as the priest spoke the words, "for this is my body," "for this is the cup of my blood," linking those words to a concrete, material, thing, rendered in stone, pigment, wood. In that moment when, the Church taught, Christ's body and blood were really present, Christians could see his body: on the walls, above their heads, and in the vestments of the priest.

The Council of Trent affirmed that the sacraments were seven in num-ber (Session 7, March 3, 1547). It affirmed and expanded the constitu-tions of Fourth Lateran on the Mass. In Session 13 (October 11, 1551), it affirmed:

> our lord Jesus Christ, true God and true man, is truly, really and substantially contained in the propitious sacrament of the holy eucharist [communion] under the appearance of those things which are perceptible to the senses . . .

> that by the consecration of the bread and wine, there takes place the change of the whole substance of the bread into the substance of the body of Christ our Lord, and of the whole substance of the wine into the substance of his blood. And the holy catholic church has suitably and properly called this change transubstantiation.[4]

In Session 22 (September 17, 1562), in which it affirmed the doctrine of the sacrifice of the Mass, the Council also affirmed both the identification of Christ as priest and the necessity that a priest celebrate the Mass. In Session 23 (July 15, 1563), it affirmed "sacrifice and priesthood are so joined together by God's foundation," that the one was not separable from the other.[5] For the Council, the Incarnation was inseparable from the priesthood, which, in turn, was inseparable from the sacrament of communion, when Christ was really present.

The evangelical accusation of "idolatry" marked a fundamental rethinking of the Incarnation and its meaning for living communities

---

[4] *Decrees of the Ecumenical Councils*, edited by Norman P. Tanner, S.J., vol. II (London: Sheed & Ward, 1990), pp. 693, 695.
[5] *Decrees of the Ecumenical Councils*, vol. II, p. 742.

of Christians. For evangelicals, human nature, which they held to be essentially sinning, severed human beings from the person of Christ, God Incarnate. That sense of human nature was the underpinning of their broad distrust all things human-made, including the elaborate movements and rhythms of the medieval Mass. It led evangelicals to reject, absolutely, the role of the priest: No human being could ever stand for Christ – neither mendicant, nor peripatetic preacher, nor priest. No human reenactment of the sacrifice of the cross, evangelicals wrote, could ever approximate, let alone reproduce, the sheer magnitude of God's sacrifice of his only son on the cross. "Idolatry" – whether the Mass or religions of the western hemisphere – accorded human beings agency that God alone possessed and human understanding an authority that was God's alone.

For evangelicals, the single most important consequence of the Incarnation was God's Word, that locus where living Christians might look to discern God's will. God's Word – its words, its narratives, its books – and not the stories of Christ's life circulating in medieval sermons, plays, and images should be the direction, in many senses of the word, for faithful Christians. It should be the focus of their devotion: where they looked in order to find God. It should be the wellspring for answering all questions: How does one live? What is an upright life? What does a true Christian do, in evangelicals' words, to honor God? True Christians placed themselves in absolute obedience to God's Word: What it commanded, true Christians did. Nothing more. And nothing less. God had revealed his will in this place, this physical locus, where each Christian might turn, direct his or her attention.

Sacraments Reconceived

Christ had, evangelicals preached, commanded, his disciples to do very little, most fully, after his crucifixion, when he appeared to them:

> And Jesus came and said to them, "All authority in heaven and on earth has been given to me. Go therefore and make disciples of all nations, baptizing them in the name of the Father and of the Son and of the Holy Spirit, and teaching them to obey everything that I have commanded you. And remember, I am with you always, to the end of the age.
> Matthew 28: 18–20[6]

---

[6] *The New Oxford Annotated Bible*, Third Edition, edited by Michael D. Coogan (Oxford, 2001). Unless otherwise noted, all quotations are from this translation.

Within his life, Christ had commanded his disciples to "do" but once:

> While they were eating, Jesus took a loaf of bread, and after blessing it, gave it to his disciples, and said, "Take, eat; this is my body." Then he took a cup, and after giving thanks he gave it to them, saying, "Drink from it, all of you; for this is my blood of the covenant, which is poured out for many for the forgiveness of sins.
>
> Matthew 26: 26–27

> Then he took a loaf of bread, and when he had given thanks, he broke it and gave it to them, saying, "This is my body, which is given for you. Do this in remembrance of me." And he did the same with the cup after supper, saying, "This cup that is poured out for you is the new covenant in my blood."
>
> Luke 22: 19–20

For evangelicals, these texts were definitive. Following them, evangelicals eliminated five of the seven sacraments the medieval Church had recognized: confirmation, penance, marriage, ordination, and last rites.

In this, evangelicals broke with the medieval understanding of sacraments. With Augustine, evangelicals acknowledged that a sacrament comprised words and matter – the material "sign" of which Augustine had spoken. But unlike Augustine, they did not allow that those "signs" were unlimited. For evangelicals, a sacrament was an action, involving matter, that Christ had commanded. If Christ had not commanded an action, it was not a sacrament. Even if Christ had done something – blessed a marriage – if he did not command his followers to do it, it was not a sacrament.

For all evangelicals, Christ had commanded two sacraments: baptism and what they came to call "the Supper." They shared the fundamental conviction that a sacrament, in order to be a sacrament, must be Christ's command. The Augsburg Confession also included the sacrament of Absolution, but Luther's *Large Catechism* of 1529 did not include it among the sacraments. Indeed, the *Large Catechism* spoke of "the sacrament," which was the Supper. Each existed in its own distinctive relationship to a human life.

All evangelicals agreed that baptism initiated a human being into the community of Christians. While Anabaptists agreed that baptism initiated, they held – against persecution and execution – that an adult chose baptism when he or she had arrived at a full commitment to a Christian life. In their first years, when all European Christians had been baptized as children, Anabaptists therefore rebaptized adults and did not baptize infants. Other evangelicals held that baptism should happen but once, in the infancy of each human being, and that it therefore initiated a human being into a life in which faith grew over time. All called for the use of water – the material sign – though they disagreed on the degree to which it could wash away anything spiritual, foremost sins.

If baptism was to occur only once in a human life, all evangelicals agreed, the second sacrament – what his followers were to "do in remembrance of me" – was to be a praxis, done consistently and repeatedly over the course of each human life. Evangelicals did not agree on frequency, but they agreed that this sacrament was to be done again and again and again. "Worship" for all Christians encompassed many different kinds of praxis: prayer foremost; not simply listening to, but attending to sermons; for many evangelicals, singing. But among all those practices, only one consistently brought God, humankind, and matter together in a moment that, evangelicals and Catholics agreed, transformed each Christian. They divided, and divided irreparably and to the present day, on how that moment transformed each Christian, but for all, in communion, God was "present," and the faithful "received" that presence into their persons.

For medieval Christians and for Catholics, communion was the fulfillment of the Mass, that moment when Christians took Christ's real body into their mouths. For them, it was the exact moment when the world of matter dissolved into the world of divinity. If for some such as Andreas Bodenstein von Karlstadt and Kaspar von Schwenckfeld communion could be laid aside, for the great majority – Lutherans, Reformed Christians, and Anabaptists – those words, "this do in remembrance of me," leapt from the page, spoke to each Christian who wished to be obedient to God. The words of the Gospel narrative, "this is my body," "this is the cup of my blood," seemed so simple, tiny and familiar. But they proved the most volatile of all, because in them, Catholics and evangelicals alike found the precise definition – in places far removed from Jerusalem, 1,500 years after Christ's Crucifixion – of the relationship among God, matter, and humankind.

Reading a Mystery

If anyone should contend, however, that Christ has not commanded us to say these words, "This is my body," in the Supper, I reply: It is true that the text does not read, "You shall say 'This is my body,'" and there is no printer's index pointing to the command; but I dare them, no matter how bold they may be, to leave these words out as if they were not commanded! We do not read in the text, either, "You shall say, 'take and eat.'" Again, we do not read, "You shall take the bread and bless it," etc. But let us see who would dare to say, "Do not take the bread and bless it," or "Do not say, 'Take and eat'!" Am I really being told that Christ must spell out these words, "Thus shall you say and do," letter by letter, and that it is not enough that he said in conclusion, "Do this in remembrance of me"? If we are to do what he did, then indeed we must take the bread and bless it, and break it and distribute it, saying, "This is my body." For all this is included in the imperative word, "Do this," and we must not leave out these words. For St. Paul also says that he received from the Lord what he delivered to us [I. Cor. 11:23]. Surely these are words of command, and they do not permit us to tear out or alter a single point.

Martin Luther, Confession Concerning Christ's Supper (1528)[7]

Evangelicals' universal, insistent, at times violent, repudiation of the Mass, the doctrine of transubstantiation, and the medieval understanding of the sacrament of communion arose from their particular reading of Scripture. It was not that the Mass had no scriptural foundation – as the Council of Trent stated, Jesus's words were the foundation for the doctrines of real presence and transubstantiation the Council decreed. Evangelicals brought to Jesus's words a different way of reading the Bible: each book from its beginning to its end, and all the books gathered together as "God's Word" – and a swirl of resonances. It fostered a different sense of the text, at many levels.

Question:
With which words did the Lord hold and institute his holy Supper?

Answer:
This the holy evangelists describe for us: Matthew, Mark, Luke, and Saint Paul.

Our Lord Jesus Christ, in the night he was betrayed, took the bread, gave thanks, and broke it, and gave it to his disciples, and spoke: Take, eat, this is my body, which is given for you. Do this in remembrance of me.

In the same manner, he also took the chalice after the Supper, gave thanks, and gave it to them, and spoke: Take and all of you drink from it. This chalice is the New Testament in my blood, that is spilled for you, for the forgiveness of sins. Do this as often as you drink in remembrance of me.

Johannes Meckhart, Catechism (1557)[8]

---

[7] Martin Luther, "Confession Concerning Christ's Supper, 1528," *Luther's Works*, vol. 37: *Word and Sacrament III*, edited by Robert Fischer (Minneapolis: Fortress Press, 1961), p. 187.

[8] Johannes Meckhart, *CATECHISMVS. Ain kurtze Christliche Leer und underweysung für die Jugent* (Augsburg: Philip Ulhart, 1557), pp. Diii^v-Diiii, my translation.

Their reading of Scripture embedded Jesus's words, "this is my body," "this is the cup of my blood," in a particular moment in the chronology of his life. For Reformed Christians and Anabaptists, the words were spoken within the context of a meal – a sense that led them, among other things, to hear cannibalism in the Catholic understanding and to replace altars with tables, chalices with cups, hosts with bread. The Last Supper took place – in a room – among a specific group, and "in the night he was betrayed."

> . . . It is written: 'Take, eat; this is my body.' Thus one must above all things do it and believe. One must do it. . . . Christ gives himself to us in many ways: in preaching, in baptism, in brotherly consolation, in the sacrament. Again and again the body of Christ is eaten, for he himself commands us so. If he ordered me to eat manure, I would do it, since I would altogether know that it would be to my salvation. Let not the servant brook over the will of his Master. We have to close our eyes.
>
> Martin Luther, Marburg Colloquy, 1529[9]

Holding the authority of Scripture supreme brought evangelicals face to face with a mystery. As John Calvin remarked, Jesus was living when he spoke those words. What, then, was the "body" of which he spoke? Was it the same as human bodies, of the western as well as the eastern hemispheres: material, of height, weight, solidity? Did that word link humankind and God Incarnate? What was that "body's" relationship to the bread he had in his hand? What was the "blood," which the Gospel text placed in a cup? What was its relationship to the wine in the cup? Did such mundane matter – foodstuffs, really – have the potential to become, in lived reality, the living flesh and the flowing blood of Christ? What, exactly, were his disciples to "do"? These questions were no trivial game, but spoke directly to the relationship between God and matter, God and humankind. Could Christ be there – be fully "present," a person one could touch, see, taste, know through the senses? Could humankind, some 1,500 years after Christ's death and resurrection, still know his body? Unite his body and their own, physically, body with body? Thus had the medieval Church taught. And missionaries of the western hemisphere had voiced deep unease on precisely the nature of that union. Were all human bodies the same, east and west? Did human beings, in consuming the host, always integrate Christ's body into their own? How?

---

[9] Excerpts from a reconstruction of the proceedings of the Marburg Colloquy, in *The Reformation in its Own Words*, edited and translated by Hans Hillerbrand (Chatham, Kent: Harper & Row, 1964), p. 160.

In the 1520s, evangelicals and Catholics fought bitterly over "body," "this is," "this do." For all evangelicals, the words, the spoken words of Christ, were the entry, the portal, into the most intimate of experiences: the relationship between each individual Christian and God. Europeans brought no common education to those words. Luther was a Doctor of Sacred Scripture. Calvin was a lawyer. Huldrych Zwingli had been trained as a humanist, learning Greek as well as Latin. Balthasar Hubmaier, one of the leaders of the Anabaptists, was a Doctor of Theology. Nor was it only that their professional training differed from person to person. They had all come of age in a world that neither offered nor sought a uniform education such as we now know. They were not required to learn what the modern world calls biology, anatomy, or physics. Indeed, the modern "sciences" might, arguably, be said not to exist in the early sixteenth century. Europeans might, in the course of an education, read the great classical authority, Aristotle, but then again, they might not. They might also read accounts of western cannibalism, or they might not. They brought, therefore, to their intense and intimate readings diverse experiences and educations. And among those words, none proved more intimate, or more fragmenting, than "body."

"body"

> There is indeed one universal church of the faithful, outside of which nobody at all is saved, in which Jesus Christ is both priest and sacrifice. His body and blood are truly contained in the sacrament of the altar under the forms of bread and wine, the bread and wine having been changed in substance, by God's power, into his body and blood, so that in order to achieve this mystery of unity we receive from God what he received from us. Nobody can effect this sacrament except a priest who has been properly ordained according to the church's keys, which Jesus Christ himself gave to the apostles and their successors.[10]

In 1215, in seeking to still debate on the nature of Christ's presence in the sacrament of communion, the Fourth Lateran Council set forth in succinct language the doctrine of transubstantiation. For the next 300 years, the decree instead engendered a multitude of understandings as well as criticisms of the doctrine. Influential thinkers such as John of Paris, Thomas Aquinas, Giles of Rome, Duns Scotus, William of Ockham, and Gabriel Biel each grappled with the nature of Christ's body there

---

[10] *Decrees of the Ecumenical Councils,* edited by Norman J. Tanner, S.J., Volume I: Nicea to Lateran V (London: Sheed & Ward, 1990), p. 230.

on the altar, the body that the faithful received into their mouths. In some ways, the proliferation of understandings might be said to echo in the sixteenth century. But the sixteenth-century debates differed in one fundamental way: They were anchored, as medieval debates were not, to one text that all evangelicals held to be both normative and definitive. Medieval theologians had accorded no one text such status, and no theologian saw himself as the sole true arbiter of the meaning of Christ's words. In the sixteenth century, the intimate encounter with God's Word for evangelicals brought a visceral intimacy to the "body" Christ named at the Last Supper.

In 1529, at the Colloquy in Marburg, that Philip, Landgrave of Hesse, had convened to address the proliferating divisions among evangelicals, Zwingli said, "It is wonderfully consoling to me, each time I think of it: Christ had flesh like I do."[11] That body, like all human bodies, Zwingli explained, could only be in one place at a time: "Holy Scripture shows us Christ always in a single, specific place, such as in the manger, in the temple, in the desert, on the cross, in the grave, at the right [hand] of the Father."[12] For Zwingli, the word Christ spoke, "body," was a point of somatic connection between a Christian and Christ: For Zwingli, his own body was a means of knowing Christ, his experience of his own body, a way to enter into Christ's life.

Perhaps it was his own experience, a life that had carried him away from home early, to tutors and ultimately to the University of Vienna, before settling in the city of Zurich, that led Zwingli to attend so closely to location. For him, it mattered that the Gospel narratives located Christ: When Jesus was in Bethlehem, he was nowhere else; when Jesus was in the Garden of Gethsemane, he was nowhere else; when Jesus sat at the table in the upper room, he was nowhere else. For Zwingli, all bodies – human and Christ's – had location.

Nor was he alone in thinking about Christ's body in this way. Other evangelicals, such as Karlstadt, held that Christ had location and that he was now, following the Apostles' Creed, after his death and resurrection,

---

[11] "Es ist mir wundersam tröstlich, so oft ich's bedenke: Christus hat Fleisch wie ich – das tröstet wundersam," *Das Marburger Religionsgespräch 1529. Versuch einer Rekonstruktion*, edited by Walther Köhler [Schriften des Vereins für Reformationsgeschichte 148] (Leipzig: M. Heinsius Nachfolger Eger & Sievers, 1929), p. 14, my translation.

[12] "Die h. Schrift zeiget uns Christum allweg an einem sondern Ort, als in der Krippen, im Tempel, in der Wüste, am Kreuz, im Grab, zur Rechten des Vaters. Darum meine ich, er müsse allweg an einem sondern Ort sein." *Das Marburger Religionsgespräch 1529. Versuch einer Rekonstruktion*, p. 30, my translation.

to be found only "at the right hand of God the Father Almighty." For them, "the Incarnation" meant that Christ had taken on a human body, with all its physical properties: height, weight, dimension, and location. For them, that word, "body," had an immediate, material referent: human bodies.

Luther and Calvin rejected absolutely and adamantly that connection. Both severed the word in the Gospel narrative completely from human experience. For both, the same word, "body," did not signify the same thing in reference to Christ's person as it did in reference to humankind. For both, human experience of their own bodies offered no access to the meaning of the word in the Gospel text or to the sacramental moment that text instituted. Both also rejected, vehemently, Zwingli's and Karlstadt's notion that Christ's two natures divided so cleanly between a human body and a divine spirit. For Luther and for Calvin, the Incarnation had bound the two worlds – human and divine, physical and spiritual – together, though they disagreed as to how.

> How do we become certain, good gentlemen, that a body may not through the power of God be at the same time in heaven and in the Supper, since the power of God has neither measure nor number, and does things which no mind can comprehend but must simply be believed? When he says, "This is my body," how shall I calm my heart and convince it that God has no means or power to do what his Word says? And perhaps, even if a body is not now visibly present at several places, he may well know of other ways by which he might render a body invisibly present, indeed, even visibly in many places at the same time. If he could do this, would you not have deceived us woefully by saying No before you knew for sure? Have you also proof from the Scriptures that they do not concede this possibility to the omnipotence of God?
>
> Martin Luther, *That These Words of Christ, "This is My Body," etc. Still Stand Firm Against the Fanatics* (1527)[13]

For Luther, the meaning of the word "body" in that place was governed by divine omnipotence. No word, no matter how seemingly familiar, could ever constrain God's power or Christ's agency – the meaning of the word, "body," in that place in Scripture was, therefore, utterly singular. It had no referent beyond the Word of God itself – no human bodies, no human experiences of any kind. Both opponents and followers found in his sense that God could be anywhere he chose a notion of "ubiquity" – that is, a sense that Christ was bodily everywhere where communion was

---

[13] Martin Luther, "That These Words of Christ, 'This is My Body,' etc. Still Stand Firm Against the Fanatics," *Luther's Works*, vol. 37, p. 47.

being offered – an understanding grounded in their own very different understandings of body and Christ's person. And yet for Luther, defining Christ's body in that place began with obedience to the Word of God, no matter how inscrutable it might be, and the acknowledgment of God's power to do as he chooses, unconstrained by any laws of matter or physics. Only placing one's own understanding in radical obedience to the text, setting aside all human referents – of one's own body, of the world of matter, of the natural world – and listening to God's Word could open the meaning of the word for a Christian.

> And this remains for us an established fact: whenever Scripture calls our attention to the purity of Christ, it is to be understood of his true human nature, for it would have been superfluous to say that God is pure.... No wonder, then, that Christ, through whom integrity was to be restored, was exempted from common corruption!
> John Calvin, *Institutes of the Christian Religion*, Book II, Chapter XIII[14]

In his *Catechism* and the *Institutes*, Calvin came last to the Supper: For him, understanding that word, "body," was among the most difficult things for a Christian. It did not come through human knowledge – not science, not the study of Scripture, not the experience of one's own body. Even as Calvin, like Zwingli, held that Christ's body shared with all human bodies location, a spatial specificity, he rejected any connection between human experience and Christ – Christ's perfection separated his body from all human bodies, even as the specificity of its location made impossible any notion of its ubiquity. Understanding the content of the word, "body," in the narrative of the Last Supper came only over time, gradually, in a dialectical process, in which "Christ grows in us and we in him." For human beings to understand the content of that word, "body," in the Gospel narrative, they must, for Calvin, "do this" – follow Christ's command. Receiving Christ's "body" in communion was the necessary process for coming to an understanding of the word. For Calvin, the content of that seemingly familiar word existed in dialectical interdependence with "this do."

> As we now have communion with one another in this bread and drink of the Christ meal, so also should the body and blood of all of us be shared with each other, just as the body and blood of Christ is shared with us all....
> ...We conclude that the bread and wine of the Christ meal are outward word symbols of an inward Christian nature here on earth, in which a

---

[14] John Calvin, *Institutes of the Christian Religion*, edited by John T. McNeill, translated by Ford Lewis Battles (Philadelphia: The Westminster Press, 1960), vol. I, p. 481.

Christian obligates himself to another in Christian love with regard to body
and blood. Thus as the body and blood of Christ became my body and
blood on the cross, so likewise shall my body and blood become the body
and blood of my neighbor, and in time of need theirs become my body and
blood, or we cannot boast at all to be Christians. That is the will of Christ in
the Supper.

> Balthasar Hubmaier, *Several Theses... To All Christians Concerning
> the Instruction of the Mass* (1525)[15]

Three years after publishing this treatise, Balthasar Hubmaier was himself martyred: captured, tortured, and burned at the stake; his wife, a
stone around her neck, thrown into the Danube River. Few of the first
generation of Anabaptists had the luxury of developing their thought on
the body of Christ over years. In contrast to Zwingli, Karlstadt, Luther,
Martin Bucer, and Calvin, each of whom wrote extensively, over years, on
the Gospel text, many of their Anabaptist contemporaries left but tantalizing traces of their understanding of that one word. But such writings
as survive suggest that Anabaptists held fundamentally different understandings – in the plural – of Christ's body than other evangelicals had
articulated. They also suggest Anabaptists broadly shared among themselves what we might now call a metaphorical understanding of Christ's
body: The same word, for them, brought together their own persons, the
community of all faithful, and Christ. Christ's "body" was not bounded
in the ways it was for Zwingli, nor was it "there" in the same way as it was
for Luther, but, for those moved by the Holy Spirit – the third person
of the Christian trinity so centrally important to Anabaptists – body and
blood united Christ and his followers, as Hubmaier said, shortly before
his own death, in sacrifice and martyrdom, as well as in communion. For
him, martyrdom, the breaking of the body and the shedding of blood,
was inseparable from communion.

"blood"

Over time, out of concern that Christ's sacred blood might be spilled, the
medieval Church had come, in its terms, to "reserve the chalice." Over
time, the Church permitted only the religious, its definition, to receive
the chalice with its sacred blood. The laity were permitted to receive

[15] Balthasar Hubmaier, "Several Theses by Dr. Paltus Fridberger of Waldshut To all Chris-
tians concerning the instruction of the mass, 1525," *Balthasar Hubmaier: Theologian of
Anabaptism*, edited and transalted by H. Wayne Pipkin and John. H. Yoder (Scottsdale,
PA: Herald Press, 1989), pp. 75–6.

the host, which the priest had broken into pieces – symbolizing Christ's body broken – but not the chalice. In the sixteenth century, lay men and women said the Church "withheld" the chalice – a term that speaks to the spiritual power of the event. They wanted both body and blood.

And as evangelicals debated the "body" in the Gospel narrative, they reunited body and blood: Their focus, more often than not, was the body, but the body was not, for them, a thing apart from the blood. The medieval separation of host and chalice, evangelicals preached, was unnecessary; for some, it was yet another manifestation of clerical arrogance, "withholding" that which should belong to all. All evangelicals called for both the bread and the wine to be offered to the faithful. All agreed that the medieval Church had arbitrarily divided what the Gospel text did not: Christ offered both bread and wine to his disciples.

> The more detestable is the fabrication of those who, not content with Christ's priesthood, have presumed to sacrifice him anew! The papists attempt this each day, considering the Mass as the sacrificing of Christ.
> John Calvin, *Institutes of the Christian Religion*, Book II, Chapter XV[16]

In reuniting bread and wine, evangelicals elided the material distinction the medieval Church had made in the Mass between body and blood. That rejection was twinned with their rejection of the medieval understanding of the Mass as "a sacrifice," a sacrifice that, following medieval teaching, the priest reenacted with each Mass. Evangelicals all rejected, on the same principle of the divide between divine perfection and human sinfulness, the notion that a living human being could in any way capture Christ's "sacrifice." For them, that sacrifice was "once for all time." Christ's divinity made of his death a singular, extraordinary, supranatural, and inimitable act – human beings were mortal, death was normal for each and every human being. God had chosen to die, and to die "for all humankind." For no evangelicals could or should Christ's sacrifice be reenacted in worship services.

As Hubmaier suggested, "blood" was no esoteric notion. As the persecution, prosecution, execution, and exile of religious minorities intensified, the "blood" of the Last Supper acquired not new valences – there had been Christian martyrs from the apostles forward – but a density of referents: friends, family, "brothers and sisters in Christ," who had been decapitated, hacked into pieces, executed, their own spilled blood through those acts of violence flowing into Christ's. For many Christians,

---

[16] Calvin, *Institutes*, vol. I, p. 503.

in western and eastern hemispheres, "the cup" had been "passed," the blood of his faithful a living testimony to Christ's own blood.

"is"

> We know, however, that these words, "This is my body," etc. are clear and lucid. Whether a Christian or a heathen, a Jew or a Turk hears them, he must acknowledge that they speak of the body of Christ which is in the bread. How otherwise could the heathen and the Jews mock us, saying that the Christians eat their God, if they did not understand this text clearly and distinctly? When the believer grasps and the unbeliever despises that which is said, however, this is due not to the obscurity or the clarity of the words, but to the hearts that hear it.
>
> Martin Luther, *Confession Concerning Christ' Supper*, 1528[17]

If evangelicals divided on the relationship between their own bodies and Christ's, they severed relations with one another – relations that princes and city councils were seeking to preserve in order to present a united front to Habsburg power – over the smallest word, "is." All evangelicals rejected the doctrine of transubstantiation, in which the bread which had been in that place was changed into the body, which now occupied the same space. All but Karlstadt agreed that "this" referred to the bread – Karlstadt resolved the mystery of the sentence, "for this is my body," by arguing that Christ pointed to his own body when he spoke aloud the word, "this." And it was a mystery. Or a puzzle. As evangelical after evangelical recognized, by any measure of human experience, the sentence made no sense. How could "this," bread, be, that word, "is," Christ's "body"? How could "this," a cup of wine, be "my blood"? Hence Luther's rejection of all scientific explanations. And yet, Christ had said, according to the Gospel text, the Word of God, exactly that. For all, Catholic and evangelical alike, that tiny word, "is," marked the relationship between matter and God. At Marburg, Luther and Zwingli broke permanently over that one small word.

> In the first place, the holy council teaches and openly and without qualification professes that, after the consecration of the bread and the wine, our lord Jesus Christ, true God and true man, is truly, really and substantially contained in the propitious sacrament of the holy eucharist under the appearance of those things which are perceptible to the senses.
>
> Chapter 1, Decree on the most holy sacrament of the eucharist, Session 13, Council of Trent, 11 October 1551[18]

---

[17] Martin Luther, "Confession Concerning Christ's Supper, 1528," p. 272.
[18] *Decrees of the Ecumenical Councils*, vol. II, p. 693.

For medieval Christians, following the decree of the Fourth Lateran Council, and for Catholics, following the 1551 decree of the Council of Trent, "is" marked a transition from the world of mundane matter to God's Incarnation. By 1500, theologians had developed a complex doctrine to explain what "happened" on the altar. Drawing on concepts the Greek philosopher Aristotle had developed long before Christianity, they distinguished the "accidents" – outward attributes such as color, texture, shape, weight, dimension – from "substance," the essence of a thing. Thus, as the priest spoke the words, the substance of the bread became, was changed into, the substance of Christ's body; the substance of the wine was changed into the substance of Christ's blood; and the accidents of bread and wine, and particularly the bread – its shape, texture, weight – remained, but they were only "accidents," not essential. For Catholics, in other words, Christ was "really" there, his real body, his real blood, on the altar immediately after the words were spoken – even as the appearance of wafer and wine abided. Outward appearance and inner reality could be separated from one another. Matter could change from mundane to divine in an instant.

> All right, I will show that the words "This is my body" must be understood figuratively. Listen to John 6. Christ speaks here to the Jews and also to his disciples of the eating of his body and the drinking of his blood. When they, understanding it as bodily eating, shuddered, he answered, "It is the spirit that giveth life, the flesh profiteth nothing." Thus it is clear that he dismissed once and for all the carnal eating of his body.
> Johannes Oecolampadius, Marburg Colloquy, 1529[19]

For Johannes Oecolampadius and Zwingli, as for Karlstadt, given their particular sense of the materiality of Christ's body – its dimension, its location – "this" could not equal the bread. It was physically impossible: Whereas bread, that common matter, could be everywhere human beings gathered, the single body of God Incarnate could only be in one place at any one time, and that body was, as the Apostles' Creed taught, at the right hand of God the Father. For Zwingli and Oecolampad, the puzzle was resolved through a different understanding of "is." Zwingli and Oecolampad argued that "is" did not mark an equality: bread ≠ body. No, they argued, "is" served to designate a "symbol": Christ had designated bread and wine as symbols of his body and blood. For them, and for Churches, such as the Anglican Church, influenced by this resolution of the puzzle, Christ's body was no longer to be found on earth, but

[19] *The Reformation in its Own Words*, p. 158.

he had designated for the faithful material signs that, with the study of God's Word, acquired powerful content and connotations. For Zwingli, taking those signs into one's person "nourishes the spirit," in ways directly parallel to the ways food nourishes the body.

> In the year following [1525] it occurred to me, as often as I handled the bread and wine in the mass, that they were not the flesh and blood of the Lord. I thought that the devil was suggesting this so that he might separate me from my faith. I confessed it often, sighed, and prayed; yet I could not come clear of the ideas.
>
> Menno Simons, *Reply to Gellius Faber*, 1554[20]

> Secondly, that the real body of Christ the Lord is not present in the sacrament...
>
> Michael Sattler, Confession before the Court of Ensisheim, 1527[21]

Anabaptists shared with Oecolampadius, Zwingli, and Karlstadt the conviction that Christ's physical body was not there. They were wary, however, of formulations drawn from literary study. The bread and wine remained for Anabaptists simple foodstuffs that Christ had designated his followers to "take," "eat" or "drink" in remembrance of him. For them, the presence of the Holy Spirit, who was there among the faithful, transformed not the things themselves, but the meaning of the eating. For them, Christ had brought the mundane world of the simplest material things into a world of spiritual meaning, for those illumined by the Holy Spirit. The matter remained what it was, bread and wine, but for those moved by the Holy Spirit, eating it placed them at Christ's table.

> I do not ask how Christ is God and man and how these natures can be united. God can do more than our imagination presumes. One must accept the Word of God. It is up to you to prove that the body of Christ is not here, when the Word says, "This is my body"! I do not want to hear reason. Carnal and geometrical arguments I repudiate altogether... God is above all mathematics. The words of God are to be adored and observed with awe. God commands, "Take, eat; this is my body." I desire a persuasive proof from sacred Scripture.
>
> (Luther writes the words 'This is my body' with chalk on the table and covers the table with the cloth.)
>
> Martin Luther, The Marburg Colloquy, 1529[22]

---

[20] Menno Simons, "Reply to Gellius Faber," in *The Reformation in its Own Words*, p. 267.
[21] *Martyrs' Mirror*, p. 465, in *The Reformation in its Own Words*, p. 239.
[22] Excerpts from a reconstruction of the proceedings of the Marburg Colloquy, *The Reformation in its Own Words*, pp. 156–7.

Luther rejected all efforts to make the words of the Gospel text fit human understanding. For him, the faithful were to listen to God's Word, to seek understanding, not impose it. For Luther, God could be wherever and whenever he willed, as Luther said, again and again; this was the testimony of Scripture. If Christ said, this is my body, then this is my body, an equation that exceeded human understanding. Luther rejected the doctrine of transubstantiation on the grounds that the biblical text did not call for a transformation of substance. Christ's real body and blood, Luther argued, were "in, around, and under" the bread and the wine – both were present at the same time in the same space. Both substances. Faith and faith alone could grasp the mystery of that coexistence in space and time – reason, science, experience could never make sense of that sentence.

> Blame not on eyes the error of the mind
>
> Lucretius
>
> Quoted in Michel de Montaigne, "Apology for Raymond Sebond"[23]

Each evangelical position called attention to the witnessing Christian. In the same years, accounts of the New World were circulating. Most immediately, those accounts problematized European understandings of "body": Were European bodies the same as the bodies of the western hemisphere? In substance, if not in appearance? More deeply, they called into question the relationship among the seen world, the seeing eye, and the human mind. In debates on both sides of the Atlantic, Europeans confronted directly fundamentally volatile questions: What makes that form I see "human"? Is the texture of hair, a tactile and visual value, a mark determining "humanity," or is it, following Aristotle, simply an accident, something superficial? Is the green that I am seeing the same as the green that absent eyes are imagining? Does "human" name the same thing in both hemispheres? All these questions placed attention on the witnessing human being: his or her eyes, his or her mind, his or her perception.

It is possible that Reformation might have occurred without the Encounter. We shall never know. But the two reverberated powerfully. Would the word "body" have proven as volatile, had not Taino bodies called attention to human bodies? Would the relationship set by the medieval doctrine of transubstantiation been challenged so widely and

---

[23] Michel de Montaigne, "Apology for Raymond Sebond," *The Complete Essays of Montaigne*, translated Donald M. Frame (Stanford: Stanford University Press, 1976), Book II, Chapter 12, p. 446.

so effectively – it had been challenged before, but not so effectively – had not Europeans questioned the reality of what their eyes were seeing? These questions may never be answered, but they provide the necessary backdrop for approaching Calvin's difficult conceptualization of the relationship between God and matter.

> For this reason, the apostle, in that very passage where he calls the worlds the images of things invisible, adds that through faith we understand that they have been fashioned by God's word [Heb. 11:3]. He means by this that the invisible divinity is made manifest in such spectacles, but that we have not the eyes to see this unless they be illumined by the inner revelation of God through faith.
> John Calvin, *Institutes of the Christian Religion*, Book I, Chapter V[24]

Calvin posited a notion of "sign," explicitly taking up Augustine's term. Lutherans, then and now, found in it the same notion of "symbol" Zwingli had articulated. They did not hear, perhaps could not hear, because of the fundaments of their own thinking, what, for Calvin, the "signs" encompassed. Calvin came to his notion of "sign" in the *Institutes* after he had laid out his understanding of human perception, most centrally to his conceptualization of "sign," his argument that human eyes were enabled to see revelation in the physical and material world through God-given faith. That sense of being able to see God where others could not, which became so central to Reformed Christians' sense of themselves in the world, informed Calvin's approach to those puzzling sentences.

> the sacred mystery of the Supper consists in two things: physical signs, which, thrust before our eyes, represent to us, according to our feeble capacity, things invisible; and spiritual truth, which is at the same time represented and displayed through the symbols themselves.
> John Calvin, *Institutes of the Christian Religion*, Book IV, Chapter XVII[25]

For Calvin, the content of the signs was inseparable from the witnessing Christian – in this he broke with medieval doctrine. But the witnessing Christian could not simply find the meaning of the signs in Scripture – for Calvin, in contrast to Zwingli, the Gospel text was anything but clear or transparent in its meaning. For him, understanding the relationship of "this" to "my body," and "this cup" to "my blood" was a process in which the Christian became able, over time, to see the spiritual truth "which is at the same time represented and displayed through the symbols

---

[24] Calvin, *Institutes*, vol. I, p. 68.
[25] Calvin, *Institutes*, vol. II, pp. 1371.

themselves." Calvin, in other words, rejected both the medieval division of appearance from reality and Zwingli's notion that material signs were a thing apart from the world of the spirit. For Calvin, God revealed himself in and through the material world.

Calvin's understanding of the "signs" of the Supper transformed the Reformed sense of the world: God revealed himself, and through faith, which God alone gave to humankind, human beings could discern God in the world. Calvin directed Reformed eyes outward: to look at God's splendor, to seek God in the visible world, to discern God in the heavens and on the earth. For Calvin, seeing God in the world did not occur instantly, but over time. Receiving the bread and the wine, over time, nourished a Christian's ability to understand the sentence; understanding the sentence was a process, not a toggle switch, on or off; and with understanding came a changed perception of the world – as God-filled and divinely ordered. That sense, which Calvin articulated, "Christ grows in us and we in him," posited a different relationship between God and humankind, in which matter helped humankind come to a deeper understanding of Incarnation. The mystery of the sentence, for Calvin, was complex, inviting Christians into a lifelong engagement with the deeper meaning of Incarnation. Christ's signs, so seemingly simple, were the material entry into the mystery of Incarnation.

Calvin's sense of the "sign" underwent changes in specific Reformed communities. For Scots Reformed, for instance, the "sign" became that to which members of the community, who had been examined beforehand, had access. Most Reformed communities were concerned that those who participated in the Supper brought neither a Lutheran understanding of the words nor, more horrifyingly, a Catholic understanding of the words. Because the words, for Reformed Christians, acquired their meaning within the witnessing Christian, "this," "my body," "this cup," and "my blood" were not mere words, but cognitively complex "signs" whose content was as somatically real as anything in the world. Thus, for Reformed Christians, could Catholics be cannibals: If they hold in their minds, as Léry said of Villegagnon and Cointa, that "the words 'This is my Body; this is my Blood' cannot be taken other than to mean that the Body and Blood of Jesus Christ are contained therein," then indeed "like the savages named Ouetaca . . . they wanted to chew and swallow it raw."[26]

[26] Léry, *History of a Voyage to the Land of Brazil*, p. 41.

"This do"

On Christmas 1521, Karlstadt offered the first evangelical communion. In plain dress, without vestments, "Brother Andrew" read not the Canon, but the Gospel text, not quietly in Latin, but loudly in German. He did not elevate bread or wine. He eliminated all references to sacrifice. He offered both bread and wine to all congregants.

When evangelicals turned to instituting collective worship based on Scripture, they agreed on many aspects of the Mass they rejected and held to be "abuses." They offered both bread and wine to congregants. They turned to face the congregation. Most shed whatever clerical vestments they might have had and wore the simple black robes of a scholar of Holy Scripture. As evangelicals dismantled the dense aggregate of practices in the Mass, they confronted the question: What is the relationship among Christ, his command, "this do," and the living community of Christians?

All evangelicals agreed that the priest could not stand for Christ – that the "doing" of the command in the present was not a point of identification between Christ and the human actor. If, for Catholics, the priest remained a living connection to the person of Christ – his clothing, gestures, and office linking him to the living Christ – all evangelicals rejected the role that the Fourth Lateran Council had accorded priests. Christ, evangelicals taught, was not present through any continuum of action or office.

The human role in communion, evangelicals agreed, was narrator of sacred text, not agent for sacred action. They called those who would "administer" the sacrament of communion "ministers" – rejecting anything that might imply that the living human actor approximated Christ. Those who would come to be called Anglicans retained vestments, as a part of the singular dignity of the worship service, but they, too, acknowledged an essential divide between humankind and Christ. There was and is no evangelical counterpart to the Catholic missal, a text intended to provide not simply the words the priest is to read, but direction for the enactment: when the priest is to speak quietly; when he is to chant; when to speak words so that they are heard; when he is to kneel; when he is to bless; when he is to elevate the host, the chalice; when the priest is to face the altar; when he is to face the congregation. For Catholics, those who had been ordained – undergone the sacrament – in their persons, the precise sequence of movement and word, recalled the person of Christ, as priest, embodied him, as priest. The Anglican Book of Common Prayer comes closest to the missal, but its model was a prayerbook. For evangelicals, the divide between humankind and God severed the realm of human action from divinity.

Evangelicals agreed that the "do" encompassed the leader among the congregation, pastor or minister, taking bread and then a cup of wine into his hands. Only the Anabaptists allowed the possibility that a woman could lead in the celebration of communion. All evangelicals agreed that the bread, and then the cup, were to be passed. Anabaptists allowed for anyone to do the passing; other evangelicals held that the pastor or minister, with designated assistants or deacons, distributed the bread, then the cup. Most also agreed that Christ had blessed the bread and the cup. Most agreed that the minister should break the bread – and make explicit the connection between Christ's broken body and the gesture of breaking the bread.

Beyond that, however, evangelicals did not agree. Luther held much of the Mass to be an ancient rite of thanksgiving. Its complexity did not trouble him. That same complexity troubled Calvin very much, who urged "simplicity" in the practice of collective worship.

> Third. In the breaking of the bread we are of one mind and are agreed as follows: All those who wish to break one bread in remembrance of the broken body of Christ, and all who wish to drink of one drink as a remembrance of the shed blood of Christ, shall be united beforehand by baptism in one body of Christ which is the church of God and whose Head is Christ.
> The Schleitheim Confession of Faith, 1527[27]

The Churches' practices ranged from the Anabaptist breaking of bread to the Mass. Over the course of its deliberations, the Council of Trent affirmed the doctrinal fundaments of the Mass – the ordination of priests, the doctrines of transubstantiation and the sacrifice of the Mass. When it closed, in 1563, it called for a single missal, one text, to be used in every church, in every parish, in every diocese, around the globe. The Mass, no matter where it was celebrated, was to be uniform. It was to mark the same saints' days, the same liturgical calendar, to follow the annual cycle. Its complex parts were to be the same, whether the Mass was celebrated in Cuzco, Madeira, Goa, Brussels, Antwerp, or Cracow. And everywhere, the Mass was to be celebrated in Latin – wherever the Mass was celebrated, there was the Church universal.

[27] "The Schleitheim Confession of Faith (1527)," *The Protestant Reformation*, edited by Hans J. Hillerbrand (New York: Harper Torchbooks, 1968), pp. 131–2.

On the spectrum between the Mass's complex structure and Anabaptist breaking of bread lay the Lutheran German Mass or Supper and the Reformed Supper. Martin Luther allowed for wide variation in local practices – including the elevation and altar cloths – so long as the congregation heard the Gospel narrative. The Reformed Supper, like the Anabaptist breaking of bread, abandoned the Mass – its cadences, its movements, its actions – completely. Like the Anabaptists, Reformed Christian worship went back to the Gospel narrative and built from it – though Reformed Christians did not sit around a table, did not pass among themselves bread and a cup of wine. If they had a church, they celebrated their Supper there, ideally, beneath the pulpit. John Calvin, like Luther, allowed for local variation, which came to include a rail, for instance, in Scots Reformed churches, to separate the congregation from the table.

The sparse Gospel text, in fact, offered little guidance. No Church simply enacted the Gospel text. Most incorporated prayers at various points in the service: before, in preparation to receive communion, after. Most also brought the voices of congregants more fully into collective worship. Over time, Luther transposed a number of texts into hymns that Lutheran congregations might sing, transforming the cadences of the medieval rite into a service in which the men and women, increasingly in pews, participated far more fully. For both Anabaptists and Reformed Christians, the singing of members became a part of worship itself: psalms for Reformed Christians, songs passed from one conventicle to the next among Anabaptists.

Even as all evangelicals held the Last Supper to be an event of the past – a deep past at that point – their divergent understandings of Christ's person, of the relationship between his body and their own, and of the relationship between his person and the bread and wine led them to conceptualize the relationship between the doing and the living community of Christians divergently. One measure of their divergence was frequency of communion.

Since the Supper was instituted for us by our Lord to be frequently used, and also was so observed in the ancient Church until the devil turned everything upside down, erecting the mass in its place, it is a fault in need of correction, to celebrate it so seldom. [Add: For the present, let it be advised and ordained that it always be administered four times in the year.]

Hence it will be proper that it be always administered in the city once a month, in such a way that every three months it take place in each parish.

Besides, it should take place three times a year generally, that is to say at
Easter, Pentecost and Christmas in such a way that it not be repeated in the
parish in the month when it should take place by turn.

John Calvin, Draft Ecclesiastical Ordinances, 1541[28]

Following Fourth Lateran, medieval Christians were required to receive
communion only once a year. The most devout Christians could, depending on the priest and the endowment of Masses, receive communion
every day. Anabaptists, reading the text in ways so markedly different
from other evangelicals, took to heart the words, "as often as you do
this," breaking bread often. While there might be sermons multiple days
in a week in other evangelical congregations, communion was rarer. In
part, the frequency of communion depended on external factors, such
as political support and the presence of ministers who could administer
the sacrament "correctly" or "appropriately." In Geneva, for example,
Reformed communion was ultimately offered but four times a year. This
was not Calvin's wish – he held that communion was fundamental to
strengthening faith – but a political compromise.

But frequency was also a measure of something else. Over the 1520s,
it became clear to evangelical preachers that the Word was not going
to transform Christendom as soon as it was heard. It became clear that
those few words had opened a Pandora's Box of infinitely divergent
readings and understandings. The Last Supper went to the heart of how
Christians understood God Incarnate, Christ, to be among them in the
here-and-now. It was shaped by their understandings of his person, of the
relationship between Christ's body and theirs, of the world of matter and
its relationship to divinity, of God and his agency among humankind. In
the 1520s, as this preacher offered the bread and the wine but preserved
the chalice and the paten, that preacher offered bread and the wine in a
pewter cup, a third sat at a crude wooden table, a fourth stood before an
ancient marble altar, evangelicals heard more intensely Paul's warning
to the Corinthians:

Whoever, therefore, eats the bread or drinks the cup of the Lord in an
unworthy manner will be answerable for the body and blood of the Lord.
Examine yourselves, and only then eat of the bread and drink of the cup. For
all who eat and drink without discerning the body, eat and drink judgment
against themselves.

I Corinthians 11: 27–29

[28] "Draft Ecclesiastical Ordinances (1541)," *Calvin: Theological Treatises*, translated by J.K.S.
Reid (Philadelphia: The Westminster Press, 1954) pp. 66–7.

All, Catholic and Protestant alike, heard the great spiritual danger in eating and drinking "unworthily." Luther's translation of Paul's first letter to the Corinthians linked it to the Last Judgment – so great was the sin one risked. The King James English Bible of 1611, which drew on Calvin's biblical translations, rendered the final sentence "For hee that eateth and drinketh unworthily, eateth and drinketh damnation to himselfe, not discerning the Lord's body." Evangelicals agreed that Christians risked their souls in eating and drinking "unworthily." They disagreed on what Paul's admonition meant for communities of the faithful, foremost, how to define "worthiness."

For Anabaptists, only those who were "redeemed" – those who had, through choosing baptism again, demonstrated their membership in the "body of Christ" – could break bread, eat the bread, drink the wine. For Luther and Calvin, communion should be offered to "the weak" in faith in order "to strengthen" that faith. Understanding the nature of Christ's Incarnation and of his presence among the living community of Christians was inseparable from the growth of faith. Communion, they said, should not be withheld from the uncertain. But they invoked Paul, too, arguing that there was great danger in receiving the bread and wine, if one did not understand what one was receiving.

> Therfore if any of you be a blasphemer of God, an hinderer or slanderer of his worde, an adulterer, or be in malice or enuie, or in any other greuous cryme, bewaylle your synnes, and come not to this holy table: lest after the takynge of this holy sacrament, the diuell entre into you as he entred into Iudas, and fill you full of all iniquities, and bring you, to destruction, bothe of bodye and soule.
> John Knox, Service Book for the English Congregation in Geneva, 1556[29]

Ultimately, the Scots Reformed Church divided its congregations between those who had been examined and who would approach the table with correct understanding, and those who had been found wanting in that correct understanding – they were to remain on the other side of the rail, spatially and spiritually divided from those who received communion.

> 11. If anyone says that faith alone is sufficient preparation for receiving the sacrament of the most holy eucharist: let him be anathema. And in order that so great a sacrament may not be received unworthily, and hence unto

---

[29] *The Liturgical Portions of the Genevan Service Book*, edited by William D. Maxwell (Edinburgh: Oliver and Boyd, 1931), p. 122.

death and condemnation, the holy council establishes and declares that, granted the availability of a confessor, those burdened by an awareness of mortal sin, however much they may feel themselves to be contrite, must first avail themselves of sacramental confession.

> Canons on the most holy sacrament and eucharist, Session 13, Council of Trent, 11 October 1551[30]

For evangelicals, "worthiness" was bound up with understanding: understanding the meaning of each of the words Christ spoke; understanding the relationships they set among Christ's body, the material world, and believing Christians; understanding what the Incarnation meant for living Christians. The medieval Church had not required of those who received the host that they understand correctly what it was they were receiving. It required of them that they confess, do penance, and receive absolution before approaching the altar. The Council of Trent strengthened that requirement, binding communion and the sacrament of penance together more directly. In the sixteenth century, first evangelical Churches, and then, increasingly, the Catholic Church came to require of those who would participate in communion that they be able to articulate, usually in the precise formula of that Church's catechism, the relationship between Christ's body and the elements: commemoration, consubstantiation, sign, transubstantiation. Each Church's catechism asked of each catechumen, each person seeking to become a member of that Church, to state the precise way in which Christ was "present" in that Church's sacrament of communion, before he or she could receive communion.

Presence

In the debates on "this is my body," "this is my blood," European understandings of "presence" proliferated. All Churches claimed the word for their own communion: For each, Christ was "present" when the words were spoken – though, as we have seen, they differed enormously on the nature of that presence. With the institution of Churches, divergent conceptualizations were catechized, preached, taught, and, for some Churches, the ability to articulate a conceptualization of presence became a prerequisite for participating in communion. It was necessary for each Christian to know the meaning of the words, of the doing, in

[30] *Decrees of the Ecumenical Councils*, vol. II, p. 697.

order for him or her to conceptualize correctly how Christ was present among his or her community.

There was not one understanding of "presence," but many, even as each Church used the same term, "real presence" to speak about Christ in their midst. For each, that "presence" could only be known, experienced, within the Church that taught it. For each, that "presence" bound all members of the Church together, across the face of the globe, bound them with the body and blood of Christ. "Where two or three are gathered in my name," there was Christ. For them, and them alone, Christ was "real."

For all Churches, as they experienced exile and displacement, communion could be offered anywhere: in private chapels, in fields, as well as in churches or temples. In the moment when the Gospel words were given breath, no matter where a Christian was, he or she knew God's presence – for him or her, a "real" presence, not some abstraction or sterile concept, but a complex physical and spiritual experience of God's nearness. God was there, in ways that set each Church apart from every other church. Each Church defined carefully and distinctively the nature of Christ's body and blood, the relationship of his body to the bread and wine, and the relationship of each human body both to the matter of the bread and wine and to Christ's body. Each Church defined for its faithful, for "true Christians" as it defined them, the precise relationships between God and humankind, God and matter.

For each Church, that understanding could be taught: preached, catechized, enforced and reinforced through Consistory or Inquisition. It was not geographically bounded, not located in any one place at all. It was not limited to one language, one country, even one hemisphere. That understanding resided in each "true Christian," who could live anywhere – France or Brazil, Cracow or Lima – and who was united with Christ and other Christians precisely in his or her understanding of those words and the relationships they defined.

And for each Church, Christ was absent among all those who held different understandings of the words. Not simply wrongly conceived. Absent. For each Church, at the center of every other Church was a void. Other Churches were "empty," their members, "empty": not merely "not Christian," or even, "not human," but empty of divine presence. And just as Luther had found Zwingli's understanding of "this is" "empty," or Catholics found Reformed Christians' understanding "empty," so, too, each Church came to find every other Church's enactment of "this do" "mere ritual" – actions empty of content. For each Church, their own doing was full – Christ was present. For each Church, what other Churches did was empty: of Christ, of content, of meaning. An empty ceremony, a ritual rather than Incarnation. And for each Church, the world divided between those who were nourished and those who were empty, between those for whom God was "real" and "present" and those who were truly "godless," between those in whom Christ grew and those who practiced cannibalism, the ultimate idolatry.

Conclusion

In 1567, Gerard Mercator published a map of the globe as two half-spheres divided and defined by water. Mercator had been born fifty-five years earlier, in 1512, in Rupelmonde, a small town on the River Scheldt south of Antwerp, in the Habsburg Netherlands. In 1544, the Inquisition Charles had authorized twenty-two years earlier had Mercator arrested and imprisoned in the dungeon of a local castle. It took his friends seven months to win his release. Mercator had published no evangelical treatises, preached from no pulpit or street corner. He was suspected of Lutheranism and so arrested and imprisoned. As with so many Europeans in the sixteenth century, the Reformation changed Mercator's life – arrest, imprisonment, and flight.

In fact, we know little about Mercator's belief. He wrote a short commentary on Paul's Letter to the Romans, rejecting John Calvin's understanding of predestination. He was, by his profession, a cartographer and globe maker, someone who sought to render the world in two and three dimensions. In the wake of his imprisonment, he fled his native land, like thousands of others, and found refuge in the Duchy of Cleves, where he never took citizenship – for nearly fifty years, Mercator had no legal home.

No leader of a Church, no hedge preacher, no pamphleteer, Mercator drew visions of Europe and of the world that fundamentally reoriented Europe in relationship to the world. It is to him that we owe the notion of two hemispheres – the sense not only of a globe, a sphere, but of something round that can be logically divided into halves, each of which is equal, rendered according to mathematical principles. His maps did not center on Jerusalem, as medieval maps had done, or on Europe, as Ptolemy's maps did; they visualized the globe as an abtract whole.

The call to order the world according to God's Word reached into thousands of lives. It was voiced on street corners, along roads, in workshops and courts; it was heard in villages and towns, fields and mountains, port cities and isolated alpine hamlets. It encompassed every human relationship: families, neighbors, residents of towns and villages, subjects and lords. Printed bibles and evangelical preachers catalyzed hundreds of visions, no one of which was fully realized, each one of which faced immediately differing understandings of what a world formed according to God's Word would be. By the end of the sixteenth century, there were many where there had been a myth of a universal Church. By the end of the century, the very word "Christian" could not be taken to connote the same things from one person to another, and the word's connotations for one could provoke terrifying violence in another.

The changes set in motion did not, for any of the participants, have their hoped for outcomes. But the world was changed. Fragmentation did not simply mean many Churches where there had been one. The radical divisions called into question so much that had seemed self-evident in 1500: marriage, family, kinship; motherhood and fatherhood; the ways in which authority temporal and ecclesiastical were inscribed on the landscape of Europe; the material world; the structuring of time; how God was present in the world. By 1600, within Europe, new conceptions of jurisdiction and subjecthood had been instituted. New definitions of marriage, in the plural, had been set in law. New families had been constituted. At the end of the sixteenth century, the harrowing fragmentation of medieval Christendom had engendered new ways of thinking about space, time, the material world, as well as what it meant to be a Christian in a world so much larger and stranger than it had been.

Space

By 1600, Europe was no longer "Christian." Some places were Lutheran, some, Catholic, some, Reformed. Even if we recognize them all as Christian, they did not. Some sovereigns still looked to Rome as the head of all Christendom. One was head of a church, of England, coterminous with her jurisdiction. Others governed lands where the Book of Concord linked their subjects to those who lived in other lands confessing the Augsburg Confession.

For individuals, the terrain was discontinuous, broken according to lines of jurisdiction that were themselves shifting, uncertain. By 1600, so many places had declared all but one kind of Christianity illegal

FIGURE C1. Rumoldus Mercator, after Gerardus Mercator, *Orbis terrae compendiosa descriptio*, 1587. Library of the University of Amsterdam.

within their borders, and those caught preaching or practicing another Christianity could face the same consequences as Jews had for centuries: expulsion, the loss of property, or a public and intentionally agonizing execution. For all Europeans, the European landscape was treacherous, at times, fatal.

Space no longer divided between temporal and spiritual swords. The spiritual sword was neither universal nor universally identical with the temporal sword. The two did not exist in the same relationship from place to place, nor had any place, as it turned out, found a new, stable balance between them. The Thirty Years' War, with its salted fields, burned churches, unearthed graveyards, orphans, raped widows, and starved populations, brought home the terrible volatility of contested jurisdictions and mutually exclusive understandings of true Christianity.

And as sovereigns accorded one kind of Christianity legal status, they confronted subjects who chose not to leave, who chose to live the legal religion publicly but who did not hold it true. Early modern sovereigns also confronted religious minorities in new ways: while Jews had been a religious minority in parts of Europe for centuries, all Christian minorities, save Anabaptists, had some place in Europe where their particular understanding of true Christianity was sovereign. Religious minorities constituted an uneasy presence in early modern domains: Their sense of membership in a transregional community of true Christians at once helped them withstand the coercive powers of any sovereign and linked them through spiritual kinship to other domains, other sovereigns.

For individual Christians, some places in Europe were Christian, some were not. The Christianity of the place depended very much on the Christianity of the person: Rome was not Christian for evangelicals; neither Wittenberg nor Geneva was Christian for Catholics. Someone who was considered Christian in Geneva was at great risk in Spain, where a Catholic monarch actively sought the eradication of all but Catholic Christianity. For each Christian, where one was born might prove fatal, strange shores might provide haven, even "home." "Christian" was not a familiar landscape, but wherever "two or three are gathered in my name." Indeed, the strangeness of place became inseparable, for thousands, from living their Christianity.

Fragmentation drove Europeans from their homes in unprecedented numbers – with no certain destinations and across an uncertain landscape. Exile was the experience of tens of thousands of Europeans, as governments sought to enforce religious conformity and as those same governments changed their Church, most dramatically in England during the middle of the sixteenth century. Places such as Geneva and London became centers of refugees, where the one thing people had in common was their Church – neither language nor work, neither family nor citizenship.

If exile was one common experience, another was mission. Catholics foremost, but also some Reformed Christians viewed the globe as offering unlimited opportunities for establishing true Christianity outside the boundaries of Europe. For Catholics, the globe was God's gift: If Europe was no longer uniformly or reliably Christian, the world was the theater for God's glory. Away from Europe, Catholics demonstrated the truth of their Christianity – through martyrdoms as well as conversions. If evangelicals were not at home in London or Leiden, they could buy passage on a ship for an alien shore.

Perhaps it is no more than coincidence, but Mercator's life and the lives of other cartographers suggest a more intimate relationship between Reformation and cartography. Certainly, the information that navigators were bringing back from their voyages across the Atlantic and then around the globe inspired cartographers to integrate all that they were hearing and learning into the maps they were drawing. But in the same years that Europeans were driven from their homes, in which some rulers withdrew their lands from the jurisdiction of Rome, cartographers were seeking a new representation of space itself. Though sixteenth-century cartographers still drew on the principles the Greek geographer and mathematician Ptolemy had developed, they used those principles to render a different vision of the world, in which Europe was no longer at center, but a small extension off an enormous land mass, across an expanse of ocean from two other, large masses of land that Ptolemy had never imagined. On the maps in circulation at the end of the century, any person could locate him- or herself using mathematical principles – without reference to theology or to Europe.

Time

In medieval Europe, bells had marked liturgical time, in which hours varied according to the length of a day, from place to place and season to season, but the same hour was marked with the same rhythms of prayer and chant in every place – no matter what the belief of different residents of that place, Jewish or skeptic, monk or mercenary. Diplomatic correspondence as well as laws, economic transactions as well as sentences of execution were all dated according to Christian time. With Reformation, some evangelicals silenced bells, others set them to new rhythms. The marking of the day, the week, and the year was no longer constant from place to place, but, following the divisions of the land, broken, discontinuous.

The different rhythms of worship made audible differences in thinking about time itself that had emerged in the sixteenth century. In medieval Europe, the religious and the laity had lived with one shared day of worship, in which devout laity joined the religious in churches, but their weeks had differed: For the laity, Sunday was a day of "rest," a day set aside from the work week, which the medieval Church asked them to devote to worship; for the religious, each day had time allocated for devotion. It was not that, in rejecting the notion of an oath, evangelicals rejected the religious' notion of time. Quite the contrary, John Calvin called for all faithful, not just a minority, to live their lives as spent constantly, in waking and sleeping, conscious of God. He shared with the cloistered Teresa of Ávila a sense that all time was God's. For them, and for those who shared a sense of God's attentiveness to human lives, time did not divide between work and worship; for them, all time was to be spent mindful of God, worshipful, no matter what one was doing. For Anabaptists, for those who were godly, no time was apart from God. For Luther, the faithful were to be mindful of God, at work as well as during formal worship, in the home as well as in church. While he did not share Calvin's or Teresa's sense of

God's scrutiny, he did share their sense that, for the faithful, no time was "secular," apart from God.

The Council of Trent called for a single, uniform liturgical calendar and a single uniform liturgy for all Catholics everywhere – for Catholics, the measurement as well as the valences of time were to be constant around the globe. The moments of liturgical time were to be marked, as they had always been, in reference to the sun in that place, and the day, week, and season were to be common among all Catholics. So, too, the liturgy everywhere was to share the same cadences, gestures, and words of the liturgy – recorded in a single text, the Roman Missal, that the pope had set. Even as Trent sought to preserve a universal sense of time, Catholic minorities knew, as their petitions testified, their time was no longer the only time, the relationship they held between time and worship not the only one.

Reformed Christians who embraced Calvin's vision of largely autonomous congregations did not necessarily share a liturgical calendar or a liturgy with other congregations. For them, time was set locally, reflecting a discontinuous sense of time as well as place. For them, "where two or three are gathered in my name," in that place, Christians lived in God's time. They gathered to worship together on Sundays, but as consistories and preachers reminded them, each day was spent under God's eyes, each waking moment was to honor God.

In no place, then, was time itself unexamined, its measurement, its division into units, its organization into "days," "weeks," "seasons," and "year" – the deep structures of human life – a given. In each place, the ringing or the silence of bells, as well as the rhythms of the ringing, marked a place that had chosen to structure time in one way and not another. And in 1582, when Pope Gregory XIII sought to introduce a calendar incorporating the astronomical discoveries of the century – a more accurate calendar than the Roman that had been used – countries divided bitterly and for more than a century. The Iberian Peninsula, some of Poland, and most of Italy adopted the calendar immediately. Great Britain, as it had become, did not adopt the calendar until 1752, and Greece, marking an even more ancient division, did not adopt it until 1923.

The fragmentation of time could not hold in a world in motion. Exiled Christians might travel from place to place and live in that place's particular temporal rhythms and measurements, but merchants, diplomats, and others who traveled as a matter of course needed a means to measure time – hours, days, months, and years – constant from place to place. They had drawn on Christian time before the sixteenth century, but hourglasses and mechanical clocks, which pre-dated the sixteenth century, offered a way to measure time in units set by mathematics and mechanics. Over time, church bells were set to mechanical clocks, to a sense of time defined by mathematics, not theology. Much later, countries recognized the necessity of a single calendar, of common leap years and added days.

As with cartography, the sixteenth century witnessed a proliferation of thinking about time itself. It was not simply evangelical chroniclers' sense of time ruptured and of two parallel times of revelation, or Catholic chroniclers' lineages of tradition. In the sixteenth and seventeenth centuries, some grappled with the import of Aztec and Inka calendars. Others, such as Mercator, sought to construct chronologies that encompassed all human history – to build a sense of time at once cognizant of Christian time and apart from it. For them, time could be understood not as a broken line, but a continuous line, from a beginning to the present day, and all human events had a place on that line: the classical texts, Jesus, Paul, Columbus.

Matter

In medieval Europe, each church owned relics. These physical remains of a saint – his or her bones or clothing, now fragmented into a femur, a knucklebone, a skull – or a splinter of the cross on which Jesus had died, or a thorn from his crown, these things were the material locus for holiness, and the place, in owning them, was more intensely sacred. Christians traveled to touch, to look at, to be near these material remains, to connect somatically with holy lives and embodied sanctity.

By 1600, some places had thrown out all their relics, smashed and melted down their reliquaries, removed or stilled all but one altar, which was now the site of a very different understanding of worship. In 1600, other places were adding relics, building an ever denser site of sacred presence, increasing the altars and the Masses celebrated at them. For each, the other place was blasphemous, a site of idolatry, there in the landscape of Europe.

It was not simply that for every Christian, God was to be found some places, but not others. Nor was it simply the relationship between matter and divinity. For Catholics, matter could be a site for the greater presence of sanctity. For Anabaptists especially, matter was simply matter, but God had sanctified the world. For Lutherans, matter could, at best, aid in education. For Reformed Christians, the material world divided between human-made and divinely made: Art was essentially different from nature, its origins in human hands severing it from any revelation of any kind.

And with this fragmentation of thinking about matter came a proliferation of understandings of "representation" – the relationship among matter and the mind's eye, between matter and revelation. For Catholics, an image still could link the mind to God. For Reformed Christians, an image was a human thing, severed from God in all but the God-given talent that had guided the hand. For Catholics, the crisis of hermeneutics – the rending loss of a shared reading of Scripture – led, in the Council of Trent, to the assertion of control over interpretation, which had consequences for Catholics such as Galileo. For Reformed Christians, God was visible in the natural world; faith, not the sacrament of ordination, enabled the human eye to see the divine ordering.

By the end of the sixteenth century, all Churches recognized explicitly that the meaning of material things was not something self-evident. For some, the habit of a Franciscan signaled the poverty of Christ; for others, it signaled human arrogance; and when that habit was carried to the western hemisphere, as Franciscans found, it signaled still other meanings to those who had not grown up in a European landscape. For all, meaning depended on the eye of the viewer, which might or might not be enabled to see the meaning of an object, a structure, a color, a shape. For all, eyes were to be educated so that they might be able to discern the meaning that was no longer self-evident. Words were to teach eyes.

Each Church called things of other Churches "idols" – altars or tables, chalices or rude cups, images or blank walls – binding the world of Europe to the largely unknown and deeply strange world of the western hemisphere. Things, placed in ancient structures generations ago, now linked those places to the other world, where "barbarians" and "savages" sacrificed human beings to their violent gods. Any person might practice idolatry – the false understanding of God's relationship to the material world. Any person, in any place. Both hemispheres, as in Mercator's spatial representation, were home to idolatry, even as both were home to Christians. The meaning of matter was not anchored to any one place; its meaning resided in the eyes of its beholder.

Incarnation

With Reformation, "Christian" came to mean something very different: no longer a person baptized in a place of ancient churches and practices, but a person who entered the world, anywhere, in one way and not others. Europeans as well as people of the western hemisphere could be idolaters. Europeans as well as people of the western hemisphere could be barbarians, offering sacrifices to idols. Europeans as well as people of the western hemisphere could be cannibals. And Europeans as well as people of the western hemisphere could be Christian. By 1600, Christians were defined not by the language they spoke or the places of their birth, but by signs: clothing, food, practices, forms of worship. Jesuits could be Italian or Spanish, Goan or Chinese by birth, but joined in the union of hearts and minds. Cannibals as well as Catholics could become Reformed Christians.

For the next five centuries, the Churches formed in the Reformation grappled with the relationship between nature and Christian, on so many different levels. But in the battle for souls in the sixteenth century, a Tupi was Christian as one's Catholic neighbor was not, if the Tupi understood the horror of eating God – the Tupi was human, the Catholic was not. As Jesuits worked to convert the peoples of the western and southern hemispheres, the images they offered people in different places incorporated familiar faces: black virgins and indigenous saints. For each Church, its God worked through human beings; its God chose the instruments of divine revelation. A European face could be Christian or cannibal; a strange face could be a brother or sister in Christ. Visual familiarity did not signal spiritual affinity, and spiritual kinship bound persons from each hemisphere to persons they had never seen.

When Gian Lorenzo Bernini completed the piazza before Saint Peter's Basilica in Rome, he surrounded the space in which the faithful gathered with monumental figures of martyrs from around the globe. Martyrdom could take place anywhere on the surface of the earth. Even as each Church continued to struggle with the relationship of its converts from other parts of the globe to the body of the faithful, each embraced its martyrs, no matter where they were born, and celebrated their conversions as testimony to the Church's universal truth and God's global glory.

It was no longer possible, in 1600, to speak of "the Christian religion" as a kind of shorthand for the great majority of Europeans. The Christian religion differed in its referents, its content, depending on the person using the term. For all Europeans, "religion" was no longer marked by a simple fact of baptism – as it had served to distinguish the medieval legal categories of "the Christian religion" and "the Jewish religion" – nor was it restricted among Christians to those who took vows. In a fragmented world, one carried a sense of space, time, matter, person, and God that bound one essentially to others across the surface of an alien and treacherous world.

Selected Bibliography

Benedict, Philip. *Christ's Churches Purely Reformed: A Social History of Calvinism.* New Haven: Yale University Press, 2002.

Bireley, Robert. *The Refashioning of Catholicism, 1450–1700.* New York: MacMillan, 1999.

Blickle, Peter. *The Revolution of 1525: The German Peasants' War from a New Perspective.* Thomas A. Brady, Jr. and H.C. Erik Midelfort, trans. Baltimore: The Johns Hopkins University Press, 1981.

Blockmans, Wim. *Emperor Charles V: 1500–1558.* London: Arnold, 2002.

Boutry, Philippe, Pierre Antoine Fabre, and Dominique Julia, eds. *Reliques modernes: Cultes et usages chréiens des corps saints des Réformes aux révolutions.* 2 vols. Paris: Éditions de l'École des hautes études en sciences sociales, 2009.

Bouwsma, William. *Calvin: A Sixteenth-Century Portrait.* Oxford: Oxford University Press, 1988.

Boyle, Marjorie O'Rourke. *Erasmus on Language and Method in Theology.* Toronto: University of Toronto Press, 1977.

Brady, Thomas A. *German Histories in the Age of Reformations, 1400–1650.* Cambridge: Cambridge University Press, 2009.

Brady, Thomas A. *Turning Swiss: Cities and Empire, 1450–1550.* Cambridge: Cambridge University Press, 1985.

Bynum, Caroline Walker. *Wonderful Blood: Theology and Practice in Late Medieval Northern Germany and Beyond.* Philadelphia: University of Pennsylvania Press, 2007.

Cavallo, Guglielmo and Roger Chartier, eds. *Histoire de la lecture dans le monde occidental.* Rome-Bari: Giuseppe Laterza & Figli Spa, 1995.

Chartier, Roger. *Inscrire et effacer: Culture écrite et littéature (XIe-XVIIIe sièle).* Paris: Gallimard Seuil, 2005.

Chrisman, Miriam Usher. *Conflicting Visions of Reform: German Lay Propaganda Pamphlets, 1519–1530.* Atlantic Highlands: Humanities Press, 1996.

Christian, Jr., William A. *Local Religion in Sixteenth-Century Spain.* Princeton: Princeton University Press, 1989.

Coster, Will and Andrew Spicer, eds. *Sacred Space in Early Modern Europe.* Cambridge: Cambridge University Press, 2005.

Crick, Julia, and Alexandra Walsham, eds. *The Uses of Script and Print, 1300–1700*. Cambridge: Cambridge University Press, 2004.

Crouzet, Denis. *Les Guerriers de Dieu*. 2 vols. Seyssel: Champ Vallon, 1990.

Cummings, Brian. *The Literary Culture of the Reformation: Grammar and Grace*. Oxford: Oxford University Press, 2002.

van Deursen, A. Th. *Bavianen en Slijkgeuzen*. 3rd ed. Franeker: Uitgeverij Van Wijnen, 1998.

Dickens, A.G., and John M. Tonkin. *The Reformation in Historical Thought*. Oxford: Blackwell, 1985.

Diefendorf, Barbara. *Beneath the Cross: Catholics and Huguenots in Sixteenth-Century Paris*. Oxford: Oxford University Press, 1991.

Dixon, C. Scott, and Luise Schorn-Schüte, eds. *The Protestant Clergy of Early Modern Europe*. Basingstoke: Palgrave Macmillan, 2003.

Duffy, Eamon. *The Stripping of the Altars: Traditional Religion in England 1400–1580*. New Haven: Yale University Press, 1992.

Dyrness, William A. *Reformed Theology and Visual Culture: The Protestant Imagination from Calvin to Edwards*. Cambridge: Cambridge University Press, 2004.

Ehrstine, Glenn. *Theater, Culture, and Community in Reformation Bern, 1523–1555*. Leiden: Brill, 2002.

Elliott, J.H. *Empires of the Atlantic World: Britain and Spain in America 1492–1830*. New Haven: Yale University Press, 2006.

Estenssoro Fuchs, Juan Carlos. *Del paganismo a la santidad: la incorporación de los indios del Perú al catolicismo, 1532–1750*. Lima: IFEA Instituto Francés de Estudios, 2003.

Finney, Paul Corby, ed. *Seeing Beyond the Word: Visual Arts and the Calvinist Tradition*. Grand Rapids: Wm. B. Eerdmans Publishing, 1999.

Gelderblom, Arie-Jan, Jan L. de Jong and Marc Van Vaeck, eds. *The Low Countries as a Crossroads of Religious Beliefs*. Leiden: Brill, 2004.

Gordon, Bruce, ed. *Protestant History and Identity in Sixteenth-Century Europe*. 2 vols. Aldershot: Ashgate, 1996.

Grafton, Anthony, with April Shelford and Nancy Siraisi. *New Worlds, Ancient Texts: The Power of Tradition and the Shock of Discovery*. Cambridge, MA: Belknap Press, 1992.

Gregory, Brad. *Salvation at Stake: Christian Martyrdom in Early Modern Europe*. Cambridge, MA: Harvard University Press, 1999.

Grell, Ole Peter, ed. *The Scandinavian Reformation: From Evangelical Movement to Institutuionalisation of Reform*. Cambridge: Cambridge University Press, 1995.

Israel, Jonathan. *The Dutch Republic: Its Rise, Greatness, and Fall 1477–1806*. Oxford: Clarendon, 1995.

Kaplan, Debra. *Beyond Expulsion: Jews, Christians, and Reformation Strasbourg*. Stanford: Stanford University Press, 2011.

Kaufmann, Thomas. *Türkenbüchlein: Zur christlichen Wahrnehmung türkischer Religion in Spämittelalter und Reformation*. Göttingen: Vandenhoeck & Ruprecht, 2008.

Kelley, Donald R. *The Beginning of Ideology: Consciousness and Society in the French Reformation*. Cambridge: Cambridge University Press, 1983.

Kingdon, Robert M. *Adultery and Divorce in Calvin's Geneva.* Cambridge, MA: Harvard University Press, 1995.

Kingdon, Robert. *Myths about the Saint Bartholomew's Day Massacres, 1572–1576.* Cambridge, MA: Harvard University Press, 1988.

Lara, Jaime. *City, Temple, Stage: Eschatological Architecture and Liturgical Theatrics in New Spain.* Notre Dame: University of Notre Dame Press, 2004.

Luebke, David M., ed. *The Counter-Reformation: The Essential Readings.* Oxford: Blackwell, 1999.

MacCormack, Sabine. *Religion in the Andes: Vision and Imagination in Early Colonial Peru.* Princeton: Princeton University Press, 1991.

Martin, John Jeffries. *Venice's Hidden Enemies: Italian Heretics in a Renaissance City.* Berkeley: University of California Press, 2003.

Matheson, Peter. *The Imaginative World of the Reformation.* Minneapolis: Fortress Press, 2001.

Matheson, Peter. *The Rhetoric of the Reformation.* Edinburgh: T & T Clark, 1998.

Melion, Walter. "The Art of Vision in Jerome Nadal's *Adnotationes et Meditationes in Evangelia.*" Introduction to *Annotations and Meditations on the Gospels.* vol. I: The Infancy Narratives. Frederick A. Homann, S.j., trans. Philadelphia: St. Joseph's University Press, 2003.

Mentzer, Raymond, ed. *Sin and the Calvinists: Morals Control and the Consistory in the Reformed Tradition.* Kirksville: Sixteenth Century Studies, 1994.

Mentzer, Raymond, and Andrew Spicer, eds. *Society and Culture in the Huguenot World, 1559–1685.* Cambridge: Cambridge University Press, 2007.

Mills, Kenneth, and Anthony Grafton, eds. *Conversion: Old Worlds and New.* Rochester: University of Rochester Press, 2003.

Muir, Edward. *Ritual in Early Modern Europe.* 2nd ed. Cambridge: Cambridge University Press, 2005.

Naphy, William G. *Calvin and the Consolidation of the Genevan Reformation.* 2nd ed. Louisville: Westminster John Knox Press, 2003.

Nischan, Bodo. *Lutherans and Calvinists in the Age of Confessionalism.* Aldershot: Ashgate, 1999.

Oberman, Heiko A. *Luther: Man between God and the Devil.* Eileen Walliser-Schwarzbart, trans. New Haven: Yale University Press, 1989.

O'Malley, John W. *The First Jesuits.* Cambridge, MA: Harvard University Press, 1993.

O'Malley, John W., et al., eds. *The Jesuits: Cultures, Sciences, and the Arts, 1540–1773.* Vols. I & II. Toronto: University of Toronto Press, 1999, 2006.

Pagden, Anthony. *European Encounters with the New World.* New Haven: Yale University Press, 1993.

Pagden, Anthony. *The Fall of Natural Man: The American Indian and the Origins of Comparative Ethnology.* Cambridge: Cambridge University Press, 1982.

Pardo, Osvaldo F. *The Origins of Mexican Catholicism: Nahua Rituals and Christian Sacraments in Sixteenth-Century Mexico.* Ann Arbor: University of Michigan Press, 2004.

Parker, Geoffrey, ed. *The Thirty Years' War.* 2nd ed. Abingdon: Routledge, 1997.

Pelikan, Jaroslav. *Jesus Through the Centuries: His Place in the History of Culture.* New Haven: Yale University Press, 1985.

Pelikan, Jaroslav. *The Reformation of the Bible; The Bible of the Reformation.* New Haven: Yale University Press, 1996.

Pereira, Jos, and Robert Fastiggi. *The Mystical Theology of the Catholic Reformation: An Overview of Baroque Spirituality.* Lanham: University Press of America, 2006.

Racaut, Luc. *Hatred in Print: Catholic Propaganda and Protestant Identity during the French Wars of Religion.* Aldershot: Ashgate, 2002.

Richardson, Brian. *Printing, Writers and Readers in Renaissance Italy.* Cambridge: Cambridge University Press, 1999.

Roper, Lyndal. *The Holy Household: Women and Morals in Reformation Augsburg.* Oxford: Oxford University Press, 1991.

Roth, John D., and James M. Stayer, eds. *A Companion to Anabaptism and Spiritualism, 1521–1700.* Leiden: Brill Press, 2007.

Schwartz, Stuart B., ed. *Implicit Understandings: Observing, Reporting, and Reflecting on the Encounters Between Europeans and Other Peoples in the Early Modern Era.* Cambridge: Cambridge University Press, 1994.

Scribner, R.W. *For the Sake of Simple Folk: Popular Propaganda for the German Reformation.* 2nd ed. Oxford: Clarendon, 1994.

Scribner, R.W. *Popular Culture and Popular Movements in Reformation Germany.* London: The Hambledon Press, 1987.

Smith, Jeffrey Chipps. *Sensuous Worship: Jesuits and the Art of the Early Catholic Reformation.* Princeton: Princeton University Press, 2002.

Southern, Richard. *Western Society and the Church in the Middle Ages.* Hammondsworth: Penguin, 1970.

Spence, Jonathan. *The Memory Palace of Matteo Ricci.* New York: Viking, 1983.

Stayer, James. *The German Peasants' War and the Anabaptist Community of Goods.* Montreal: McGill University Press, 1991.

Sunshine, Glenn S. *Reforming French Protestantism: The Development of Huguenot Ecclesiastical Institutions 1557–1572.* Kirksville: Truman State University Press, 2003.

Wandel, Lee Palmer. *The Eucharist in the Reformation: Incarnation and Liturgy.* Cambridge: Cambridge University Press, 2006.

Wandel, Lee Palmer. *Voracious Idols and Violent Hands: Iconoclasm in Reformation Zurich, Strasbourg, and Basel.* Cambridge: Cambridge University Press, 1995.

Wiesner-Hanks, Merry. *Christianity and Sexuality in the Early Modern World: Regulating Desire, Reforming Practice.* New York: Routledge, 1999.

Zinguer, Ilana, and Myriam Yardeni, eds. *Les deux réformes chrétiennes: Propagation et diffusion.* Leiden: Brill, 2004.

Index

absence, 12, 52, 62, 216, 224, 226, 253
altar, 26, 27, 30, 55, 210–214, 215, 224,
    234, 236, 261, 262
  altar cloth, 30, 38, 214, 215, 223, 224
  attacked, 202
  construction, 30
  Lutheran reduction to one, 212–213
  main or high, 27, 30
  side altars, 30
altarpiece, 26, 27, 213, 215, 223, 228
Amsterdam, 130, 158, 160, 165, 169, 172,
    200, 224
Anabaptists, 81, 95–97, 103, 105, 108,
    121, 130, 140, 152, 153, 166, 167,
    172, 185, 231, 249, 257, 262
  Acts of the Apostles, 96
  baptism, 96, 231
  breaking of bread, 216, 234, 248
  communion, 238–239, 243, 248, 250,
    251
  conventicles, 96, 216
  family, 131
  Holy Spirit, 198, 243
  Kingdom of Münster, 153, 165. *See also*
    Münster
  marks of, 96
  marriage, 124
  oaths, 96
  polygamy, 96, 124
  Schleitheim Confession, 166
  and the ordering of the world, 95–97
Anders, Uli (d. 1520), 14, 205, 210
Antichrist. *See* polemics
Antwerp, 30, 32, 104, 130, 158, 165, 169,
    195, 202, 210, 248
  iconoclasm, 201–202

apostasy, defined, 143
apostles, 26, 55
Apostles' Creed, 8, 57, 126, 146, 179, 197,
    237, 242
Aquinas, Thomas (1225–74), 208,
    235
Aristotle (384–322 BCE), 40, 44, 48, 59,
    60, 72, 235, 242
Augsburg, 34, 83, 85, 98, 100
Augsburg Confession, 1530, 100–102, 154,
    156, 167, 256
  content, 166
  defined, 101
Augustine (354–430), 36, 86, 112, 231,
    245
  definition of a sacrament, 36
Augustinian friars, 34, 84
Ave Maria, 57
Aztecs, 48, 57, 226
  cannibalism, 60

baptism, 48, 55, 57, 58, 221, 231
  Anabaptist, 96
  Calvin on, 105. *See also* Reformed
    Church, the
  fonts, 221
  forced baptism, 57
  infant, 231
  Lutheran, 101
  sacrament of, 35, 36
  within three days of birth, 36
barbarian/barbarism, 59, 60, 61, 62, 204,
    262, 263
  as a justification for slavery, 59
Barton, Elizabeth, the Holy Maid of Kent
    (?1506–34), 147, 150, 151